MERCHANTS OF MISERY

MERCHANTS OF MISERY

VICTOR MALAREK

Macmillan of Canada
A Division of Canada Publishing Corporation
Toronto, Ontario, Canada

Canadian Cataloguing in Publication Data

Malarek, Victor, date.
    Merchants of misery

ISBN 0-7715-9429-1

1. Narcotic habit — Canada.   2. Narcotics and crime — Canada.   3. Narcotics, Control of — Canada.   I. Title.

HV5840.C3M34 1989   363.4'5'0971   C89-094933-6

Printed and bound in Canada
by T.H. Best Printing Company Limited

Design: Don Fernley

Macmillan of Canada
A Division of Canada Publishing Corporation
Toronto, Ontario, Canada

Contents

Preface

The widespread use of illicit drugs has become a national tragedy. It has broken homes, wrecked lives and destroyed promising careers. It has invaded schools, playgrounds, businesses and government offices. It has tainted politicians, corrupted policemen and disgraced national heroes. It has unleashed a cycle of escalating crime and violence, and sucked billions of dollars out of the national economy. The drug traffickers have literally overrun our first line of defence, law enforcement, and the government seems powerless to stop them. On May 28, 1989, the Royal Canadian Mounted Police released its annual National Drug Intelligence Estimate. The findings contained in the 110-page document are alarming.

- Cocaine will remain widely available throughout Canada in the 1990s. Toronto, and especially Montreal, will increasingly serve as the main importation and distribution points for cocaine destined for all regions of the country.
- The abundant supply, greater availability and dropping prices will make cocaine more affordable and accessible to a larger number of people from all socio-economic groups.
- Crack-cocaine use is expected to escalate in Toronto and become more visible in other major Canadian centres. As a result, crime rates in these cities will climb and more cocaine-related deaths will occur.
- Marijuana and hashish continue to be the most widely available and used illicit drugs throughout Canada and will remain the principal drugs of abuse well into the next decade.
- Foreign sources will continue to provide the majority of

cannabis products on the Canadian drug market, although
domestic cultivation, especially hydroponic and indoor
growing operations, will account for a greater share of the
market in the coming years.
- Outlaw motorcycle gangs continue to play a leading role in
the financing, manufacture and trafficking of chemical
drugs.
- There has been an overall increase in heroin abuse in
Canada in recent years, with the vast majority of users
concentrated in Vancouver, Toronto and Montreal.
- Organized crime syndicates will continue their involvement in heroin supply and distribution networks operating in Canada. The sophistication of the criminal
organizations and their ability to deal in large quantities of
narcotics will continue to ensure their monopoly of the
Canadian market.

Once considered a victimless crime, drug abuse imposes a
staggering burden on society – one that we simply cannot
afford to carry. At one time, drug users were thought to
belong to a fringe of the lower economic classes. Today, this is
no longer the case. Up to two million Canadians regularly
smoke, snort, shoot or swallow illegal drugs. Drug abuse has
spread to all levels of society – from welfare recipients and
high-school dropouts to factory workers, yuppies and the
well-to-do.

The image we have of sleazy drug dealers hanging around
schoolyards enticing youngsters to buy a gram of grass or a
vial of crack-cocaine is not far from reality. What it does not
show, however, is the vast, invisible networks that place those
drugs on the street. Most drug users do not think about the
violence and weapons, or the bribery and intimidation, or
the armed thugs and bands of terrorists that are part and
parcel of the drug trade.

No doubt the most frightening aspect of the trade is that it
snares those who are most vulnerable – young people. Drugs
offer a powerful appeal to those who are just beginning their
quest for independence and self-identity. Curiosity and the

drive for new experiences make them particularly susceptible to the co-called drug experience.

An added deadly risk connected with the drug scourge is the ever-present danger posed by intravenous drug users contracting AIDS. It is estimated that 10 to 15 per cent of AIDS sufferers in Canada are intravenous drug users. As the spread of drug abuse increases, so will the number of AIDS carriers.

Every year, hundreds of millions of dollars are spent in Canada on law enforcement in what appears to be a futile attempt to stem the drug tide. Police forces could double and triple their expenditures and it would not make an appreciable dent in the supply. The drug war will not be won by police ramming down doors, arresting dealers and throwing them behind bars. The only hope lies in reducing the demand through prevention and education programs. This formidable task will require a major shift in the public's attitude toward drugs. That is already happening across Canada, although in a disjointed way, from high-school education programs to angry citizens' action committees fighting to close down the drug markets flourishing in their apartment complexes and neighborhoods.

The failure in the past of the government and the schools to communicate accurate information to the public on the dangers of drug use is one reason why the problem has reached crisis proportions today. The myriad problems associated with the drug trade will not be solved next year and perhaps not even in the remainder of this century. Years of permissiveness and laissez-faire attitudes have allowed the problem to root itself deeply in our society. From crack houses and shooting galleries to posh nightclubs and middle-class suburban homes, Canada has become, by some accounts, one of the most drug-oriented countries in the Western world.

I have come away from writing this book with a profound sense of concern and worry. Until recently, I never thought the drug problem was as serious or widespread as some had claimed. I have gone into garbage-strewn laneways in downtown Vancouver and found street kids curled in a tight ball too stoned on chemical drugs to stand up. In Toronto, I spoke with frightened senior citizens who were viciously mugged for the $20 in their purses or wallets by youths who wanted just enough cash to buy their next hit of crack-cocaine. I met with convicted drug traffickers in Canadian penitentiaries, many of whom now preach the evils of drug abuse. In Montreal, I saw dozens of young heroin addicts lying on blood- and urine-stained mattresses in cockroach-infested flats with only two or three used syringes scattered on the filthy kitchen counter. I have looked into scores of drug cases involving violence and murder, and spent many nights with drug squad police officers across the country following the activities of small, medium and big-time drug dealers, traffickers and couriers. And I dug into the financial worth of several known drug kingpins in Canada and traced their money-laundering schemes to off-shore havens and then back to legitimate enterprises in Canada.

My investigations have taken me into the United States for a frightening, first-hand look at the drug epidemic there. I also visited the Golden Triangle in Southeast Asia to look into the first link in the heroin chain. I then went to Hong Kong to investigate Triad gangs which control the international China White heroin trade.

As a result of my research, I am absolutely convinced that Canadians face an urgent situation, one that must be dealt with in a major way. The drug problem will not be solved by building more prisons and filling them with drug dealers. It will only be resolved by a serious and concerted effort in the areas of prevention, education and treatment.

Lastly, this book focuses on certain drug gangs which have been identified by their national or ethnic backgrounds. People who know my work in the areas of human rights and refugee issues will understand that I mean no disrespect to the groups to which these individuals belong.

Victor Malarek
June 1989

Acknowledgements

I would like to thank my wife, Anna, for her continuing support and love, and my daughter, Larissa, for keeping me supplied with bushels of hugs and kisses. I would also like to thank my editor, Anne Holloway, for her direction; my brother, Peter Malarek, for his invaluable assistance; and Grant Lowery and Brenda Cane for their help. A special thanks to *The Globe and Mail*. Much of the research would not have been possible without the assistance of many people and organizations. In particular, I would like to thank the Royal Canadian Mounted Police, the Montreal Urban Community Police force, and the Metropolitan Toronto Police Department. I would also like to thank the U.S. Drug Enforcement Administration, the Royal Hong Kong Police Department, the Office of Narcotic Control Board in Thailand and the Metropolitan Bangkok Police drug squad.

1
Losing the War

Heroin dealers openly sell their poisonous product in downtown Montreal video arcades. Marijuana and hashish dealers make home deliveries to customers in Vancouver suburbs. Chemical drugs with alluring names such as Ecstasy, Strawberry Fields and Purple Haze are being sold in schoolyards in Halifax, Moncton, Hamilton and Winnipeg. Cocaine dealers have set up shop in bars and nightclubs in Edmonton and Calgary. And Toronto is caught up in a crack epidemic that is devastating the city's poorer neighborhoods.

Federal Health Minister Perrin Beatty recalled in an interview for this book how, as Solicitor General in 1984, he became aware of the nation's drug problem in a most profound way during a trip to Canada's Arctic. "I remember landing in Frobisher Bay, speaking to the RCMP there and asking, 'What sort of problems do you have here?' And they said, 'Drugs.'. . . They said it normally comes from Montreal. The price in Frobisher Bay was twice the landed price in Montreal and you could go through the north through community after community and the price would simply continue to double as you went up, always available if someone is prepared to pay the price. And what it brought home to me was that even in the most remote and inaccessible parts of Canada's Arctic, if there is someone who is willing to pay, there is always someone to fill the demand."

Canada's front-line troops in the war on drugs are throwing up their hands in despair and openly admitting that they are losing. Drugs pour into this country at an alarming rate and the authorities can't stop the flow. Canadians, it appears, have developed a voracious appetite for illicit drugs and are willing to run considerable risks for new and dangerous highs.

1

"It's like standing in a line at McDonald's," said Staff Sergeant Smokey Stovern of the RCMP's Vancouver drug squad. "It never seems to let up. Despite our best efforts, and I feel we're doing an awful lot of good work, drugs are continuing to pour into this country from around the world. The fact is, we lost control of the situation years ago. I can't for the life of me see where we are winning this thing. We win the odd skirmish. We put periodic dints into it when we make big seizures. But the reality is it's out of control and I don't think the police can solve the problem. We simply lack the manpower, the resources and the ability to solve it, not only in Canada, but around the world."

Stovern's comments are anathema to his superiors in Ottawa, and he knows it. But the affable 50-year-old, who has been with the RCMP Vancouver drug squad for more than a dozen of his thirty-two years in policing, is fed up with mincing words about a crisis that he believes requires urgent public attention.

"The candyman is everywhere," Stovern lamented. "He's on the street corners, in laneways, in high schools and universities, and in the nightclubs. He even makes deliveries to customers in middle-class suburban homes and downtown office towers."

Undercover drug cops in cities across Canada agree, privately and publicly, with Stovern's grim assessment. They point to the massive seizures involving large weights of heroin, hundreds of kilograms of cocaine, thousands of microdots of LSD, and tons of marijuana and hashish as hard evidence that the war is being lost. A major bust with bales of hashish trotted out for the cameras makes for good press conferences and gives the public the feeling that something is being done, but it's only an illusion, police admit. In reality, these seizures do not represent success. They represent failure.

Sergeant Ken Ross, who heads the drug squad in Victoria, has been involved in seizures of motherships carrying tons of marijuana. "I look at all those bales and I think, sure, we did one hell of a good job, but then I ask myself, who the hell wants all these drugs? In the 1960s and '70s, we would make ounce busts and occasionally we would hit it big and seize a few kilograms, and for a while it would be hard to get the stuff on the streets. The price would go up a bit and then some more would make it in. Today, we make a 50-kilogram seizure of cocaine and the street price goes *down*. It makes you wonder how many loads got through and are stashed around the country," Ross said.

Jacques Duchesneau, director of the organized crime unit for the Montreal Urban Community Police force, likened the drug war to the classic struggle of David and Goliath. "We've doubled our staff and increased our seizures by 400 per cent in the last year and we haven't made a dent in the traffic. The demand is out there and the supplies just keep coming and coming."

Staff Inspector Jim Clark, who heads the drug squad for the Metropolitan Toronto Police, complained angrily that dope dealers are back in full swing within days after a major drug sweep through certain areas of the city. "Judges are giving crack dealers seven days, fourteen days in jail. That does a lot for our morale and it sends a bad message back to the streets."

One frightening aspect of the nation's so-called war on drugs is that Canada's police forces are fighting on the front lines with woefully outdated technology, while their enterprising adversaries have equipped themselves with the latest high-tech gear.

In the middle of a virtually deserted parking lot outside a sprawling suburban shopping mall in Montreal's east end, a red Corvette sat idling. Inside, two well-dressed drug dealers scanned the area for anything that smelled or looked like a cop. What they didn't know was that their rendezvous had been set up by two undercover drug cops. After a brief wait, the undercover team pulled up alongside the sports car.

In the lot on the flip side of the mall, an unmarked police car slid into position. One of the officers inside this backup unit immediately radioed the command centre. There was no response, just the loud crackle of static. He tried again and was met with another burst of ear-splitting static.

"Those bastards have a cellular phone in their car and they've probably got an electronic scanner to pick up police radio bands. We can't even get through to our office and now I've got to leave the car and use a pay phone to contact my office. You got a quarter?" the officer shouted, angrily slamming his fist into the dashboard.

For dope dealers, a long-time essential tool of the trade has been the paging beeper with its staccato tweet, but now they are increasingly turning to the cellular telephone. While the phones are far more expensive than the pagers, they allow greater mobility and are harder for law enforcement officers to track. The dealers' high-tech arsenals also include computers, satellite tracking dishes, fast cars, speedboats, planes, trucks, surveillance cameras, and a wide array of electronic gadgetry from police radio band scanners to equipment to detect whether a telephone is bugged or a room has been wired to pick up conversations.

"We're in a game now where we can't even compete," the RCMP's Stovern said. "We still have to revert to smoke and hand signals. Our communications are totally antiquated compared to what the bad guys have.

"Look at our vast coastlines. They can be virtually penetrated at will. On the west coast, the Queen Charlotte Islands have become a haven for drug smugglers. And what do we have out there to help us look for ships smuggling in drugs? The Canadian Coast Guard only does search and rescue, so unless a drug ship is sinking and sends out an SOS, they won't do anything. Canadian Fisheries vessels will only stop boats if they suspect illegal fishing. It doesn't matter to them if the boat is carrying tons of marijuana. And the Canadian Navy is always in dry dock or in some part of the Atlantic or Pacific Ocean on NATO manoeuvres. All the RCMP has in British Columbia is two 53-foot police boats and that is simply not enough to patrol the entire West Coast.

"One of the jokes out here is that we should call Gorbachev in Moscow and ask him to help us by ordering his navy to 'up periscope!' because the Russians are out there anyway," Stovern said wryly.

Even if the police were given all the gadgets and toys they requested, they admit these wouldn't be enough to turn the tide in the drug war. Even the strongest enforcement activity, they say, is at best a stopgap measure. It can put certain aspects of the trade into temporary remission, but it does nothing to cure the malignancy.

Anyone who doubts this assumption should take a look at the study done for the Rand Corporation called "Risks and Prices: An Economic Analysis of Drug Enforcement". Authors Peter Reuter and Mark Kleiman examined the incredible police effort mounted by the U.S. government over the past five years against cocaine and marijuana, and concluded that "despite the increased enforcement effort, which has yielded substantial results in terms of drug and asset seizures, arrests, and lengthy prison sentences, it appears that both marijuana and cocaine are still readily available. Indeed, the street price of cocaine, the best single short-run indicator of the efficacy of enforcement, has declined since the enforcement effort intensified."

The authors noted, however, that their "pessimistic" findings should not be interpreted as condemnations of drug enforcement. "It simply points to the limits of what can be achieved with certain instruments aimed at these two markets."

In a second Rand study commissioned by the U.S. Defense Department called "Sealing the Borders: The Effects of Increased Military Participation in Drug Interdiction", Peter Reuter devised a mathematical model to estimate the impact that increased spending on interdiction would have on drug consumption in the country. The study concluded that an even more stringent policy would not cut cocaine consumption by 5 per cent.

The aim of drug enforcement is threefold. First, the intention is to disrupt the drug market by making dope dealing an expensive and risky business. The thinking is that if the cost is high, the curious and the casual user will be deterred from becoming an addict, and, in turn, the addict population will stay low. Secondly, enforcement makes the search for drugs by users, and the search for buyers by dealers, a nerve-racking venture. Neither side ever knows if it is dealing with an under-cover cop or if it is under police surveillance. And thirdly, drug enforcement makes neighborhoods safer by not permitting them to be used as open-air drug markets.

Notwithstanding these worthy goals, there has been far too much emphasis and dependence on enforcement as the cure to the problem. Enforcement has an important role to play in the overall picture, but alone it will not stop the spread of drugs. Recent experience shows clearly that an astounding rate of drug busts throughout North America has hardly affected the volume of consumption. In fact, even with intense police surveillance and raids, prices have declined. In the case of cocaine, despite the seizure of hundreds of kilo-grams annually in Canada since 1986, the price has dropped anywhere from 50 to 80 per cent.

Donald Heaton, assistant commissioner of the RCMP, told a Parliamentary Committee on National Health and Welfare in 1987 that the "strongest enforcement activity is really only a holding action, and the ultimate solution to Canada's drug problem will have to be found somewhere else." Greg Stevens, chairman of the Alberta Alcohol and Drug Commission, told the same committee that while it is important that firm mea-sures be in place to make life difficult for drug traffickers, further investment in "supply-side initiatives" will produce diminishing returns.

In addition to all the practical stumbling blocks in their path, Canadian drug enforcement officials face fierce inter-agency rivalry and battles that serve only to damage their common objectives. RCMP investigators are widely reputed to be extremely territorial, often refusing to cooperate in investigations mounted by municipal police forces.

In February, 1989, *Globe and Mail* reporter Peter Moon

unearthed a confidential federal government report which stated that working relations between the RCMP and Canada Customs are severely strained, particularly in the field of drug enforcement. The report noted that long-standing and unnecessary competition between the two agencies has wasted government money and reduced the effectiveness of the federal government's customs enforcement program.

"There appears to be misunderstanding, some suspicion of each other's motives and conflicting ideas about what each other's role should be," the report says. "The situation is long-standing and many well-intentioned attempts have been made on both sides to break out of the deadlock, but these have largely been unsuccessful because of the subtle influence of outside factors."

The strained relations were traced back to 1984 when Customs officers were assigned to full-time drug enforcement work. Apparently, a number of senior Mounties felt the move amounted to encroachment on their exclusive domain. Nevertheless, Customs formed its own drug interdiction teams across the country and went to work. Since then, they have been in the forefront of some of the most impressive drug busts made in Canada. In fact, Canada Customs drug teams and inspectors seized more drugs between 1985 and 1988 than all the country's police forces combined. In the same period, the bitter animosity between the RCMP and Customs intensified.

The report, which was completed in 1986, cited constant feuding over who should be in charge of investigations between the Mounties and other federal agencies responsible for enforcing federal statutes. This destructive rivalry, the report noted, severely impaired the effectiveness of the law enforcement effort. It also found that the RCMP did not trust the competence of many of the other law enforcement agencies, and, in turn, many of them complained about lack of cooperation from the Mounties. All sides said they were working closely together on solving the disputes. But a top-ranking drug detective in Toronto maintained in an interview for this book that rivalry between the RCMP and city and provincial police forces continues. His sentiments were echoed by several investigators attached to municipal police forces across the country.

"We can't stand the elitism and arrogance and bureaucratic red tape we have to put up with in dealing with the RCMP," the Toronto detective said. "The Mounties hate Canada Customs because they [the RCMP] got caught with their pants down on the drug crisis. They weren't acting on their mandate. And now, they rely on Canada Customs' busts and tips from the U.S. Drug Enforcement Administration to justify their existence. And I can tell you, the animosity between the Ontario Provincial Police and the RCMP is so deep. They hate each other with a passion, and if the OPP knows that the RCMP are going to be included in an operation with the Metro Toronto Police drug squad, then they're out. They won't have anything to do with it. But on the record, they'll tell you the relationship is peachy-keen.

"The fact is, you can't take a guy from Gander, Newfoundland, or Flin Flon, Manitoba, make him a Mountie, give him a six-week course on drugs and then put him out onto the streets. It just doesn't work in Toronto, Montreal or Vancouver," the detective said.

Barbara Edwards was at her wits' end, her voice hoarse from yelling at Jason, her rambunctious four-year-old. In less than thirty minutes, he had turned the living room into a disaster area and was now in the kitchen jamming with the pots and pans. Jason wanted to go to the park and was hellbent on getting his mother to take him. Barbara, a single mother, was trying to get a few household chores done on her day off. It came down to a tug of wills, and Jason won. Hand in hand, the duo headed for Christie Pits, a sprawling park on the western fringe of Toronto's downtown core.

Sitting on a park bench that was tattooed like a biker's arm with initials, dates and hearts, Barbara was reading a magazine while her son gambolled on a gentle slope above. She looked up lazily when her beaming child scampered over to her with a newfound treasure, and then reeled with revulsion and fear when her eye registered the translucent object Jason was holding. Clutched in his tiny hand was a used hypodermic syringe. A yellowish-red liquid stained the inside of the narrow plastic tube. She lunged and snapped the syringe out of the little boy's grasp, hurling it onto the embankment. Jason began to cry as his mother feverishly inspected his hands and arms for any sign of a puncture wound. The outing was over, ruined by a junkie with no regard for anyone or anything but his own need for a fix.

"That creep. That rotten creep. That bastard. He could have given my child AIDS," Barbara recounted over a coffee at a local donut shop. "I'm getting out of this neighborhood. There's just too many drug pushers and dope addicts around here. It's too dangerous. I don't want to bring my son up in this environment."

Alone, Barbara simply did not have the courage or the energy to take on the pushers and the users that had muscled into her neighborhood over the past year. More to the point, she was afraid of reprisals if she dared to speak out.

Throughout several working-class neighborhoods bordering on the main drug-dealing thoroughfares of the city, residents are afraid for their safety as drug dealers and users brazenly carry on their business on nearby streets. The residents are sickened by the constant discoveries of used hypodermic needles tossed onto their lawns, into their flower beds, and strewn all over nearby parks and playgrounds. They are horrified at the sight of junkies injecting themselves in broad daylight in the alleyways behind convenience stores and local public schools. They are fed up with finding stoned addicts sleeping on their lawns, and with manoeuvring baby carriages around belligerent pushers and strung-out junkies when they go out for an evening stroll.

Time and time again, they call the police, anonymous voices on the telephone screaming hysterically that something must be done to rid the community of the riffraff. A patrol car is dispatched and cruises up and down the side streets. The next day, more used needles are collected from the parks, school-yards, alleyways and lawns. These once-pleasant neighbor-hoods have become drug war zones. How could this have ever happened in Toronto, the residents wonder.

On a busy weekday morning in early August, a contingent of heroin addicts began converging on Bloor Street West and Ossington Avenue. They paced furtively as they waited for their supplier. Many of them looked uneasy, their faces mir-roring the painful cravings gnawing deep inside their abdo-mens. They needed their fix.

At about 10:30 a.m., a rusting grey van moved along Bloor Street. The junkies immediately took notice. The word moved swiftly through their bedraggled ranks. In the front of the truck, two men, dressed in designer T-shirts and jeans, intently surveyed the street scene. A young woman and man sat perched on a bench in the rear of the van peering out the back window. The driver circled the area several times, check-ing and rechecking for cops and corralling his anxious clients in a tighter circle before turning off Bloor Street one last time and parking in an alley behind the Ossington subway station.

The junkies scurried over to the vehicle like famished fla-mingos. The back doors flew open and the foursome hur-riedly dispensed capsules and syringes to outstretched hands clasping crumpled ten- and twenty-dollar bills. Within min-utes, the business transactions were completed, the metal doors slammed shut, and the van sped off into the city traffic. Some of the junkies couldn't hold on any longer and darted behind a dumpster at the rear of a donut shop where they hastily prepared their potent concoctions in spoons, tied rubberbands tightly around their arms and cranked up.

A few days later, the same van circled the area for several minutes before stopping alongside a park on Bloor Street. This time, there were five drug entrepreneurs in their twen-ties and early thirties in the vehicle. The back doors had just swung open when a platoon of plainclothes police officers who had staked out the park charged the van. Four of the dealers grabbed handfuls of plastic packets of heroin and shoved them into their mouths in a frantic attempt to destroy evidence. The police managed to seize a small quantity of heroin, twenty-five syringes and various drug paraphernalia, and charged the quintet with trafficking in drugs and obstructing police in an investigation.

That evening, the junkies began their trek to Bloor and Ossington to wait for a connection and, within an hour, another dealer arrived on the scene to fill the demand. After a series of hand signals and facial gestures, the nattily attired Pied Piper of Smack led his followers to a concrete play yard behind an elementary school. His stash was hidden in a tin can buried in a corner of a children's sandbox.

In the late summer of 1988, outraged residents living in the St. Clair Avenue West and Old Weston Road area of Toronto decided the time had come to strike back and wrest control of their neighborhoods from the dealers and the junkies. Carrying placards and sporting "Say No to Drugs" buttons and T-shirts, about 200 men, women and children paraded down neighborhood streets chanting "No drugs!"

Dennis Fatino, an organizer of the march, shouted that the demonstrators were giving the drug pushers and users a very clear message. "Get out! This is our community. We want our parks back and our streets back without having to wade through the drug dealers to buy a quart of milk." Fatino argued that politicians have failed to recognize the seriousness of the drug problem because they are too busy debating the finer points of the rights of criminals or the dilemma of what to do with the city's garbage. "The immediate problem is drugs. Let's deal with that first and then we can deal with the garbage problem. We have a garbage problem, but it's a human garbage problem. These bums are peddling death."

Scores of residents in the Christie Pits area quickly followed suit with a boisterous weekend rally of their own. Standing on a makeshift podium in a corner of the park, speaker after speaker vented outrage and frustration over the sad state of their community. "We're now saying to the sellers and buyers, we're not going to sit by anymore," a local municipal politician vowed. "To you pushers and buyers, we're saying we will find out who you are. We're going to be watching you and we're going to take down your licence plate numbers and give this information to the police."

Steve Peconi, an undercover drug squad officer who persuasively mimics the spaced-out appearance of a drug user, happened into Christie Pits during the rally and calmly asked a man standing at the edge of the crowd what was going on.

"A bunch of do-gooders against drugs," the man shot back.

"Yeah, tell me about it," Peconi muttered.

"You looking?" the man asked.

Always ready to make a drug buy, Peconi placed his order – a gram of cocaine. The two men left the Pits and headed for a local "coke bar". The dealer darted inside the club while Peconi waited outside. Moments after the deal was made, the man, protesting his innocence, was hustled into an unmarked police cruiser by two detectives.

Throughout the maze of Toronto's subsidized public housing projects, tenants were pleading with Metro Toronto Housing Authority (MTHA) officials to put an end to the rampant drug dealing in the beleaguered highrises. They were tired of gangs of dope dealers prowling the hallways harassing and intimidating residents and housing employees. In a bid to combat the drug scourge, the housing authority instituted a controversial policy in late 1988 to evict all members of a family of anyone suspected of illegal drug activities. The housing authority estimated that at least 1,000 of the 125,000 people living in its 33,000 apartments were involved in the drug trade.

Housing officials used Section 109(1)(b) of the Ontario

Landlord and Tenant Act which states that a tenant may be evicted if he or she "exercises or carries on, or permits to be exercised or carried on, in or upon the residential premises or any part thereof, any illegal act." The get-tough move, which resulted in eighty-nine individual and family evictions in 1988, triggered sharp criticism from civil libertarians, lawyers and some community activists, who charged that civil eviction proceedings do not adhere to the strict rules of evidence used in criminal courts and that the tenants' rights were being violated.

In response to the critics, Ontario Housing Corporation (OHC) chairman David B. Greenspan defended the policy, arguing that he had heard the pleas from elderly and frail tenants and from exhausted and frightened single mothers for help against ruthless and strung-out dealers who intimidate, mug and rob them. "It is unconscionable," Greenspan argued, "that our society would allow criminals to operate their profitable and tax-free business from heavily subsidized housing units. The tenants and the MTHA are within their rights to deny public shelter to these criminals and their families. . . . Poverty denies our tenants any choice about where they live. We recognize that the OHC is the housing of last resort for the drug dealers. But it is also the housing of last resort for the victims – the single mothers they terrorize and the children they often lead into addiction or otherwise recruit. These people cannot just move out when the drug dealers move in. So the drug dealers have to go."

On March 21, 1989, Ontario's Divisional Court dismissed the first of a series of appeals from individuals evicted under the policy. In upholding a District Court ruling, three judges gave Angela Taylor and her two young children a week to get out of their public housing apartment. In their decision, the judges did not dispute the contention by Mrs. Taylor's lawyer, Marvin Kurz, that his client had never been accused of drug dealing or any other illegal act, but they noted that evidence showed that she had permitted the activity by her husband, Wilfred. Mrs. Taylor was served with an eviction notice on

January 8, 1989, six days after her husband was charged with trafficking in cocaine. He was sentenced a year later to six months in jail after being convicted of trafficking in a narcotic.

Throughout 1987 and 1988, the more than 1,100 residents of 200 Wellesley Street in downtown Toronto lived under a veritable state of siege in their Metro Toronto Housing Authority apartment building. The 30-storey, 711-unit highrise had gained the unsavory reputation as one of the worst buildings for crime in the development known as St. James Town. It was infested with drug dealers, users, hookers and pimps, and so strong was their nasty grip on the building that ordinary residents were afraid to venture outside their apartments after dusk.

In 1988, Metro police raided the building several times, arresting scores of people, mostly drug dealers and addicts. In the process, they shut down at least a dozen crack houses. The police were somewhat surprised when residents standing on apartment balconies and in the main lobby cheered them as they hauled away the drug refuse.

Vickie Rennie, who has lived in the building with her mother, Kay, for nineteen years, was one of those applauding on the sidelines, and it wasn't long after a raid in June, 1988, that she decided that she had had enough. "I was just tired of being held captive. We couldn't use any of the stairwells because they were controlled by drug dealers and users. The elderly were so scared to go out that they hibernated in their apartments and relied on other tenants and friends to buy them their groceries. Children were constantly freaking out their parents by bringing used syringes home that they found in the stairwells and in the park outside."

Vickie recalled that when the drug dealing first began in earnest, it was carried out behind closed doors. "But as the fear grew in the building, the more control the dealers got. At one point there were fifteen crack houses in the building. The dealers had a whole network set up so that when one place was busted they would move their operations to another apartment. They were all affiliated with each other."

Despite the increasing drug menace, the 31-year-old woman did not want to move. She liked her apartment and the location. The only problem was the drug dealers. So she decided to phone the police and ask what she could do. "I was only one person but I was determined to do something," she recalled. At the urging of Constable Hans Jewinski, Vickie launched "Vertical Watch", a variation of Neighborhood Watch, in her apartment building. Recruiting members was not an easy task. "They were afraid of retaliation," she explained. But persistence paid off and, eventually, she managed to persuade more than 450 tenants to join the program.

"We became the eyes and ears of the building. If we saw something suspicious going on like drug dealing, we immediately called the police, and they would act on it right away. The good thing is that it is all done anonymously. We don't have to give our names so that takes care of the fear of retaliation."

One evening, an irate drug dealer placed a plastic shopping bag filled with animal and human excrement outside Vickie's door. "I was threatened more or less by certain individuals but I don't want to talk about that, except to say that what came out of their mouths would turn your face blue."

Her efforts paid healthy dividends. The tenants regained control of the building. The drug dealers were evicted, chased out or arrested, and the crack houses were shut down. "The apartment dwellers now like this place once again. The seniors sit outside and chat with their friends and the kids are running around playing again," Vickie said, beaming with pride. Since Vertical Watch went into action, apartment break-ins, purse snatchings, auto thefts and muggings have dropped dramatically. "If every highrise apartment building and community did what we did," Vickie said, "the problem would go away. The bottom line is that our gang is bigger than any two-bit drug gang and we've also got the police on our side."

While all the parties involved in waging the war against drugs are sincere and dedicated in their efforts, their strategy has focused too exclusively on the so-called supply side of drugs, the suppliers and traffickers, and their method of arrests and seizures has proven ineffective against the billion-dollar international drug trade.

In a search for new weapons against drugs, Douglas Lipton, research director of Narcotic and Drug Research Inc. in New York, has come up with the novel suggestion that the U.S. government should simply purchase all the opium and coca crops that are grown each year and then destroy them in a blazing bonfire. He calls his scheme "pre-emptive buying" and estimates the annual price tag for the entire coca crop grown in Peru and Bolivia at about $3 billion a year. Khun Sa, the opium warlord who controls 70 per cent of the opium and heroin produced in Southeast Asia's Golden Triangle, has offered to sell his entire crop to the American government over the next five years for $48 million a year. The price tag may sound steep, but when pitted against the annual multi-billion-dollar budget of drug enforcement in the U.S. alone, it would be a steal.

"There are any number of dealers who control the traffic who couldn't care less who they sold the stuff to. The thing is we could buy it, save an enormous amount of money and destroy it," Lipton explained, stressing that such a program would complement and not replace drug enforcement, education and prevention initiatives. He also countered arguments that a cash-for-crops program would almost certainly entice large numbers of Third World peasants into growing coca and poppies. "The thing is, you can't grow opium and cocaine everywhere. It takes a certain altitude, climate and soil conditions. So there's a limit to that."

Lipton acknowledged that crops would still be siphoned off into the drug trade, and noted that even if the entire drug crop was eliminated, "there still are the designer drugs, the chemicals that are manufactured in laboratories that could be used as substitutes. The problem wouldn't go away necessarily, but certainly the major aspect of the smuggling issue, the whole interdiction and international problems related to that, would decline dramatically."

All those involved in the drug war now acknowledge that the time has come for the various forces to focus more attention on the consumer or demand side by discouraging drug use through treatment, prevention and education. While the Canadian public is wringing its hands in despair over the drug crisis, there is a critical shortage of treatment centres. Some professionals estimate that perhaps only 10 per cent of hard-drug users get treatment of any kind, and studies have found that only a small portion of drug users actively seek treatment.

Yet more than ever before, existing treatment centres are facing a crushing demand on their limited and under-funded resources, and waiting lists just for preliminary interviews stretch from four to six months. The shortage is so acute in Ontario that every year hundreds of residents are treated outside the province, most in treatment programs in the United States. In 1987, 918 Ontarians were treated in out-of-province programs at a cost of more than $4 million to the Ontario Health Insurance Plan. However, the effectiveness of this approach is highly suspect because it does not provide adequate support services, relapse-prevention components and effective follow-up for patients released from these programs.

Staff Inspector Jim Clark of the Metro Toronto Police wonders how anyone can expect a drug addict who has been convicted of a crime to stay out of trouble after being released on probation or given a suspended sentence by a judge in return for a commitment to seek treatment. "What is a serious drug addict going to do in the four to six months he is waiting to get into a treatment program?" Clark asked, shaking his head. "This whole thing is ridiculous."

The well-heeled who can pay for treatment can get it almost immediately. For about $9,000, an upscale cocaine addict can get into a private twelve-week residential program that boasts an 80 per cent success rate while offering its clients a country club retreat, complete with exercise rooms, whirlpools, saunas and tennis courts. The less fortunate might be able to squeeze into an out-patient counselling program operated

at a local downtown shelter for the homeless. The success rate
there will probably peak at 10 per cent. The actual program
may be just as good, but the harsh reality of the street junkie's
life is that he will return to the same neighborhood and
friends when his treatment is concluded, and sooner or later
end up joining them in using drugs.

Surveys have identified a patchwork of drug treatment programs scattered across Canada. Some centres have seemingly
impressive programs in place, but many lack effective backup
and support services following the release of the patient. In
rural and remote regions of the country, treatment is
nowhere to be found.

Another serious shortcoming of drug treatment programs
lies in assessing their effectiveness. Many private centres
claim success rates that cannot be taken seriously. Numerous
studies have shown that recovery from serious drug abuse is a
long, costly and taxing process, full of pitfalls. Rarely does an
addict go back to a straight, drug-free life after just one
drying-out period. Relapse is a cruel fact of life.

In September, 1986, Prime Minister Brian Mulroney told a
hushed audience in Vancouver that drug abuse in Canada
had "become an epidemic which undermines our economic
as well as our social fabric." In May, 1987, the federal government responded to the prime minister's concern by launch-
ing a $210-million National Drug Strategy to combat the drug
epidemic. One-third of that money was earmarked for treatment and rehabilitation programs, administered by provincial governments over a four-year period. Fully two years after
announcing the drug strategy, not one penny of treatment
money had reached the street. Federal officials attributed the
delay to complex and difficult negotiations with their provincial counterparts and promised that the cheques would soon
be in the mail.

Like treatment, prevention and education programs
receive more lip service than hard cash from our governments. "Just Say No" campaigns may sound impressive when
extolled in front of television cameras by dour-faced politi-

cians, or when chanted by toothy sport celebrities in media advertising campaigns. No doubt they are popular with the middle class, but they do not address the real issue. Most drug users are not even awake when the "Just Say No" rallies are being held and the sugar-coated speeches are being delivered.

So far, the attention of drug prevention and education programs has been focused mainly on a captive audience – school kids. There is some evidence that this approach is beginning to yield positive results. Biennial surveys by the Addiction Research Foundation (ARF) indicate a slow but steady decline in smoking, drinking and drug use among Ontario high-school adolescents throughout the 1980s. "We're seeing a reduction in the numbers of users of cannabis," Dr. Reginald Smart of the ARF noted. "In our 1987 survey, 15.9 per cent reported using cannabis. That is half of what we saw in our 1977-1979 survey. And so far, we see no increase trend in cocaine use with only 4 per cent reporting use in 1987, and no trend either in LSD use, which peaked in 1981 at 10.2 per cent. Our 1987 survey showed LSD use at 5.9 per cent.

"The overall picture is a stabilization of reported drug use or a downward trend which bodes well. We are seeing a conservative trend with students in high schools," Dr. Smart said. However, because their surveys rely on voluntary self-reporting by the individuals questioned, the ARF readily concedes that the findings are likely to be an under-estimation of the problem.

Not included in the ARF surveys is the army of high-school dropouts. In a study of the school system for the Ontario Ministry of Education in November, 1987, George Radwanski concluded: "We can confidently state that roughly one-third of young people in Ontario drop out of high school before graduating from grade 12." Dr. Smart noted that when surveys have been taken among the dropout population, "we see drug use rates that are three to four times higher than those we find among teenagers who remain in school."

A study by Dr. Alan King of Queen's University in Kingston,

Ontario, surveyed more than 38,000 young people across Canada in grades 7, 9, 11 and the first year of college and university during the 1987-88 school year. It also included adolescents who had recently dropped out of school and street kids in large cities. The study, which was carried out for the Federal Centre for AIDS, found that use of cannabis products increased from 3 per cent at grade 7 to 25 per cent at the university level. Use among dropouts was 33 per cent. Dropouts reported heavy use of cocaine and LSD; 29 per cent and 51 per cent respectively reported use of these substances.

The study also found that street youth heavily abuse alcohol and drugs. "About one-half of the youth surveyed supported weekly or daily drug or alcohol habits." Sixty per cent reported using marijuana and hashish, 24 per cent on a daily basis; 23 per cent said they used acid and 11 per cent used cocaine fairly regularly with 19 per cent saying they used the drug on "special occasions". Twelve per cent of the street drug users, of whom almost half were prostitutes, injected drugs, as did 5 per cent of dropouts. Nearly half of the adolescent intravenous drug users said they had shared needles with others.

The study concluded that "there is a significant proportion of injection-drug users among the young people at great risk of acquiring AIDS." Later the report stressed that street kids "are most likely to contract and spread AIDS and other STDs [sexually transmitted diseases] because they take more risks with respect to sexual activity and many regularly share drug-injection needles. Their anti-authoritarian attitudes make street youth especially difficult to reach with relevant and timely messages." The study also noted that the availability of syringes is not the only problem. "Sharing needles is part of a ritual that acts to maintain group solidarity."

Dropouts drink, smoke and use drugs more frequently than teenagers in school, the study concluded. "They are beyond the influence of school-based programs and most, having achieved a certain level of independence, will not respond to many types of community-based programs. Their sphere of influence extends well beyond their own group, often to a younger population, and this influence may have a detrimental effect on programs for school-based youth. For these reasons the importance of reaching school dropouts cannot be underestimated."

Teenage dropouts and street kids are seen by police as the major irritant in the drug war. If they did not use drugs, the supply side would simply wither in the fields of Third World countries. If they did not become addicted to drugs, they wouldn't need to commit crimes in order to get money to feed their expensive habits. Grant Lowery, executive director of Central Toronto Youth Services, has argued for decades that not enough is being done for the kids on the street. "They are worse off now than they were fifteen years ago in terms of our capability in setting up effective outreach programs. Federal and provincial funding has been dramatically reduced in this area. They don't see it as a priority. And in times of restraint, these programs are the first to be cut because they are labor-intensive and they are not visible because you can't point to a building and say 'This is where it's happening.'"

An intense back-room brawler and outspoken advocate on issues affecting young people, Lowery cannot understand why politicians and bureaucrats have difficulty in accepting the fact that community-based outreach programs are an important and urgent component in the drug war. "These kids are the hardest hit by the drug problem. This is the group where the real tragedy occurs and the high economic costs come into play. They are the ones who cause the most serious trouble and create economic havoc by committing crimes in order to get money to buy their drugs. And these are the kids that are missed in the numbers game when people talk about preventive education in the schools. We're making a gigantic and costly mistake by not doing something for them, by not putting together an effective outreach program to get to them," Lowery insisted.

Community-based prevention is difficult to implement because no one has the attention of the target population long enough to carry out effective counselling. At best, most outreach programs are fragmented, again because of serious under-funding and a lack of commitment from the public and private sectors. Yet, street youth are the one segment of our society who could benefit from the types of services offered by such an approach. These are the young people who feature prominently week in and week out in news media stories highlighting the drug epidemic in Canada.

Unless serious community-based programs are developed and properly funded for the large number of street kids, runaways and dropouts who fall through what Lowery describes as "society's safety net", the tragic human, social and economic consequences of the drug war will continue to increase our feelings of helplessness.

The drug crisis is not simply a problem of dealers and users. It is a complex issue into which play a host of psychological, social, economic and political factors. Accordingly, the solution will have to be a complex mix of international cooperation, enforcement options, treatment, education and prevention programs, and economic reform. Such a solution requires committed political leadership. Until then, the drug crisis will continue along its devastating course.

Packets of California Gold, Hawaiian Extra Mild, Jamaican Menthol and Thai Thins are being sold in cigarette stores across the country. In tiny bold lettering on the side of these packs of marijuana is the standard Health and Welfare Canada warning that the product can cause cancer and can significantly impair judgement and coordination. Tastefully packaged one-gram baggies of Colombian cocaine, plastic vials containing tiny tablets of LSD, and China White, Afghan Beige and Mexican Black heroin in capsule form – all these can be found on the "mental health" shelf at the corner drugstore. Once illicit, these drugs are now selling over the counter at prices well below what they once sold for on the street, and they carry a worry-free guarantee of purity.

The government is reaping a fortune in newfound revenues, and the deadly drug wars have stopped. Cities are no longer terrorized by vicious gangs fighting for control of a piece of asphalt on which to sell their illegal products, because the government has finally solved the dope dilemma. It has become the nation's drug kingpin, and in doing so it has virtually put the mobsters out of business.

This once unthinkable scenario may sound farfetched, but it is now being debated by a growing number of influential political and community leaders throughout North America. At the root of the debate is deep frustration over an admittedly failed policy on dealing with the drug epidemic. That frustration has led some people to suggest that decriminalization of illicit drugs may be the only way to end the impasse.

And, at first glance, the arguments for legalization are seductive. Billions of dollars in tax revenue would pour into government coffers instead of into the numbered Swiss bank accounts of drug warlords. International drug syndicates and cartels would come crashing down as organized crime is driven out of the drug business. Impoverished Third World farmers growing illicit crops would get more for their backbreaking labor as Wall Street traders bid for poppy, coca and marijuana futures on the stock exchange. Homicide rates would decline dramatically as violent drug gangs disintegrated. Muggings, armed robberies, break and enters, purse snatchings and shoplifting would also drop astronomically. A small army of corrupt judges, prosecutors, police officers and lawyers would be looking for other work. Tens of thousands of street pushers and peddlers might put their entrepreneurial skills to better legitimate use. Addicts would be protected from the risk of accidental deaths and overdoses due to poisoning from tainted illicit drugs. Best of all, ordinary Canadians and Americans caught in the crossfire of the senseless drug war would feel safe in their neighborhoods.

Proponents of legalization argue that it would take the immense profits out of the drug trade. It would allow society to deal openly with the drug problem by properly treating it as a social disease and a health issue, rather than as a crime. To buttress their arguments, they point to the hypocrisy of banning marijuana, cocaine and heroin while allowing the sale of alcohol and cigarettes – two substances which wreak more havoc and kill more people every year than all illicit drugs combined.

Professor Ethan Nadelmann of Princeton University's Woodrow Wilson School of Public and International Affairs argues, in a paper prepared in 1988 on U.S. drug policy, that the case for legalization is particularly convincing when we realize that ". . . the health costs exacted by illicit drug use pale in comparison with those associated with tobacco and alcohol use." Nadelmann noted that alcohol has been identified as the direct cause of 80,000 to 100,000 deaths annually in the United States since 1983, and as a contributing factor in an additional 100,000 deaths. That same year, alcohol abuse cost American society, which currently has an estimated eighteen million alcoholics, more than $100 billion. And in 1984, more than 320,000 deaths were attributed to tobacco consumption. According to the National Council on Drug Abuse in Washington, D.C., only 3,562 people were known to have died in 1985, from the use of illegal drugs.

In a study published in early 1989, the Canadian Medical Association reported that diseases caused by smoking, such as lung cancer and heart disease, claim 35,000 Canadian lives each year. It also reported that sidestream or secondhand smoke annually kills an estimated 330 Canadians, and that smoking costs the Canadian economy $7 billion a year in health care and lost job productivity, while generating a total economic activity of $5 billion. Smoking is now recognized as the leading cause of preventable death and disease in North America.

By conservative estimates, there are about 600,000 adult alcoholics in Canada, representing one drinker in twenty-five, and, according to Addiction Research Foundation figures, about 1.6 million Canadian adults regularly indulge in "hazardous" drinking. Research also shows that Canadians spent more than $11 billion in 1988 on buying alcoholic beverages, and a 1988 ARF study found alcohol directly responsible for an extra $6 billion in health-care costs, $2.5 billion in lost job productivity, and $1.8 billion in law enforcement nationwide. The ARF study estimated the economic burden exacted by illegal drug use in Canada at $2.7 billion in terms of excess health cost, $1 billion for lost job productivity, and $849 million for law enforcement.

Professor Nadelmann stressed that there is no valid basis for distinguishing between alcohol and tobacco, on the one hand, and most of the illicit substances on the other, as far as relative dangers are concerned. "If degree of immorality were measured by the levels of harm caused by a dealer's products, the 'traffickers' in tobacco and alcohol would be vilified as the most evil of all substance purveyors," the professor noted. "That they are perceived as respectable, even important, members of the community while providers of the no more dangerous illicit substances are punished with long prison sentences says much about the prejudices of most Americans with respect to psychoactive substances but little about the morality and immorality of their activities."

It is difficult to argue with proponents of drug legalization when presented with arguments like this. There is some truth in most of the points, but the legalization debate collapses under serious analysis. Alcohol and tobacco do kill more people than grass, crack and heroin, but that is because more people drink and smoke than use illicit drugs. If we legalize hashish, in no time it will kill just as many people as cigarettes, if not more. Legalize cocaine and it will kill just as many people as hard liquor.

Douglas Lipton of Narcotic and Drug Research Inc. cited two reasons why he is strongly opposed to legalization. The first: "Heroin and cocaine are the most seductive drugs that we know of. Heroin is the most powerful anxiety reliever. You're essentially anesthetized from not only physical pain but psychic pain. And cocaine makes you feel like a king and that you can do anything you want. It gives you a supreme kind of confidence and exhilaration. Those drugs are incredibly seductive. Because you're not hooked by the first or second episode, you believe that you're in control even though you're gradually going out of control and then you're hooked.

"There are a lot of people who do not use illegal drugs out of the moral conviction that since they're illegal they shouldn't be used. I say that there are a lot of those people who, in the event that these substances became legalized, would try them if they became available. I believe that these drugs – they're not like smoking cigarettes and they're not like alcohol – are so seductive that many people would begin using them because of the way they make them feel and the eventual loss of these people, as they become addicted, to the productive workforce and to their families and their loved ones would be incredible. It would be a real movement toward decadence and hedonism."

Lipton noted that one significant hurdle in buying illegal drugs is that they are sold by criminals. "That deters a lot of people from getting involved. They just don't want the hassle. They don't want to associate with the sleaze who deal drugs. If you legalize drugs then that whole deterrence is gone. And even with legalization, there will always be a black market. Youngsters will never be allowed legal access to heroin or cocaine. So there still will be the black market for distribution."

But the real argument in the drug debate should not be over stringent laws that criminalize possession of marijuana; or increased taxes and newfound wealth for government coffers; or the obvious hypocrisy behind the sales of alcohol-tobacco versus the banning of illicit drugs; or the terrifying reality that drug gangs are terrorizing our communities. The real debate should focus on one fundamental question: what kind of society do we want for ourselves and our children? Most psychoactive drugs – legal and illegal – rapidly damage and destroy the mind and body. If we legalize illicit drugs, we will see more marriage breakdown, child abuse and child neglect. More babies born retarded, addicted and with congenital defects. More high-school kids dropping out because they're too stoned to concentrate. More people killed in car crashes and dead from overdoses. More job accidents and absenteeism. This alarming scenario is all too real to the people who should be listened to – the men and women who work in treatment centres with drug addicts. Day in and day out, they witness the shattering effects of legal and illegal drugs. They know the devastation and human misery that legalization will bring.

Inevitably, the decades-old debate on the decriminalization of marijuana is trotted out by proponents of legalization as a compromise. They argue that pot is a "soft drug", not nearly as dangerous as cocaine and heroin and, they maintain, certainly not nearly as destructive as alcohol. Pot smokers do not become violent and beat their wives and children, legalization proponents say. But scientific studies have found that marijuana impairs judgement significantly. Coroners working on the bodies of people killed in traffic mishaps have found tetrahydrocannabinol, the active ingredient in marijuana, in the blood of many of the drivers. Furthermore, studies have found that pot has a much higher cancer-causing tar content than tobacco.

Some critics have warned that, under legalization, drug use would double, triple and possibly quadruple, encouraged by free and open access and low prices. Just how many people will turn into addicts, and what will be the cost in human terms? While legalizing drugs might save the government millions of dollars in law enforcement, a doubling of drug use will certainly mean that other costs, especially in health and social care, will rise dramatically. Some proponents have countered that there will be no significant increase in drug use, that the number of users will remain stable, that those who are not users simply won't change under legalization. This argument is incredibly naive. The lure of legal highs will most certainly draw more people – especially impressionable youngsters – into the drug net.

There is also an underlying, insidious prejudice to the legalization debate. Serious drug abuse is seen by many to

reside in the ghettos or in the welfare slums among the poor
and the uneducated. By legalizing illicit drugs, the advocates
argue, we would reduce the ills associated with crime in the
ghetto. Ghetto kids would no longer have neighborhood
drug-peddling heroes to idolize. They wouldn't need to amass
small fortunes to get their daily fix. They wouldn't be forced
to spend their waking hours breaking into middle-class
homes, mugging senior citizens or stealing women's purses to
get enough cash to keep them high for a few hours. But this
concern for ghetto dwellers is often only a mask for an attitude that says that if addicts want to destroy themselves, then
why waste money trying to stop them? Because they are not
usually nice, white, middle-class members of society, they are
considered expendable.

Whether drugs are sold legally by the government or in some
back alley by a drug pusher, the product will still require money,
and few drug addicts can hold down a regular job. Under legalization, they would still continue to steal or to prostitute themselves for money to buy drugs and to survive. And the
economically disadvantaged will continue to commit crimes as
long as the root causes of their collective misery are ignored.

The legalization debate raises other questions. Who would
be allowed to buy the drugs? Recreational users? Anyone over
the age of eighteen? How would we keep them out of the
hands of youngsters? How would they be distributed? By pre-
scription or freely over the counter at a corner milk store or
pharmacy? What would be the allowable dosage? Do you ban
drug advertising, even though the products are now legal?
Will Carla's Coke Emporium or Marijuana Slims be prohibited from sponsoring track-and-field events? How do you
enforce testing of individuals suspected of being under the
influence while driving a vehicle?

The bottom line is that we won't solve crime or the social
problems associated with the current illegal drug trade by
legalizing it. To argue otherwise would be to submit the Canadian public to a dangerous social experiment whose consequences would devastate the country.

2
Smack in Montreal

NEWS ITEM: TEHRAN (AP) – Seventy drug smugglers were hanged across Iran yesterday (Feb. 14, 1989) in a ferocious anti-narcotics crackdown. Sixty-seven men were hanged in public at dawn in a blinding snowstorm and three women were executed inside prisons. Seven men were hanged in Tehran squares in a public spectacle that underlined the government's determination to eliminate drug smuggling.

John Westlake rummaged through his briefcase, retrieved a packet of glossy color photographs, and tossed them onto the corner of his desk. "Take a look at these while I make a few phone calls," he grumbled.

In the first photograph, a young man lay dead on the floor near the doorway of an apartment. There were two gaping bullet wounds in his chest and one in his head. His eyes stared blankly at the ceiling. The next was of another man. He had been shot at point-blank range in the head.

"Those guys are history," Westlake growled sardonically, cupping the palm of his hand over the phone. "They're in the ground full of worms."

The shootings had occurred on Saturday night, March 5, 1988, in an apartment in Montreal's west end. The apartment had served as a "shooting gallery" where heroin addicts went to buy smack and shoot up, and as a retail outlet for heroin. It was run by an Iranian drug gang.

Ahmad Koshniat, who had arrived in Montreal in 1984 asking Canada to give him protection as a refugee fleeing persecution in his homeland of Iran, had rented the second-floor apartment in a nondescript lowrise building on

29

Prudhomme Street in Notre Dame de Grâce. Jacques Theriault, a 27-year-old junkie, ran the shooting gallery, which was
furnished with an old, stained mattress and a television set.
He was given free drugs for his services.

Westlake, a no-nonsense, tough-talking drug squad investigator for the Montreal Urban Community Police force, said
the one-room apartment had been under occasional surveillance, and was just one of many heroin houses which moved
from one apartment building to another every few months to
avoid detection by police. Surveillance teams monitoring the
activity at this shooting gallery had reported that during the
operating hours of noon until the 10 p.m. closing time –
which junkies refer to as their "last call" – roughly thirty
regular customers showed up to buy smack. Estimates were
that the daily take was $3,000 to $5,000.

Just before noon each day, Koshniat and a fellow Iranian
expatriate would arrive with the day's supplies – tiny packets
of heroin, tightly wrapped in bond paper in what is known as
"the drug store fold", and a box of syringes. Koshniat would
rattle off any instructions he might have for the dealer and
then he and his colleague would leave, returning just before
the closing hour to collect the day's receipts.

On that fateful Saturday evening in March, Koshniat
showed up around 9:30 p.m. with Awilfar Behroz, another
Iranian refugee claimant. Minutes before the last call, the
doorbell buzzed. Following established security precautions,
Theriault got the password on the intercom in the outside
lobby and buzzed the caller in. A moment later, there was a
rap at the door and Theriault peered through the peephole.
Recognizing the two men standing outside as regular customers, he removed a four-by-four "New York" stop and unbolted
the door. In the dimly lit corridor, the men quickly pulled ski
masks over their heads and burst in as the door swung open.
One of the men was armed with a 9 mm pistol, the other with
a butcher knife. They ordered Behroz and Theriault to lie on
the floor, and demanded the day's receipts and the leftover
heroin.

Koshniat, who was in the washroom, charged into the room to investigate the commotion, startling the two intruders. The man with the gun opened fire, hitting Koshniat once in the head and twice in the chest. The man with the knife began slashing at Behroz, who feverishly tried to protect himself with his arms as he writhed on the floor. After Koshniat collapsed in a lifeless heap, the gunman turned to Theriault, put the pistol to the terrified junkie's head and pulled the trigger. The two men then grabbed the money and fled. In their panic, they forgot about the leftover heroin.

Bleeding profusely, Behroz stumbled out of the apartment. A block away, on busy Sherbrooke Street West, he flagged down a taxi and went to his own apartment in the suburb of Lachine. He spent only a few minutes there and then managed to get himself to a nearby police station where he reported the shootings. He was rushed to the Verdun General Hospital for treatment, and was released the following day. Behroz gave homicide detectives little to go on. He had no idea who the masked attackers were.

Theriault was unconscious and barely alive when the police got to the apartment. He was rushed to the Royal Victoria Hospital in the city's downtown core, where he was hooked up to life-support machines. He died two weeks later without ever regaining consciousness. Police combed the apartment for clues. Oddly, they found no heroin.

A week after the shootings, the Iranian heroin gangs staged a lavish Mafia-style funeral for their fallen comrade. Twenty-two Cadillac limousines pulled up outside the funeral salon before proceeding to a nearby Islamic mosque for the funeral service. After the ceremony, a reception was held at the apartment of Shari Alahzar's sister. Alahzar, nicknamed the Godfather, was sentenced to twelve years in prison in 1987 for attempting to import several kilograms of heroin into Canada.

Koshniat's body was flown to Tehran, where it lay unclaimed in an airport warehouse for more than a year. His relatives, who lived in a remote village near the Afghan bor-

der, could not retrieve it because of the fierce fighting
between Iran and Iraq.

"We've got a good idea who did the hit," Westlake said bluntly
as he put down the phone. "Two Italian junkies from the east
end. But there's a slight hitch: we can't prove it."

Westlake had been working heroin investigations for the
MUC drug squad for three years. Tall, bearded, solidly built
and streetwise, he takes his work seriously and harbors a deep
hatred for heroin dealers. His partner, Gaston Pitre, had been
working heroin for four years. A man of few words, he looks
like someone who would feel more at home behind a plow or
in a lumber camp than busting down doors looking for heroin traffickers. Both men know the steamy underbelly of
Montreal. Westlake worked the rough-and-tumble, English-
speaking western downtown core, pounding a beat for most
of his twenty-four years with the force, while Pitre, a nineteen-
year veteran, walked a flipside beat in the gritty, French-
speaking eastern core.

"When we go into the east end, I talk," Pitre said. "When we
go into the west end, Westlake does the talking."

Westlake spat out a chewed toothpick and jammed another
into his mouth. "The boss told me to take you around and
show you everything," he said. "I'm going to show you what
has happened in this city with heroin over the last couple of
years. I guarantee it will blow your mind." He began rummag-
ing through his briefcase again and retrieved more photographs. "These are the bastards that we're going to take
down." He placed a number of pictures in a row on his desk.

"This is the leader of the gang, Shahrokh Amadzadegam.
He's known as the Shah. An Iranian. One of these so-called
refugees," Westlake muttered caustically. "All these guys are
Iranian and they all work for the Shah. They all deal in smack
and they're all 'refugees'. We're going to bust every one of
these bastards, and put them in the pen where they belong."
He spat out the second toothpick.

Pitre glanced over at his partner's desk and stuck a thick index finger in the face of the color photograph lying third in rank below the Shah. On the back of the picture was scribbled Ali Reza Oraki. The 24-year-old had come to Canada two years earlier as a refugee. He was a draft dodger fleeing the Iran-Iraq battlefields. "I want him. I arrested that fucker last year for dealing smack and his lawyer got him off on a technicality. That little creep gave me the finger when he walked out of the courtroom. I want him. He won't get away from me this time."

"It's going to take us a bit of time to bring down the Shah and his gang," Westlake interjected. "We just got the okay from the big boss to plan the project. I figure by sometime in the fall, the Shah and his boys will be behind bars where they belong."

The Shah, he explained, was reputed to be the man who brought Iranian heroin trafficking to Montreal. The 31-year-old came to Canada on a student visa on April 12, 1980, and immediately asked for refugee status. It has not been granted, nor did he have landed immigrant status. Amadzadegam had remained in the country without status under a ministerial permit. In less than a year, the Shah set up a drug-dealing operation in Reggie's Bar on the sixth floor of the Hall Building of Concordia University on de Maisonneuve Boulevard, in the heart of the city, and on almost any weekday, he could be seen sitting like a Mafia don at his usual table in a corner of the cafeteria with an attaché case that contained mostly hashish, hash oil and chemical drugs like LSD and MDA. He also kept a stash of drugs safely concealed in a student locker somewhere in the seven-storey building.

The Shah soon commanded a small band of drug runners who fanned out nightly to comb the downtown bars for customers. For years, he operated with relative impunity. He was first arrested in the summer of 1982, charged with simple possession and fined $800. On October 11, 1983, he was fined $200 and given two years' probation on an assault charge. Two months later, he was back in court, where he was sentenced to three months for obstruction of justice. He had warned the victim in the assault case to drop the charge.

The Shah's scrapes with the law continued to escalate. On March 24, 1984, he was arrested during a drug deal that went sour. The Iranian did not like the quality of the hashish that was delivered to him from one of his dealer contacts, so he kidnapped the dealer's courier in a bid to get his money back. Amadzadegam was charged with kidnapping, extortion and conspiracy to possess hashish. He was released on bail. Three months later, on June 13, the Shah was arrested while in possession of 18 kilograms of hashish. Again he was released on bail. On September 23, a police wiretap taped Amadzadegam giving instructions to one of his henchmen to beat up the courier in the kidnap and extortion case as a warning not to testify in the upcoming court case. He was immediately arrested and charged with obstruction of justice. On April 17, 1985, the Shah was sentenced to two years less a day on the charge of possession of 18 kilograms of hashish. He was brought back to court in late November of that year on twenty-eight charges stemming from the other incident involving kidnapping and extortion. After some razzle-dazzle legal footwork by his lawyer and the Crown prosecutor, he pleaded guilty to three charges. On December 6, he was sentenced to a further ten months consecutive. With this much time added to his previous sentence, the Shah should have been transferred from provincial prison to a federal penitentiary. But in a bizarre twist, the paperwork that accompanied Amadzadegam back to prison simply indicated ten months, which prison authorities assumed was to be served concurrently. The Shah ended up not serving a single day of the ten-month sentence.

When he was finally released in the summer of 1987, Amadzadegam, who has a fondness for fine Italian silk suits, bought a modest home in St-Colomban in the Laurentian foothills, which he shared with his French-Canadian girlfriend. He also bought a small jewellery boutique on Ste. Catherine Street near the Montreal Forum, a convenience store in Lachine, and a couple of cars.

The Shah's trusted lieutenant was Kambiz Yazdani, who had the unassuming demeanor of a chartered accountant. He came to Canada on January 1, 1980, and also asked for refugee status. He eventually married a Canadian and was granted landed immigrant status on October 10, 1984. Yazdani had his first run-in with Montreal drug squad officers in September, 1984. The bespectacled Iranian was arrested and charged with simple possession of hashish, and fined $50. He took a giant leap up the drug ladder when he was arrested a year later in possession of 50 grams of heroin. On March 26, 1986, he was found guilty of possession for the purposes of trafficking and sentenced to four years, six months in prison. He was paroled in early January, 1988.

With calm and painstaking attention to detail, Westlake and Pitre planned a "project" aimed at putting the Shah out of the heroin trafficking business, even if it was only for a number of years. The key to their case was netting a reliable informant to introduce an undercover cop or "double agent" to the lower echelons of the gang as a heroin buyer. Once inside, that agent would need a dependable supply of money in order to make buys and work his way into the confidence of mid-level gang members and eventually get to the top man – the Shah.

"And then, bam!" Westlake slammed his glove-like palm on the photos spread over his desk. "They're ours. We've got them by the balls and this time we're going to squeeze hard."

In mid-June, Westlake and Pitre finally got the break they were looking for. They had busted a young Iranian who was selling heroin in a video arcade on Ste. Catherine Street. The dealer, who was in his early twenties, had sold a "point" of smack (a 0.1-gram packet of heroin) to an undercover cop on three separate occasions and was now facing up to nine years in prison for trafficking. Westlake set out to "turn" him and get him to "roll over" on his drug connections. He graphically laid out the dealer's grim future in prison, portraying in fine detail what lay in store for such a good-looking young man in penitentiary. Then he dangled the one option that might keep the Iranian out of jail. His eyes fixed on his interrogator in fear and disbelief, the man agreed to cooperate.

"I'm making no promises," Westlake reiterated. "If you help us nail these bastards, I'll talk to the Crown and see if he'll reduce the charge. I promise you that. But you've got to cooperate. Any bullshit and you could say goodbye for nine years. We want you to get us good information. We want you to get our double agents in the door to make some buys. Can you do that?"

The Iranian looked down at the floor and in a hoarse whisper forced out a barely audible reply.

"Is that a yes?" Westlake asked.

"Yes," the man said.

"Good, we'll meet you tomorrow and set things up," Westlake said. "Here's my beeper number. Call me at exactly 2 p.m. and leave me a phone number to reach you."

Westlake and Pitre moved quickly to get the necessary paperwork prepared requesting the department to approve their newest informant. From that moment, the young man would never be referred to by name but only as informant 294. The next day at 4 p.m., 294 jumped into the back of an unmarked car on a quiet downtown side street. He was nervous.

Westlake got right to the point. "You know the Shah?"

Informant 294 sat bolt upright. "Yes. I know him. I know some of his friends better. But I know him."

"Do you think you can get near the Shah? Can you get him to sell to you? Can you get him to trust you?"

"I don't know. Maybe. I think so but I first have to make buys from his people. They know me but they won't bother with me if I don't deal with them. I need money to make the buys."

"We've got the money. Plenty of money. Don't you worry about that. You see that car ahead of us? In it are two double agents. I want you to take 'Joe Spaghetti' and introduce him to one of the Shah's dealers. Say you know him and he's okay. Joe will buy a gram of smack. I want him in tight with your guy and, after a few buys, you tell your dealer that Joe wants to buy 20 grams of smack. That way he'll have to introduce our double agent to the next level to deal that kind of weight," Westlake explained. Pitre signalled to the agents in the car ahead. A skinny, pale undercover drug cop came over to the car. "These skinny little guys can get away with buying smack. They look like fucking addicts," Westlake joked as the officer got into the back of the car.

"This is 'Joe Spaghetti'. You'll take him to make the buy," Pitre said in a friendly tone, putting his arm around the informant's shoulders. "You be careful. Everything will be okay. I give you my word on that."

The double agent and 294 left together for a pre-arranged sale at a busy downtown shopping arcade on the corner of Ste. Catherine and Guy streets.

The two officers slumped back into their seats and chomped on a half-dozen toothpicks each while they waited for the agent they called Joe Spaghetti and 294 to return. "You always have to keep in mind that the informer is a stool pigeon. You can't get emotional, especially with heroin dealers and junkies. They'd turn on their own mothers for a hit," Westlake said with intense disdain.

Pitre added: "What I did with that guy. You know, put my arm around his shoulder. The handshake. It's part of the game. It's all bullshit. You can't get close to these people. Three of my sources have been killed in the past four years."

"There is one thing you have to understand about heroin. You got to be a fucked-up human being to be a junkie. You've got to be a piece of shit to sell smack," his partner said, glaring into the rearview mirror.

Spaghetti and 294 returned forty-five minutes later. The double agent was beaming. The deal had gone down. In his fist, he clenched a one-gram packet of heroin. It cost him $270.

"Everything went okay," Spaghetti said. "We set up another buy in two days. The guy was nervous at first but I think he feels sure that I'm not a cop."

"I told you I could get in," the informant boasted. He was riding high on the thrill of the undercover operation.

"Yeah. You just call me in two days at 2 p.m. on my beeper and keep your nose clean. You get in any shit and the deal is off. You understand?" Westlake instructed.

"He'll be okay. You did a good job. You take care of yourself and don't get into any trouble. Call us if you need help," Pitre added in a friendly tone.

Informant 294 shook hands with Pitre and Spaghetti and left. Westlake shook his head as 294 disappeared around the corner.

That evening, Pitre got a call on his beeper. He had to meet another informant, known as 082, in "the hole", a secluded rendezvous under a crumbling elevated roadway on the fringe of Old Montreal.

"This guy helped us with a big bust a few weeks back," Pitre said. "He's going in the joint for eighteen months. We busted him last year for trafficking smack but we got the Crown to get him a reduced sentence after he agreed to cooperate with us. He is working on another deal for us."

At the rear entrance to "the hole", a black van approached cautiously. The lights flashed. Pitre flashed his lights twice and the van pulled alongside the car.

Informant 082 was a Turk. He was olive-skinned, his black hair slicked back with glimmering, perfumed gel. He was dressed stylishly and sported a solid gold Rolex watch. He appeared overjoyed at seeing Pitre again, shaking his hand warmly and slapping him on the back. He glanced cautiously at Westlake and nodded. The conversation was entirely in French. The informant told the duo that he had talked to some high-level heroin dealers in another Iranian gang about making a deal for a pound of smack.

Pitre's eyes lit up. "*Tabarnac!* A pound! You hear that, John? A pound!"

"But these guys are real paranoid," 082 said. "They are willing to deal but only on their terms. One of their guys will pick up the money from the car. The stuff will be sitting on a toilet in an apartment nearby so if anything goes wrong, they can flush it."

"No damn way. They bring the stuff to us in the car so we can test it. They see the money and we test the product. Then, *bam*!" Pitre hammered his fist onto the dashboard. "We bust the bastards."

"They won't do it. They are paranoid of a set-up."

"They want the money. They're greedy. Once they see the money, they'll go for the deal our way or we blow it off," Pitre said.

The informant lit up a cigarette and stared intently out the window as a Jeep Cherokee rumbled through the lot. As it passed, 082 covered his face discreetly with his hand.

"You know, you shouldn't be driving the van," Pitre warned. "That guy we busted with the coke last month could put two and two together and figure it was you who set him up. He might have a few friends looking for you."

"He doesn't know my real name," 082 replied confidently.

"He could have taken down your licence number and got someone to trace it. Maybe you should get rid of the van," the officer suggested.

"No one could trace it. Before we went on the bust, I put a stolen plate on my van," the informant said.

Pitre winced. "*Tabarnac*! I don't want to hear about it," he shouted, covering his ears.

"I don't even have a driver's licence. I went for the test and they refused to pass me over one stupid question."

"Which question?" Westlake asked.

"The one where they say if you are tired, do you pull over and rest, or do you take something to keep you awake? Where I come from it is normal to take a pill to stay awake when you have a long way to drive."

Everyone burst out laughing.

Jacques Duchesneau, director of the organized crime division of the Montreal Urban Community Police force, is a soft-spoken, devoted family man deeply troubled by the drug epidemic gripping the city. The most frightening change he has witnessed in the past few years has been the dramatic increase in heroin abuse, particularly among Montrealers in their late teens and early twenties.

"Heroin was always here," he said. "Prior to 1983, I would say we had about 5,000 junkies, and the trade was controlled by the Italian mob. But since that time, the number of junkies has tripled. I would say, and I am being very conservative, there are 15,000 junkies in the city today."

The result has been that Montreal has gained the dubious distinction of being Canada's heroin capital, a title previously held by Vancouver, which has an estimated 10,000 heroin addicts and users. Duchesneau laid the blame for the dramatic increase in heroin abuse squarely on the shoulders of gangs of Iranians, who, since 1983, have been arriving in larger numbers at Montreal's Mirabel International Airport claiming to be refugees. His investigators have linked at least 300 Iranians to various drug rings in the city. With the next breath, Duchesneau stressed that he did not want his comments to be interpreted in any way as an attack on the reputation of the more than 9,000 members of Montreal's Iranian community. "These drug dealers are a minority. Unfortunately, they give the majority of law-abiding, hard-working Iranians here a bad name. It's the same for any ethnic group when a minority gets involved in crime."

In the past three years, more than 100 Iranians have been convicted on heroin charges and, during the same period, these same drug dealers have been implicated in dozens of violent incidents ranging from knifings outside downtown nightclubs to grisly murders. The gangs are generally made up of young men from the same village, town or region in Iran, and many of them have links to Southwest Asia's infamous "Golden Crescent" area – a swath of sun-drenched mountains cutting through Iran, Afghanistan and Pakistan, which supplies 29 per cent of Canada's illicit heroin market.

Leaning intently over his desk, Duchesneau recounted the

arrest of a notorious gang of Iranian drug traffickers in
March, 1987, at Montreal's Mirabel airport in connection
with a seizure of 2 kilograms of heroin. The gang, headed by
Jasan Bavi, were in the arrivals lounge waiting for a "mule", a
courier who was smuggling in a shipment from New Delhi,
India, in the lining of his suitcase. The courier, Daniel Ther-
rien, a middle-aged, cherubic-looking Quebecker, had
worked as a waiter at the CP hotel adjacent to the Mirabel
complex and knew many airport employees. He was waving
cheerfully to a few of them as he sauntered into the baggage
area, but he blanched and his knees buckled when two grim-
faced Canada Customs officers ordered him to accompany
them to a back room for a thorough body search. Out in the
public arrivals area, a platoon of undercover officers moved
in on the mule's welcoming party and arrested four Iranians
and an American.

Later that evening, a second team of drug squad officers,
backed up by a heavily armed SWAT unit, smashed down the
doors of an apartment in Montreal's west end, which was
rented by an Iranian known on the streets as "the Doctor".
The officers found that the man was "very cooperative." In
fact, he was too cooperative, showing them where he had
hidden one-point packets of heroin as well as file folders
stuffed with stolen passports and travel documents. The
police tossed all the evidence into an empty suitcase they'd
found in the bedroom closet and headed for the drug squad
office. There, a sharp-eyed detective was bothered by a nag-
ging feeling in his gut about the suitcase from the raid. Then
it hit him. It was identical to the one seized at the airport. He
grabbed a screwdriver from his desk drawer and drove it
through one side. Concealed in the lining was another 2
kilograms of heroin.

Because of overcrowding at the Parthenais provincial jail in
east-end Montreal, Bavi was sent to a lockup in nearby Sorel,
Quebec. In May, while the guards were consumed by the
Stanley Cup playoffs on television, the 30-year-old gang
leader sawed his way to freedom with a hacksaw smuggled to

him during a weekend visit by his teenage girlfriend. The MUC Police did not learn about the breakout until a week later when, during a scheduled court appearance, they discovered Bavi was absent from the prisoner's dock. A telephone call was placed to the Sorel jail, and the detectives were informed that their man had escaped.

In July, Bavi's voice was picked up in a telephone wiretap on an unrelated drug investigation. One of the eavesdroppers recognized him instantly. Bavi was arranging to meet with a gang member in the north end of the city. He wanted help in getting out of the country. Drug squad officers staked out the planned rendezvous site and swooped in on a suspicious car as it slowed to a stop to pick up an Iranian man. Bavi, wearing a wig and dark sunglasses and carrying a Greek passport, was sitting in the back seat with his 17-year-old girlfriend. He was on his way to the United States. Instead, he was taken to the more secure Parthenais jail where, alone in his cell and in a fit of rage, he sewed his lips together. His associates surmised that he blamed his mouth for getting him caught. Had he not spoken on the phone, his voice would never have been picked up on the wiretap. Bavi was sentenced later in the year to nine years in penitentiary for conspiracy to traffic heroin.

"We have a real problem here," Duchesneau said despondently. "Many of the Iranians who have come here have been involved in drug dealing in their homeland or come from regions of Iran where opium poppies have been grown for centuries. They know where to get heroin. They have the connections."

Shaking his head, Duchesneau recounted how the Iranian drug gangs managed to avoid a deadly and costly bloodbath with the established mobs which dominated the city's heroin trade. "The Iranians simply went out and created their own market. They established a completely new market by getting thousands of young people hooked on heroin. They didn't take any customers away from the mob."

The police official pointed out that the crime involved in the heroin trade is far more extensive and insidious than just the importation and trafficking of an illicit drug. "Junkies need a good supply of money to support their habit, and they get that money from crime. They commit robberies, mostly break and enters. A lot of young women get involved in prostitution. If someone is using one gram of smack a day, that can cost anywhere from $270 to $550, depending on the supply and the purity. A habit like that could easily run into a couple of thousand dollars a week. There is no work these addicts can do to get that kind of money."

The drug squad is housed on the third floor of a bleak-looking, three-storey concrete building across the street from the MUC Police headquarters in Old Montreal. Entry is secured through a series of combination locks or by phoning the receptionist from a telephone on a wall in the main floor lobby. The bullpen is a large, open pit with rows of battered steel desks topped with archaic manual typewriters and stacks of police manuals, reports, forms and files.

Only a handful of the men in the bullpen look like cops trying not to look like cops. The majority could easily pass as bikers, small-time drug dealers, addicts and street riffraff. A few are well-groomed, clean-shaven and stylishly dressed. They are the Montreal squad's answer to Miami Vice – the men and women who ride around in swank sports cars posing as high rollers making "heavy-weight" drug deals. The atmosphere in the room is always charged. Each unit – cocaine, heroin, cannabis, chemical drugs – has projects constantly on the go. The phones ring and the pagers beep incessantly.

The mood on this particular afternoon is extremely high. The squad is on the alert for a possible major drug bust. All they are waiting for is a telephone call from 082 giving them the green light.

In a neat, glassed-in office overlooking the bullpen, Lieutenant-Detective Guy Bernard intently surveyed the men and women under his command. Looking more like a bureaucrat than a detective, Bernard has been with the squad since 1981 and has headed the *section stupéfiantes* since 1987. On the wall near his desk hangs a plaque bearing the emblem of the squad. For the lieutenant, it signifies what he and the squad are all about.

In the centre of the plaque is the squad's mascot, a snowy white owl. "We chose the owl because it is awake at night and that is when most drug dealing is done," Bernard explained. "It also eats rodents. Rats! We see all drug dealers as rats. The owl is white, and most of the drugs we seize – cocaine and heroin – are white powder. The owl is the only bird that can turn its head 180 degrees. For us, this is the ultimate in surveillance. We have got to see everything that goes on in a drug operation. Our lives depend on it. The owl also has exceptional hearing, and we have to use electronic surveillance from time to time in our work. The bird is perched on a branch giving it a view of the territory below, and is surrounded by a wreath of poppies, marijuana and coca plants. Again, the major drugs we deal with. To one corner above its head, you will notice a sliver of the moon. The moon gives light in the night and light gives us information. The backdrop is black, which means justice averted and tells us to make sure we hit the big and the small drug dealers. And the logo *Justum et Tenacem* means Justice and Tenacity."

The emblem was created in 1982 by a team of drug squad officers and was drawn by the police sketch artist. "I have never come into the office since that time without my pin on my lapel. It's part of me. It is my pride," Bernard declared.

The lieutenant pointed at the corner of the squad room where a number of undercover officers were chatting. "They are all double agents. They are my main preoccupation. I worry about them. About their safety. About their frame of mind. I wouldn't like to be in the situations that they confront almost every day. These officers have to have a certain quality to do that job. You have to have courage and be able to tolerate a lot of stress. You have to think like a criminal and think like a cop at the same time. And you have to be a bit of a bullshitter. We send them into situations where there is nothing but corruption, where there is a lot of money, and we ask them to come back to the office with their integrity and honesty intact. It's a tough assignment."

In the bullpen, Pitre was on the phone. He looked extremely upset. Something was wrong. After a few seconds, he threw down the receiver, sending the phone careening onto the floor. "It's off," he shouted, turning to his startled partner.

"The dealer got spooked," Westlake later explained apologetically. "That's the one rotten thing about this business. Situations change from minute to minute. Dealers are paranoid. Some little thing spooks them and the deal is off. A cop car drives by the building or they don't like the look of a plumber's van. I'm sorry about that. Maybe we could cruise around the Park and Bernard area north of Mount Royal and check out a few shooting galleries where the Greek junkies and dealers hang out. I'll get Joe Spaghetti and Tony."

Spaghetti and his sidekick cruised along Park Avenue in a car ahead of Westlake and Pitre. Westlake hadn't spoken since he left the office. Pitre, his eyes riveted to the road, was driving. As they approached St. Viateur Street, Westlake slouched down low in his seat.

"Look over there on the east side in front of the drugstore. See that kid? He's a lookout, a spotter. There's a shooting gallery in the apartment building across the street. If the doorbell rings, the guys inside will look out the window for an all-clear signal from that kid before they open the door," Westlake said. "We'll need the SWAT team to figure a way to take the place down. Tony went in there last week to make a buy. He told us the door was made of steel and had a steel bar right across it."

On Park Avenue between Bernard and Van Horne, Spaghetti entered a dilapidated three-storey apartment building and went straight to apartment 18. He knocked on the door. Someone peered out the window which was covered with a black curtain. Someone else looked out the peephole. Not the least impressed by Spaghetti's meek and slight appearance, a burly man unbolted a series of locks and opened the door. "What do you want, asshole?" he bellowed in a heavy Greek accent.

"David sent me. I want a point."

"Who's David?" he shot back.

"He lives on Hutchinson Street near Jean Talon. He's got brown hair. A skinny guy."

"Any of you guys know this asshole?" the man shouted to the back of the room. Four men were sitting around a table topped with a small mound of beige powder and a small electronic scale. They were packaging tiny doses of the substance into aluminum foil.

"No!" they shouted in unison.

The man slammed the door in the officer's face.

Red-faced, Spaghetti rejoined Tony. The two undercover cars then sped off for Beauty's Restaurant at the corner of Mount Royal and St. Urbain.

"We never allow our double agents to go on a buy without back-up," Westlake explained as he entered the restaurant. "When an agent goes in for a meet or a buy, we wait no more than fifteen minutes. Then it's decision time. Do we wait any longer or do we go in after him?"

The two double agents were sitting in a booth at the back. Spaghetti was visibly upset. "I'd like to get that jerk who answered the door. I don't like being called an asshole."

"What did you see?" Pitre asked.

"There were five men. Four were at the table cutting smack. There was probably 20 grams on the table."

Westlake whistled. "What was the security like?" he asked.

"A half-dozen locks on the door for sure, and they had a bucket of water beside the table," Spaghetti replied.

"In case there's a bust," Tony explained. "As soon as the SWAT team hits the door, they dump the smack in the bucket and then kick it over onto the floor. That way, there's no evidence, no case, and we look pretty stupid."

"These shooting galleries are going to be a long-term project," Westlake suggested. "We'll need surveillance. The guys inside are bums. Low-life street dealers. I'd like to get their supplier. They get their stuff off Iranians."

Westlake had set up a meeting at a downtown greasy spoon later that evening with a young prostitute who had become hooked on heroin by her former boyfriend, an Iranian drug dealer. She was easy to find. Wearing a black mini-dress, mesh stockings and spiked high heels, she was hunched over a cup of coffee in a corner booth puffing furtively on a cigarette. Her face was caked with makeup but it didn't do much to hid what the last few years had stolen from her. The woman, who identified herself only as Sheila, was twenty-two but looked twice her age. The conversation was strictly business.

"I started dating this guy when I was seventeen. I was almost eighteen," Sheila began in a bored monotone. "He came from Iran. A refugee. I was in love with him. He was good-looking. Very sweet. My parents hated him. They thought he was too old for me. One night, after we had gone out for a couple of weeks, he took me to this party and we got really stoned. I thought I was smoking some kind of hash but I found out later it was heroin. 'Chasing the dragon', they call it. I got sick and barfed my guts out.

"The next night, we smoked some more and I was okay. When I came down, I wanted more. I loved it. It made me feel like I had no cares in the world. My boyfriend kept giving me what I asked for. I didn't realize until later that he never smoked any of the stuff himself. He faked it. Then he rolled up my sleeve and shot me up with a needle. I was too ripped to know what was going on. At first, when I got hooked into it, I did a half-point a day, and before I knew it I was doing a point a day and then two points. Today I do ten points. That's a gram.

"My boyfriend taught me a hell of a lesson after I was hooked. Iranians never give you anything for free. I owed him and he made sure I paid him back every cent for the heroin he fronted me. When I told him I didn't have the money to pay him, he slapped me around and started throwing me around the room. He beat me up and then he shot me up. I became his slave and he put me on the street.

"One night when I was at this party, he grabbed this girl who refused to pay him for a point and stuck her in the thigh with a knife. Right down to the bone. She freaked out and he told her that was a warning. The next time, he said he was going to slice up her liver."

A pasty-skinned hooker hustled over to the booth and whispered into Sheila's ear. "I've got to go. I've got some business to do. Thanks for the coffee." Sheila disappeared into the night.

Over the summer months, Westlake, Pitre and a team of double agents worked their informants and contacts. And their long hours were beginning to pay dividends. They made significant progress up the chain of command in the Shah's heroin organization. They also built a strong case to move in on a number of shooting galleries in the Park Extension area. But they suffered a major and potentially damaging setback: informant 294 had been arrested for a vicious assault. At the police station where he was being booked, he boasted loudly to the arresting policemen that he was working undercover for Westlake and Pitre. The two officers were summoned to the precinct.

"We had to put him on ice. We had double agents out there whose lives were in jeopardy if this guy was allowed out," Westlake recounted. "Anyway, we didn't need him anymore. Joe Spaghetti was in tight with the Shah's number two man." Informant 294 was hustled off to a provincial jail outside the city and placed in a special custody cell where he would not have any contact with other prisoners.

Then came an unexpected break. In early September, Spaghetti tried to arrange a 50-gram buy of heroin but Yazdani, the Shah's lieutenant, said he couldn't fill the order right away. In passing conversation with the undercover agent, the Iranian let slip that a shipment of high-grade smack was on its way from New Delhi and would be in the city by mid-month.

It turned out that the Shah had recruited and groomed two

mules for a trip to India to pick up 3 kilograms of heroin from a dealer in New Delhi. The couriers had their travel expenses paid for by a gang leader. The man and woman, both heroin addicts and small-time drug pushers, were also guaranteed 100 grams of heroin each upon their safe return. They left Montreal aboard an Air Canada flight to Bombay in late August. Within days, Westlake and Pitre had a positive identification of the couple: Lynne Margaret Stephan, 36, and André Lafrenière, 30. The Mounties were called in to the investigation, and they in turn alerted authorities in India, who kept the duo under surveillance.

The couple's trip soon became a series of costly and nerve-jarring misadventures. Upon arriving in Bombay, they took a train to New Delhi to meet the Shah's heroin connection. It took Lafrenière three days to locate the contact, a man called O'Neil. It turned out that O'Neil was having difficulty making the 3-kilogram buy. That problem caused the couple to delay their flight back home twice. When O'Neil finally found them "samples" to test, they were of such poor quality that he was sent out to hunt for a better grade of heroin. After more delays, and at his wit's end, the frustrated contact dropped off 3 kilograms of untested heroin at the couple's hotel room and stormed out. Lafrenière and Stephan were in a panic. The Shah had told them the heroin was to be concealed in the lining of two leather coats.

Lafrenière hooked up with a second contact who was suffering from chronic jitters, believing the local police were tailing him. The couple then went out looking for leather coats and ended up having one made to measure for Stephan. At their hotel room, the strung-out couriers tried to iron the 3-kilo bags of heroin flat to get them into the coat, but no matter how hard they tried, the leather garment bulged in all the wrong places.

The second contact suggested the couple turn the heroin over to some men who could conceal it in a suitcase. A day later, the suitcase was delivered to the hotel. It smelled of glue and it was patently obvious that someone had worked on it.

Thoroughly exasperated, Lafrenière ripped out one of the heroin bags, stuffed it into a sock and gave it to Stephan to hide in her underwear. The woman travelled from India to Switzerland and then on to Canada with the sausage-shaped package between her legs. Lafrenière threw the suitcase with the rest of the heroin into a garbage heap outside the hotel.

Lafrenière telexed the Shah, informing him that he and Stephan would be arriving at Mirabel on September 17. However, their plans changed slightly and they caught a flight which arrived in Canada a day earlier. They were easy to spot at the airport. Lafrenière, sporting a funky haircut that was short on top and long on the sides, looked like someone who had been on the streets a little too long. A tall, slender, dirty blonde, Stephan had her history as a junkie written all over her face. The couple were promptly arrested and hustled off by the RCMP. In a back room, they were strip-searched, then interrogated by the police for several hours.

"The situation was explained to them," Westlake said. "They were asked if they wanted to deal. We told them they were looking at heavy time and suggested that if they were willing to cooperate and testify against the individuals they were working for, it would be considered when they were being sentenced."

The couple agreed. The beige-colored heroin was switched with milk chocolate powder and, the following day, Lafrenière called the Shah from the airport, announcing that he and Stephan had arrived safe and sound, and were heading for their apartment. The Shah said he would meet them there later that night. By this time, Stephan was not feeling well. She was suffering from withdrawal. She needed a fix. At the apartment, Lafrenière told her to lie down on the couch and went into the bedroom to get a blanket. When he pulled the blanket off the bed, he was startled to find a Mountie lying under it with a revolver in his hand.

When the Shah and Yazdani finally arrived, Lafrenière welcomed them warmly, then nervously began to explain the litany of problems he and Stephan had encountered in India.

He took a deep breath and rubbed his trembling hands over his flushed face. The Shah stared intently at the courier. He sensed something was wrong. Clearing his throat, Lafrenière blurted out that they had brought in only 800 grams.

"You were supposed to bring in 3 kilos. Where is the rest of the stuff?" the Shah shouted angrily.

Lafrenière replied in a hoarse whisper that he had thrown the bulk of the heroin into a garbage heap in New Delhi.

The Shah was livid. He hurled a string of profanities at the hapless Lafrenière, then turned to his sidekick and spat out something in Farsi. Collecting his wits, the Shah calmly instructed Lafrenière to accompany him into the bedroom for a private chat. At that moment, the police burst in and jumped the Shah, whose right hand was wrapped tightly around a stiletto in his jacket pocket.

At the RCMP regional headquarters in Montreal's west end, the Shah opted for his right to remain silent. But before clamming up, he insisted that Yazdani knew nothing about the heroin deal, that he was only along for the ride.

Westlake chuckled. "We got an ace in the hole because our double agent made three one-gram buys of heroin from Yazdani. So we still have that bastard by the balls."

On October 19, Duchesneau gave the green light to his officers to launch a major offensive on the shooting galleries infecting Park Extension. Led by heavily armed SWAT teams, the drug squad battered down the doors of five shooting galleries in the predominantly Greek working-class area of the city.

In one cockroach-infested flat that reeked of body odor, urine and rotting garbage, the police found nine young men lying on the floor nodding off in a heroin-induced stupor. The junkies, who ranged in age from sixteen to twenty-five, had shot up moments before, yet there were only three syringes on the blood-splattered living-room floor. Green plastic garbage bags covered up the windows and discarded, yellow-stained mattresses were strewn over the living-room and bedroom floors.

"Aren't any of you assholes worried about catching AIDS?" a young undercover officer shouted in disgust. "You can get AIDS sharing needles. Don't you know that?"

No one responded.

Westlake surveyed the heap of bodies handcuffed face down on the living-room floor. "They don't give a shit about AIDS. Their only concern is getting their fix. Nothing else matters. Not their families, not their friends, not even their pathetic lives. Smack controls their lives."

At another flat, the SWAT team moved in with incredible speed and precision. Using a steel battering ram, they broke down the door and charged into the narrow hallway. With automatic rifles cocked, they swept into one room after another, ordering people to lie on the floor face down. While one officer kept his assault rifle trained on the startled and terrified suspects, another SWAT member handcuffed them. In less than a minute, a half-dozen young men and women were sprawled out on the floor in various rooms throughout the flat.

One woman, her face covered with glistening beads of sweat and pock-marked with acne scars, sat alone propped up against a wall in a dank-smelling bedroom. She was in a daze, staring blankly at the ceiling. Her eyes looked dead. A rubber band hung loosely from her right arm and a used syringe lay by her side. The blood-stained needle had snagged a thick, grey dust ball.

In all, twenty-one junkies were arrested in the raids and a small quantity of smack was seized. Six individuals were charged with trafficking heroin to double agents. A 16-year-old youth, whose arms and legs were covered with needle tracks, was taken to a detention centre for young offenders.

The following afternoon, Westlake marched into the drug squad office wearing a mischievous grin. A tiny Iranian flag which he had purchased that morning for four dollars was sticking out of the breast pocket of his checkered lumberjack shirt.

"We're going to bust the rest of those bastards tonight and I'm going to wave this flag right in their smug faces when we arrest them," the detective crowed.

After months of planning and intensive undercover work, Westlake and Pitre were about to deal the final blow to the Shah's outfit. Every dealer who had sold heroin to double agents as the undercover cops worked their way into the gang's trust would be arrested that evening. Six specific gang members had been identified and their apartments earmarked for simultaneous raids to be staged at exactly 7:30 p.m.

At 5:45 p.m., fifty-one police officers gathered for a briefing at the police station in Westmount, the designated command post for the raids. Twenty-five members of the SWAT team, dressed in dark blue fatigues, bullet-proof vests and black paratrooper boots, had been pressed into service. The elite tactical squad would take care of battering down doors, and disarming and securing the occupants before the twenty-two drug squad officers and four RCMP narcotics investigators moved in to make the formal arrests and to search the premises for heroin.

"L'heure pour la frappe est 19:30," Lieutenant-Detective Claude Morin, the commanding officer, shouted out to the officers jammed into the old municipal courtroom on the second floor of the police station.

Detailed floor plans of five separate apartments on Mackay Street, de Maisonneuve Boulevard, Grand Boulevard, Terrebonne Street, and Ste. Famille Street, were pinned up on aluminum easels. The SWAT squad was broken down into five teams, and each was assigned an apartment. On individual clipboards and in their minds, each member rehearsed the take-down over and over. Their lives depended on split-second timing.

The RCMP and drug squad officers rechecked the paper work, especially the search and arrest warrants, making doubly certain everything was in order. The tension was electric.

At precisely 7:10 p.m., a small convoy of police cars and vans converged on a massive parking lot outside the Rose-bowl Lanes in Notre Dame de Grâce. Westlake and Pitre picked the apartment on Grand Boulevard as their target. It was the suspected operating base of Ali Reza Oraki, and Pitre desperately wanted to be the one to arrest him. The image of Oraki giving him the finger was still branded in his mind.

The apartment at 2095 Grand was considered the most difficult and dangerous of the five busts. The SWAT team would not be able to use their infamous steel battering ram to gain access because the door of the second-floor apartment was barricaded with a "New York stop", a four-by-four wedged between a two-by-four nailed into the floor and another two-by-four nailed into the door. After several intense discussions, it was decided that a double agent would have to surface and blow his cover to gain access to the apartment.

At 7:25 p.m., the signal came over the police radios, and the motorcade moved out, splitting off in different directions. In a vacant lot up the street from the Grand apartment building, the SWAT team jumped out of the van with the double agent in tow, and stealthily moved over lawns and fences like trained assassins. They darted into the building and raced up a back stairwell. Once they were in place on the second-floor corridor, with their backs pressed up against the walls on each side of the apartment door, the agent knocked. An eyeball squinted in the peephole. The thud of a heavy wooden object told the SWAT team that the New York stop had been removed. As the door began to open, they rammed through with blinding speed.

Seconds later, Westlake and Pitre were in the room standing over two handcuffed Iranians who were lying on their stomachs on a floor covered with a soiled, matted, orange shag rug. Towering over one of the suspects, Westlake yelled: "You! Look up! Smile for the camera!" A police photographer began taking pictures with a Polaroid camera.

"Tell him not to take pictures," the suspect moaned.

"Shut up! It's for my family album," Westlake quipped.

"I have a family too."

"Well, you should have thought about them before getting involved in drug dealing," Westlake shot back.

"I don't know what you're talking about," the man said.

"Shut up. I don't want to hear your voice." Westlake read him his rights. "You're under arrest for trafficking in heroin. You have the right to remain silent . . ."

On a filthy kitchen counter, encrusted with rotting scraps, were two syringes and a spoon which had just been used to prepare a few hits of smack. A drug squad officer pulled on a pair of medical rubber gloves and began to go through the kitchen cupboards. A swarm of cockroaches scurried across the counter as he lifted the lid on a dented yellow bread box.

"*Tabarnac*, I hate this job. Look at the way these pigs live. It's incredible," the officer said.

Pitre emerged out of a back room. He was miffed. Oraki was not in the apartment.

"Take them in. We're heading over to 2150 Mackay Street," Westlake said.

On the sixth floor of the highrise on Mackay Street across the street from Concordia University's downtown Hall Building campus, the SWAT team had no trouble ramming through the apartment door, startling the three men inside.

"What is your status here in Canada?'" a drug squad detective bellowed to one of the men who was lying on his stomach on the parquet wood floor of the tiny studio apartment with his hands chained behind his back.

"I am a political refugee," he spat with contempt.

The cop dropped to his knees inches from the suspect's face and screamed: "Don't give me that political refugee crap. You're a piece of shit. You come here to sell drugs to our Canadian kids. You're a piece of shit."

Turning to the other man, the officer yelled: "Look up! What's your name? Well, look who we have here. Ali Reza Oraki. Pitre will be very happy to see you when he gets here."

Three police officers meticulously combed the shabby apartment for heroin, finding small stashes concealed in the windowsills. While the search was underway, at least a half-dozen customers showed up, darting back into the elevator when they saw two burly SWAT paratroopers guarding the entrance to the apartment with automatic rifles.

By the end of the evening, the operation had netted a dozen people, including the six dealers the police had been looking for, and about 60 grams of heroin. One woman and her five-year-old daughter were also swept up in the raids. They were released after a couple of hours, but police learned later that the girl had been sexually abused by the dope dealer who was dating the child's mother. (Westlake, a father of two children, was disgusted when he found out later by accident that a kindergarten teacher had reported a suspicion of child abuse to Children's Aid authorities weeks earlier. The social worker assigned to the case had never bothered to call in the police to initiate an investigation.)

At the Westmount police station, the suspects were questioned well into the early morning hours. Oraki, a tall, handsome, dark-haired man, was brought in for interrogation shortly after midnight. He was seated beside a desk in the squad room on the second floor. He forced out a meek grin when he saw Pitre.

Westlake and Pitre were going to see if they could get Oraki to turn informer.

"You remember me?" Pitre asked. "A few months ago. Remember on Fort Street. We had a little fight together. I brought you to Station 25 and I told you one day I would get you with this." The detective waved a pen inches from his prisoner's face. A pen was all he needed to complete the paperwork that would put his man in jail.

Oraki smiled sheepishly.

"So you think I forgot. But now I got the charges on you. Eight fuckin' big charges for trafficking in heroin since four months. I got you by the balls. Is that clear enough?"

Oraki began to squirm uneasily in his chair.

"You ever sell heroin?" Westlake asked.

The Iranian shook his head.

"I guess you don't know what heroin is?"

Oraki nodded.

"You know what color it is?" Westlake continued.

Again the suspect shook his head.

Pitre chuckled. "I like that."

"You know the name 'heroin'? You know the name 'liar'?" Westlake shouted.

"I have you. You're my best friend in town," Pitre interjected. He was beaming.

Westlake slammed his hand onto the desk. "You sell heroin to kids, Canadian kids, to make money. Just wait. You're going to see your friend [the double agent] coming to court in the [witness] box. You're going to look. The guy is going to say, 'Oraki, One, two, three, four, five, six, seven, eight. Eight times, heroin.' And you're going to say, 'No, not him. Police? Not police.' Yeah, police."

Pitre jumped in: "You're not going to get out for ten years. Believe me. You're not getting out."

"It's too bad Canada's a good country because me, if I had my way with you, I'd hang you or shoot you, you bastard," Westlake spat. "In Iran they would hang you for dealing heroin."

"They would do that. That I know," Pitre added. "I know in Iran if they catch you with heroin, you're fuckin' dead, man."

"You a junkie? You shoot?" Westlake asked.

Oraki mumbled he didn't.

"You drink beer?" Westlake asked.

"You bright?" Pitre asked.

"What?" Oraki looked confused.

"College?" Westlake shouted. "Smart boy. We have a problem with heroin. You want to help us. We need help."

Oraki grinned. He quickly caught on that his interrogators wanted him to roll over and become an informant. He would have no part of it. After two hours, the detectives sent him back to his cell and called in the next suspect.

On November 24, 1988, Oraki pleaded guilty to trafficking in heroin and was sentenced to four years in a federal penitentiary. Westlake predicted that the Iranian would be out on parole in sixteen months.

A week after the raids, Westlake received a telephone death threat at his home. His phone number is unlisted. The following week, the body of one of Westlake's Iranian drug informants was discovered in a laneway. He had been clubbed over the head and stabbed twenty-one times. And a week later, the informant's best friend was shot to death in his sports car on a downtown street.

In mid-March, 1989, Amadzadegan and Yazdani, who had been denied bail and had been in jail since their arrest, pleaded not guilty to possession of heroin for the purposes of trafficking and conspiracy to import heroin. They were denied bail. The two men opted for a jury trial in Quebec Superior Court before Justice Louis Tannenbaum. The most damaging witnesses were Lafrenière and Stephan, who had pleaded guilty to drug importation charges in October, 1988, and were sentenced to five years each.

On March 28, after three days of deliberation, the eight-man, four-woman jury found the two men guilty. At their April 20 sentencing hearing, federal Crown prosecutor Richard Starck forcefully argued for sentences of twenty-five years to life for both men. In a tough pre-sentence submission, Mr. Starck stressed that the Shah was "a drug kingpin" and that Yazdani was his "right-hand man". The prosecutor urged the judge to send a message to the public by making examples of the duo. Judge Tannenbaum complied, sentencing each man to twenty-five years in federal penitentiary. It was one of the harshest penalties meted out to drug pushers in recent years.

Westlake and Pitre looked at each other in delighted amazement when informed of the sentences, then nodded their approval.

"For once, my friend, the justice system worked," Westlake said.

3

China White

Hong Kong is a city drunk with money. Its gleaming office towers, swank hotels, dazzling jewellery shops and posh highrise condos reverberate with the clink of cash. Elegantly suited businessmen with attentive ears glued to cellular telephones sputter through the traffic-snarled streets in their Rolls-Royces, Jaguars and Mercedes. Top-designer fashions, mink coats, diamonds, emeralds, rubies and gold – lots of gold – adorn stunning China doll starlets and strikingly refined "number one" wives. Life is lived to the height of decadence.

But in its soul, if it has one, Hong Kong is suffering. It is afflicted with the 1997 jitters – that year, Britain's lease on the Crown colony ends, and Hong Kong reverts to the People's Republic of China. Throughout the tiny island, an undercurrent of worry pinches at its seams, and furrows of concern are etched on the faces of thousands of anxious residents who, every working day, line up outside the Commission of Canada and the consulates of other Western countries hoping to get their hands on the one precious piece of paper that will guarantee them safe passage to the West in the event that life becomes too uncomfortable under the communist Chinese.

A handful of Western nations, especially Canada, is actively courting Hong Kong's upper crust. A talkative contingent of federal and provincial bureaucrats spend long hours extolling the virtues of investing in Canada. Cadres of immigration lawyers and consultants jet into the colony every week offering advice, seminars and colorful slide-show presentations in their quest for a slice of the Hong Kong pie. And they are getting results. Thousands of wealthy Hong Kong citizens have opted for a change of address, albeit in many instances they are taking their second choice. The preferred destination is the United States, but the Americans are not as receptive or as beguiled by the glitter of gold as Canada appears to be.

Part of the American government's reticence to roll out the red carpet to Hong Kong investor immigrants comes from information stored in computer data banks in the vaults of the U.S. Drug Enforcement Administration. The DEA has an active force in the colony. Their intelligence-gathering experts know full well how many of the natives have made their millions. They know a lot about the seedy underworld of Hong Kong, and they are not about to exacerbate the already disastrous drug situation in the U.S.

Hong Kong is the home base of extremely powerful and wealthy Triads – secret criminal societies that date back to the seventeenth century in mainland China. These Chinese crime syndicates have been a serious problem in Hong Kong ever since the British leased the property from China in 1842. They are involved in every conceivable criminal pursuit – corruption, extortion, gambling, assault, armed robbery, theft, prostitution, loan sharking, protection and murder. But the foundation of Triad wealth and power is "China White" heroin, which comes from a wedge of rugged mountainous rain forest in the northern regions of Burma, Thailand and Laos known as the Golden Triangle. Triad members control the global consumption of China White from the area, which produces 60 per cent of the world's opium and heroin. In fact, the modern-day story of the Triads is inseparably intertwined with the heroin trade in Southeast Asia. Heroin has given these criminal syndicates access to staggering profits and has made many of their leaders respected multimillionaires.

Hong Kong police intelligence estimates the profits pouring annually into various syndicate coffers from the sale of China White in the billions of dollars. This wealth wreaks havoc with law enforcement, they say. It can buy and sell top government officials, judges and cops with the snap of a finger.

Canadian law enforcement agencies have only recently become seriously concerned about Triads. They worry that Triad members are heading to Canada in increasing numbers, largely because gang leaders fear their activities will be severely curtailed in 1997. "These gangs have made a fortune in Southeast Asia selling China White heroin," an RCMP drug investigator said. "The wealthy gang leaders are getting jittery. They don't know what will happen when the People's Republic takes over, and they don't want to stick around to find out."

A detailed RCMP analysis of Triads notes that, in the years just after the Second World War, the gangs assisted the Chinese nationalist forces of Chiang Kai-shek, who were battling the communists headed by Mao Tse-tung. "This is something the People's Republic of China [PRC] has neither forgiven nor forgotten," says the 1987 report. "Hong Kong Triad members know this and also realize that the PRC is still enforcing criminal law in a harsh manner." When asked in an interview for a Hong Kong newspaper about Beijing's policy on criminal activity when it takes control of the colony, a senior PRC official replied coldly that the bullet had been beneficial in reducing the crime rate in China. "The Triads are not prepared to face that kind of enforcement and, most certainly, the more influential members will attempt to set up elsewhere, with Canada being one of their prime targets," the RCMP analysis notes.

A senior RCMP drug investigator in Vancouver warned: "For many powerful Triad bosses, Canada has become a prime target to move their operations and their wealth, and Canadian law enforcement is totally unprepared for them. The Triads will have a field day in this country."

What particularly irks some drug investigators is the attitude of the Canadian government toward Hong Kong investors. "Too many government officials, especially in Immigration and External Affairs, are a little too naive about what is really happening," one investigator complained. "The federal government is laying out the red carpet for any Hong

Kong businessman who has a million bucks. They're blinded by the dollar signs. What we don't know is just how much of this money is dirty money made from the sale of heroin. And we don't know just how many of these people are members of these secret criminal societies known as Triads.

"You are going to see more and more money pouring into Canada as the 1997 deadline approaches, and you're going to see more and more people buying up important businesses and amassing vast real estate holdings. Much of it may be legitimate, earned by hard, honest work. But mark my words, a lot of it will be dirty money, made by ruthless gangsters from the drug trade, prostitution, gambling and extortion. These gangsters know they will not be able to function under the communist regime so they are preparing to leave and bring their organized crime syndicates here. I would say we've got a lot to be worried about."

In its 1988 report, the Canadian Association of Chiefs of Police decided the time had come to elevate Triads to the same level as the Mafia and outlaw motorcycle gangs. "Triad organizations have gained a foothold in Canada and the United States," the report stated. "Law enforcement agencies have recognized the need to share intelligence information in an effort to effectively combat this growth. . . . It will be a continuous long-term battle."

The police chiefs also warned that Asian organized crime will become a significant problem in Canada during the next decade, not only as the gangs fight among themselves for supremacy, but also as they clash with established underworld drug syndicates for a larger share of the market outside their community. Once they are firmly established in Canada, powerful Triad leaders will use their operations here as a power base from which to direct their international criminal activities.

Fuelled by staggering profits from the heroin trade, Chinese Triads have established a virtually impenetrable crime underworld in Hong Kong. They have invested billions of dollars into legitimate businesses – hotels, construction companies, office towers, clothing factories, exclusive jewellery stores and posh restaurants. And through these legitimate enterprises flow the gains of their illegal pursuits. It is a world where no whites are allowed. And it is a world that few Western law enforcement agencies have given any serious attention to, simply because they cannot and do not understand it. "We've left it alone for just that reason. We don't understand the language or the culture. We can't infiltrate it so we ignore it, hoping that it will simply go away," a member of the Asian Organized Crime Squad in Metropolitan Toronto confessed.

The difficulty for Canadian police is that these Triads are a world unto themselves. They are shrouded in 300 years of mythology and ritual. The word "Triad" refers to the society's symbol – an equilateral triangle which represents the mystical relationship among Heaven, Earth and Man. The Chinese name for Triad is the "Black Society".

The Triads evolved from noble beginnings. Legend has it that they were formed in 1674 during the second Manchu Emperor K'ang Hsi's reign. During that period, the country was invaded and the Emperor called for volunteers. The temple abbot in Shao Lin, in Fukien province, had trained his Buddhist monks in the martial arts. They responded to the Emperor's call and, because of their superior fighting skills, soundly defeated the attackers. The abbot was endowed the imperial seal, which gave any document he signed the force of a royal decree, and his 128 monks were showered with honors. Later, the Emperor grew fearful of the monks because of their popularity and their extraordinary skills in the martial arts, and ordered his armies to destroy them and the temple. Only five monks survived the purge and they came to be known as the Five Ancestors of the Triad. They underwent a number of mystical ceremonies and became united by one common goal – to destroy the Manchu dynasty. The surviving monks split up and founded five lodges in the five main provinces of China. During the eighteenth and nineteenth centuries, the Triads flourished throughout China, adhering strictly to their original goal of assisting those in need. In China and throughout the world where Chinese communities sprang up, Triad lodges were formed so that their members could protect their interests in an often hostile environment. In many countries, Chinese immigrants found that they simply could not get any help unless they joined a secret society. Between 1840 and 1910, the Triads began to fall under the control of greedy individuals and they rapidly degenerated into merciless, profit-driven criminal organizations that preyed on the Chinese community.

To become a Triad member, certain initiation rites must be followed. First, the ceremony must be held in a designated Triad lodge decorated with the appropriate flags, banners and ancestral titles. The recruits are required to recite thirty-six oaths of loyalty. Those oaths are written on a yellow paper along with the names of all the participants at the ceremony. The "burning of the yellow paper" is a solemn and important feature of the rite. The ashes are mixed into a bowl of wine with blood drawn from the left index finger of each recruit in a blood-brotherhood ritual, which is drunk by all those present. The bowl is then smashed to symbolize the fate of anyone who is a traitor to the oaths. One oath states that traitorous acts such as disclosure of the society's activities will result in the execution of the member and his entire immediate family. The recruit pledges unwavering loyalty to the cause.

Lee Cheung (not his real name) was only fourteen years old when he was initiated into the Sun Yee On Triad. "It was very late, after midnight, and it was very hot and muggy," the Vancouver restaurant worker, who is now fifty-eight, recalled. "There were about a dozen of us. All quite young. Some were twelve and thirteen. It was a very long ceremony held in a very large cavern under a building. There were probably fifty adult Triad members in attendance. They wore white head-bands. The Incense Master read aloud many oaths and made us swear to many things including eternal allegiance to the Triad. And then he pricked our finger, drew blood and mixed it in a cup with wine and we all drank."

Cheung said he remained an insignificant cog in the secret

society, and maintained he never committed any criminal acts for his group. His job, which he performed for more than two dozen years, was to act as a floorman for illegal gambling houses.

At the head of the traditional Triad hierarchy or chain of command is the Dragon Head or Shan Chu. He is given the number 489. The deputy head or Second Route Marshal, who is also the assistant Mountain Lord, is Fu Chan Chu. He is accorded the number 438. The Vanguard is Sing Fung and he is responsible for recruiting new members. Heung Chu is the Incense Master. Both he and Sing Fung, who also are 438s, officiate at Triad ceremonies. Hung Kwan, 426, is the Red Pole, the enforcer, head fighter and battle strategist. He is the most feared as he is often a master of the martial arts, and the group's discipline master.

Cho Hai, 432, is the Straw Sandal. He acts as the liaison or messenger, communicating with members. He also assists the Red Pole in developing battle strategy and organizes summits with other Triads. His tasks involve the delivering of ransom notes and the collection of protection money. His number breaks down into 4 x 32, which equals 128, the original number of monks at the Shao Lin temple. Myth has it that it was the legendary Sandal who miraculously changed into a boat to carry to safety the surviving monks who were being pursued by the Emperor's army. Pak Sze Sin, 415, is the White Paper Fan. He is the general administrator and advisor to the Triad. The rank and file are known as Sze Kau and are assigned the number 49.

All members must learn a myriad of secret hand signs, signals and code phrases. Certain hand gestures indicate the member's rank within the Triad, and in times of trouble code signs can be used to find shelter and protection. For example, a member needing help puts a full cup of Chinese tea in front of the pot. If a brother can help, he will drink the tea. Otherwise, he will throw out the contents and refill the cup.

Because ordinary conversation might reveal too much to prying ears, Triads use code phrases. For example, "a draught of wind" means a cop or informant has just drifted in. "Wash a body" is to kill someone; "wash a face" is to cut off the head; "bite clouds" is to smoke opium; "wave the willow" is to urinate; and "son of a leper" refers to a non-member.

As with all criminal organizations, the long arm of the law has put the Triads on the defensive. It has been illegal to be a member of a Triad in Hong Kong since 1952, so the gangs are extremely careful about holding meetings. Triad leaders are now worried about police raids on their secret lodges. As a result, traditional initiation ceremonies, which are long, elaborate and complicated, have been shunted aside for a significantly abbreviated version called Lighting the Blue Lantern. The casting aside of ritual has caused distress among old-time members who argue that it has led to the disintegration of once-powerful Triads by younger, money-grubbing members who care little about such attributes as loyalty and a code of honor.

Hong Kong police estimate that there are some 100,000 members in some 55 Triads in the tiny British colony of 5.6 million people. About 15 Triads are known to be active in criminal pursuits. In comparison, the U.S. President's Commission on Organized Crime in 1986 concluded that there were 24 Italian organized crime families in the United States with 2,000 lifetime members and upwards of 35,000 associates.

The Triads have much in common with the Mafia. During the 1850s and 1860s, patriotic Mafia families played a key role in the unification of Italy and, during that same period, Triad rebels in China were leading the Taiping rebellion against the Ching Dynasty. Both groups began as secret societies with political agendas, and both eventually became corrupt, using their power to further criminal activities. The Mafia and the Triads value silence and use secret rituals to promote loyalty and bonding. They value honor and family. Both increased their power base by preying on their own immigrant communities in countries like Canada and the U.S. As newcomers, both groups faced discrimination and felt they needed a strong organization to protect their interests and resolve disputes.

Canadian police believe there are at most six Triads operating in the country with a core membership of about 500 people. At present, these societies largely exploit their own community, whose members are too afraid to complain to the police. As a result, there has been little attention focused by police on the growing crime threat in Canada's Chinatowns, and certainly no pressure on politicians to deal with it.

RCMP intelligence warns that with 1997 fast approaching, many wealthy Hong Kong families have already moved huge sums of money and established their children in countries around the world, particularly in Canada and Australia. RCMP reports also highlight federal immigration statistics which show that, throughout the 1980s, Hong Kong has continued to be one of the highest intake areas for immigrants to Canada. "With this increase, a heightened vigil awareness within the law enforcement community is required to identify Triad members attempting to emigrate to Canada," wrote RCMP Corporal R.B. Hamilton, who is attached to the Asian Organized Crime Squad Joint Forces Operations with the Metropolitan Toronto Police force in Toronto.

In a lengthy and detailed analysis written in 1987 on the Triad threat, Corporal Hamilton noted that since many Triad officials would not meet Canada's basic immigration criteria as independent immigrants, "they are looking for other ways" to get into the country. The Mountie pointed out that "three separate reliable information sources have indicated that many Hong Kong executive-level Triad members plan to emigrate to Canada" under the federal government's highly touted entrepreneur program. While acknowledging that the entrepreneur program benefits Canada, Corporal Hamilton stressed that "a high degree of vigilance is necessary to identify organized crime figures using such programs as a means to enter Canada. The vast majority of immigrants of course are good, honest, hard-working people who will be able to contribute to Canadian society. But, there will be a small percentage of hard-core criminals who will continue their lives of crime here," he warned.

Since 1984, Hong Kong power brokers have moved billions of dollars in cash and assets to Canada, and the source of much of the money, police say, is almost impossible to trace. Long ago, Triad financial wizards established a money-laundering scheme that has baffled the most highly trained chartered accountants. Referred to as the Chinese underground banking system, it operates through gold shops, money changers and trading companies, which are often controlled in various countries by the same family. Through this banking system percolate the profits from China White sales around the world.

This underground network grew out of political instability in countries where large Chinese communities suffered under communist take-overs. It is used to transfer funds from one country to another by simply depositing money in a family-controlled business in one country, and receiving it (less a transaction fee) at a family-controlled business in another country. What is particularly bothersome to law enforcement agencies around the world is that record-keeping under this system is practically non-existent, leaving no audit trail to follow. Coded messages on a chit authorize the delivery and pickup of huge sums of cash.

Hong Kong is also one of the most important banking centres in the world, where, according to a confidential CIA report, more than $50 billion (U.S.) is exchanged on an average business day. The colony has no central bank, no currency exchange controls and no reporting requirements for cash deposits. A confidential U.S. Department of Justice report notes that Hong Kong "has become an important collection point for cash from Southeast Asian heroin. Also, a growing number of South American drug traffickers are using Hong Kong for their money-laundering needs. Meanwhile, a lot of this money is returning to the U.S., and one indication that returning money has been laundered is the small denomination of the bills. According to a Treasury Department study, approximately 35 per cent of the cash repatriated from Hong Kong is in bills of $50 or less."

In late 1987, the U.S. Customs Service completed an examination of currency transactions reports, which are required by law to be filled out on all cash transactions in the U.S. involving $10,000 or more. It found that between January, 1983, and August, 1986, a total of $1.7 billion came into the U.S. from Hong Kong while only $60 million went out to the colony. "The difference consists of laundered funds returning to the U.S. plus the effects of capital flight from Hong Kong," the Customs Service concluded.

The U.S. Justice Department report points out that "most of the incoming money . . . is being invested in commercial property: office buildings, shopping centres, apartment houses, restaurants, etc. For dirty money, this represents the end of its movement." The report also notes that "the wave of buying with front-end cash and no leverage has pushed up real estate prices in all large Chinese population centres. . . . In Toronto, real estate prices have doubled in three years because of Chinese investments."

Intelligence gathered on Triads in North America shows that close ties are maintained between these secret societies in Hong Kong, Vancouver, Toronto, New York and San Francisco. Toronto and Vancouver have been identified by investigators with the DEA and the U.S. Justice Department as major links in the heroin-smuggling syndicates controlled by various Triad interests, individual gang members and Chinese criminal organizations operating in the U.S. and Canada.

DEA intelligence indicates that key members of various Triads based in Hong Kong control the flow of heroin at every step of the process, moving large shipments from remote jungle laboratories in the Golden Triangle to distribution networks throughout North America, Western Europe and Southeast Asia, and ultimately into the thirsty veins of hundreds of thousands of heroin addicts.

Every autumn in the Golden Triangle, thousands of impoverished hill-tribe peasants slash and burn hundreds of acres of prime forest to clear a patch of land in which to plant tiny, black poppy seeds. After a few months, the steep hillsides are covered in a lush, floral tapestry of crimson reds, dusty pinks, lemon yellows and deep violets. Once the poppy petals fall to the ground, the peasants swarm over the fields with small, three-pronged carving knives, making shallow horizontal incisions into the green, egg-sized poppy pods protruding from spindly four-foot stems. Within seconds, a thick, milk-white sap begins to ooze onto the surface of the pod. As it congeals, it turns brownish-black. The next morning, the peasants flock back to the fields to scrape the hardened residue of raw opium off the pods. The work is gruelling; an entire acre yields only about 2 kilograms of raw opium. For the impoverished hill-tribe peasants, opium represents their most lucrative cash crop, paying up to $1600 for 10 kilograms.

In March, 1989, the International Narcotics Control Strategy Report, released by the U.S. Department of State Bureau of International Narcotics Matters, estimated that the Golden Triangle produced between 1,298 and 1,833 tonnes of opium in 1988.

The thunderous clap of helicopter blades ricocheting off the mountain walls sent a dozen hill-tribe men, women and children scurrying to a safe distance on a nearby hill. A Thai army helicopter hovered over a field covered with the bulging heads of flowering poppies and disgorged forty-seven heavily armed paratroopers belonging to the elite Border Patrol Police (BPP). The operation was swift. The BPP, dressed in deep blue fatigues and wearing black berets, descended on the field like a plague of locusts, slashing down the half-metre-tall poppy plants with deliberate fury. Under the vigilant eyes of several border police armed with M-16 assault rifles, the hill-tribe people sat passively watching the destruction. On that day in late December, 1988, the border patrol levelled five plantations.

With the help of the U.S. government and the United Nations Fund for Drug Abuse Control, Thailand has made tremendous strides in the past decade in eradicating opium production with crop substitution programs in its northern regions. Opium production in that country was estimated at 22 tonnes in 1988. Just a decade ago, it was well over 100 tonnes a year. Today, the real problem lies in Burma and Laos, which, according to DEA figures, produced 1,200 and 260 tonnes respectively in 1988. The DEA also predicted no reduction in production of the 1989 opium crop. In fact, early estimates based on U.S. spy satellite photographs indicate it will be a bumper year.

A report by the U.S. Department of State Bureau of International Narcotics Matters in March, 1989, lamented that continuing civil turmoil in Burma has resulted in the suspension of the Socialist Republic of the Union of Burma's annual aerial opium eradication program, triggering increased and unchecked opium production in that country. "There has also been no reduction in opium production in Laos and there continues to be information that the extensive involvement of LPDR [Lao People's Democratic Republic] military and civilian government officials in the narcotics trade suggests this is a matter of *de facto* government policy."

Once the raw opium is collected, it is then picked up by bands of armed mercenaries commanded by opium warlords who control vast regions in the Golden Triangle. The opium is transported by porter, mule and horse caravan along winding, treacherous trails cut through dense rain forest and taken to remote jungle laboratories. There, ethnic Chiu Chau Chinese chemists transform the raw opium into morphine base. The chemists and their apprentices are brought into the jungles on a fee-for-service basis or for a percentage of the profits on the wholesale market. The term "chemist" does not imply any academic knowledge or qualification. In fact, the chemists are more like chefs mixing prescribed ingredients to a set recipe. Deviating from the recipe can result in variations of strength, taste and color. One crucial stage involves ether, and a mistake can trigger a violent and deadly explosion, which will level the lab and destroy the heroin. During the refining process, the opium is reduced to one-tenth its original weight.

At a sprawling, dusty military complex outside Chiang Mai in northern Thailand, the commander of the Border Patrol Police described the refining process at a makeshift jungle lab set up in a large conference room adjacent to his office. First, he said, the chemist heats water in a large steel drum. When it reaches the right temperature – the chemist usually knows this by testing it with his finger – the opium is dumped in and stirred until it dissolves. Lime is then added, causing the morphine to bubble to the surface in a white froth and the vegetable materials to sink to the bottom of the drum as sludge. The froth is quickly scooped out and filtered through flannel cloth into a nearby drum. At this stage, ammonium chloride is added, causing the morphine to solidify and sink to the bottom. After separating and drying, the morphine looks like finely ground coffee, and still possesses the distinct, pungent odor of opium.

The chemist must now decide whether to produce heroin number 3, a smokable form preferred by the majority of heroin addicts in Asia, or heroin number 4, the injectable form preferred by the more than 750,000 addicts in North America. Number 3 is beige in color, granular in form, and normally has a purity of about 40 to 60 per cent. It is not water-soluble and cannot be injected. Number 4 is a fine, fluffy, white powder with a purity of anywhere from 85 to 99 per cent.

Notes seized from a Chiu Chau chemist show that the recipes for both types of heroin are almost identical, except for the final "crystallization" stage producing number 4 heroin. The process involves heating the morphine with a slightly more than equal weight of acetic anhydride in an enamel bin or glass flask. After about six hours, the morphine and the acid become chemically bonded, creating diacetylmorphine (the chemical name for heroin). After being allowed to cool, the compound is treated with water and chloroform to dissolve the impurities which sink to the bottom of the container. The top aqueous layer is then drained off by decanting or siphoning into another drum. Sodium carbonate or ammonia is added to this liquid to neutralize the acetic acid, making the solution alkaline. After standing for a while, the heroin will slowly precipitate and is then removed by filtration. At the end of this stage, the product is heroin number 3.

The same steps are followed in the manufacture of number 4 heroin up to and including the point where the heroin is separated from the solution by the addition of sodium carbonate. At this point, it is dissolved in ethyl alcohol, then filtered through a layer of activated charcoal and filter paper to remove impurities. In the final stage, concentrated hydrochloric acid is added to the alcohol solution along with an amount of ether equivalent to at least twice the volume of alcohol. The pure heroin hydrochloride, which is not soluble in ether, then precipitates from the solution. At this stage in the process, the recipe seized from a Chiu Chau chemist states: ". . .add 2-3 mugs of ether, and a few minutes later when flashing like golden stars is seen, add more ether slowly. Meanwhile, stir evenly with a bamboo spatula until the crystals are completely formed. (Add faster if it forms quickly, slow down if it forms slowly.)"

On a cool evening in late December, thirty-two BPP troops were assembled at the border patrol complex outside Chiang Mai and briefed on the location of a jungle refinery operating in Thailand several kilometres from the Burmese border. Under the cover of darkness, the troops moved out in a convoy of military pick-up trucks which took them as far as the crude back-road networks would allow. They then marched throughout the night through mountainous terrain. At dawn, they sighted the laboratory secluded in dense brush near a stream. It was guarded by two dozen heavily armed men. A 25-minute gun battle ensued before the insurgents and chemists fled into the jungle. Two BPP soldiers were wounded. When the soldiers finally overran the camp, they quickly realized they had hit a very large refinery. They seized 46.3 kilograms of wet heroin number 4 and another 3.1 kilograms of number 4 heroin packed in bricks. They also found 143 kilograms of opium cooking in chemical solutions; 22 kilograms of chemicals; a large quantity of ammunition; and a vast array of pots, pans, funnels, flasks, stoves and hoses.

In 1988, the BPP raided and dismantled ten clandestine heroin refineries operating in Thailand near the Burmese border. Several Thai soldiers and refinery guards were killed or wounded in those raids.

Chiang Mai, in northern Thailand, was the thirteenth-century walled capital of a former independent kingdom. Today, it is a colorful, bustling tourist town. It is also the principal centre for consummating heroin deals in Southeast Asia. At the end of the opium harvest, narcotics dealers in the upper echelons of various Triads send their middlemen into Chiang Mai to get their orders filled and to hammer out the finer details of delivery with middlemen working for seemingly untouchable heroin kingpins.

In swank hotel suites, guarded by heavily armed local thugs, deals involving several tons of China White are sealed with a handshake and a quick trip to a local bank where millions of dollars are transferred with a simple phone call. A lot of that money will be channelled into the accounts of any of a score of opium warlords who control rival free-lance insurgency groups totalling more than 40,000 armed men holed up in the mountains of the Golden Triangle. Although many of these insurgent armies claim to be fighting for loftier ideals, like independence and democracy, the reality is that their struggles have little to do with any noble cause. They are in the insurgency business for the money.

The most notorious warlord is Chang Chi-Fu, and he is on the most-wanted list of practically every drug enforcement agency in the world. He calls himself Khun Sa. Khun means "lord" in Burmese. His claim to royalty comes from his mother's side. She apparently remarried a Shan *sawbwa* or prince. Sa is his stepfather's name.

Half Shan (an ethnic minority in northern Burma) and half Chinese, the 56-year-old opium warlord, who has been called the Prince of Darkness and the King of Opium, is reputed to control 70 per cent of the opium and heroin trade in the Golden Triangle. Like a medieval lord, he has ruled his mountainous fiefdom with an iron fist for more than a quarter-century. Khun Sa is the commander of his own private, well-armed and tightly disciplined 15,000-man private force called the Shan United Army (SUA), which is financed totally by drug money. A millionaire many times over, he is clever, politically astute and ruthless. Villagers suspected of being government informers are buried alive. Deserters from his army are tracked down and shot.

As elusive as he is powerful, Khun Sa is rarely seen by westerners. Born in northern Burma, he turned to soldiering at a young age. His checkered and colorful career is a series of mishaps, defeats, incredible comebacks and bizarre alliances in the netherworld of the Golden Triangle. In 1963, the Burmese government authorized Khun Sa to form a local militia of several hundred men in the Shan States to combat Shan rebels. The militia, called Ka Kwe Ye or KKY, was given few weapons, and no money, rations or uniforms. As payment for their support in rooting out rebels, the Burmese government turned a blind eye to their opium-smuggling enterprises. A year after forming his KKY, the ambitious rebel warlord parlayed the small fortune he had amassed from the opium trade into a well-armed militia of 800 men. He then abandoned the Shan States for the Wa States near the Thai border, where poppy growing was more bountiful. He also built the first crude jungle laboratories inside Thailand for refining opium into morphine bricks, and was, by this time, exporting large quantities of opium into the country. By 1966, he had expanded his KKY to 2,000 men, but, despite the size and might of his army, he still controlled only a small portion of the opium traffic.

The Kuomintang generals, remnants of Chiang Kai-shek's nationalist Third and Fifth armies, were the real opium warlords, controlling 90 per cent of the trade in the Golden Triangle. In fact, the KMT generals almost wiped out Khun Sa in what has become known as the 1967 Opium War. Khun Sa angered the KMT when he challenged their dominance in the opium trade by sending a well-armed, 300-mule caravan carrying 14 tonnes of opium through KMT-controlled territory in June, 1967. The shipment was purportedly worth $500,000 wholesale in Chiang Mai, and Khun Sa was reportedly going to use his profits to further expand his army by 1,000 men, thereby challenging the 3,200-man force of the combined KMT Third and Fifth armies. The KMT generals moved against the caravan as it crossed into Laos. The ensuing battle was fierce, and the so-called Shan prince was the big loser. In beating a hasty retreat, he left behind 14 tonnes of opium, thousands of dollars in weapons and mules, and much of his influence and prestige.

Two years later, he was arrested by the Burmese government and jailed. Khun Sa was thought to be eliminated as a major player in the opium trade once and for all. Then in 1973, one of his loyal and trusted lieutenants kidnapped two Soviet doctors in Rangoon and exchanged them for his jailed leader. Khun Sa hastily reassembled his ragtag army and dubbed it the Shan United Army in hopes of improving his political image. He then went to work to take over the opium market in the Golden Triangle, forging alliances where necessary and turning his back on others when it suited his goals. That same year, he moved his headquarters into Ban Hin Taek in northern Thailand, a rugged, mountain-top frontier village near the Burma border. For almost a decade, he operated his opium empire with impunity and increased his army to more than 4,000 men.

The Thai government refrained from ordering an all-out military assault on his stronghold as long as Khun Sa did not threaten Thailand's national security. But the warlord continued to grow more cocky with his increased wealth and success, and Thai officials began to see him as a serious national security problem. By 1980, he had gained so much notoriety that the U.S. government put pressure on the Thai government to do something about the imperious opium warlord. The situation exploded later that year when Joyce Powers, the wife of a DEA agent stationed in Chiang Mai, was kidnapped and murdered. Thai police attributed her death to a botched robbery attempt, but one of the top drug investigators in the country concluded that the killing was the work of Khun Sa – an accusation that the opium king flatly denies. The U.S. government demanded that the Thais retaliate. It even placed a reward on the head of Khun Sa of 500,000 baht ($25,000 Canadian). The warlord countered with a similar reward on the heads of DEA agents stationed in the Golden Triangle.

In a feeble effort to save face, the Thai government launched an attack on one of Khun Sa's heroin refineries in October, 1981. An elite force, known as the Rangers, was dispatched to the area, but word of the attack was leaked to Khun Sa by one of his many corrupt Thai officials. The Rangers were ambushed by Shan rebels, and more than half were killed or wounded before the Thai army finally went in and rescued them. This open clash on Thai soil so enraged the government that it finally decided the time had come to rid the country of Khun Sa and his private army.

In January, 1982, the Thai government sent in eight companies of the Border Patrol Police to oust Khun Sa from his plush hilltop stronghold. The three-day battle left 16 Thai soldiers dead and more than three dozen wounded. More than 70 rebels were killed and another 200 wounded. Khun Sa, who again had been tipped off about the surprise attack, retreated 25 kilometres inside Burma, leaving behind 13 tonnes of weapons, including 700 automatic rifles and pistols, 25 grenade launchers, 300 grenades and 53,000 rounds of ammunition. The Thais also found bags of acetic anhydride, the essential chemical for refining opium into heroin, and a storage room containing enough plastic bags with the infamous Double U-O Globe brand label to package sixty thousand, 800-gram units of China White.

Still nursing his wounds, Khun Sa and his SUA troops were quickly drawn into another battle. This time, he went up against the Burmese Communist Party (BCP) forces and Wa insurgents. Hundreds of troops on each side were killed before a truce was finally called in late 1983.

Again, observers thought Khun Sa's days were numbered and again he confounded his detractors. A rabid anti-communist, he forged an unholy alliance with the Burmese Communist Party, agreeing to buy their opium and refine it into heroin. The BCP were desperate for money. In 1980, the People's Republic of China had reduced its arms and financial support to the BCP, in part because of the party's failure to rally Burma's minorities and in part because China wanted to improve its international image by cutting off support to communist rebel groups operating in several countries.

Over the next few years, Khun Sa virtually forced many of the once-powerful KMT opium warlords out of the drug trade while consolidating his power in the region to a point where today he is the undisputed opium king of the Golden Triangle.

Lately, the crafty warlord, who has a keen sense of public relations, has taken to issuing press releases from his mountain retreat in an attempt to upgrade his image from drug kingpin to nationalist Shan leader and freedom fighter. He now claims he is involved in the opium trade because it is his only means of raising money to finance his noble struggle for Shan independence. Like a modern-day Robin Hood, he maintains that if his people didn't grow poppies, they would starve. "My people do not know what happens to the opium after they sell it. All they know is that they have money to buy grain," he has declared.

Drug enforcement officials in Chiang Mai shake their heads and laugh. "He's not involved in the production of opium and heroin in order to provide a better way of life for his people," a U.S. drug enforcement agent said emphatically. "This man is a drug dealer, a criminal, and he doesn't give a damn who gets hurt in his almighty pursuit of money, power and greed."

In the spring of 1989, Khun Sa made an offer to U.S. president George Bush to sell his entire opium crop to the American government for the next five years for $48 million a year. He had made a similar offer in 1977 and repeated it five years later to former President Ronald Reagan, who responded with just one word. No.

"If Mr. Bush does not throw my offer in the waste basket like the others, I will do it," Khun Sa said. But he also attached two other conditions. The Shan hill-tribes would get training in growing other crops, and roads would be built to get them to market.

As in the past, his bizarre yet provocative proposal has been met with a wall of skepticism. Hardline U.S. Congressmen shot back that they will not deal with "bums" who try to blackmail or shake down the American people. A DEA official said the U.S. government would gain nothing in acquiescing to his demands. "You simply cannot pay criminals to get them to stop their criminal activities," he said.

Khun Sa laughed at the tough stand. "If you want to stop the opium king, then you should approach the opium king and negotiate with him. If you keep doing things in the same old way, then you will never stop the heroin. Not for a hundred years!"

The opium warlords of the Golden Triangle maintain a cadre of heroin dealers in Chiang Mai, where they operate, almost with impunity, out of legitimate businesses, such as jewellery stores and clothing shops. They are the vital middle link to the international drug markets. Once the deals are struck and the money is in the bank, the heroin begins to move out of clandestine jungle refineries to the street drug bazaars around the globe.

About 7 tonnes a year with an estimated street value of $20 billion is earmarked for North American veins, the lion's share going into the United States to feed the habit of its vast army of addicts. A small portion remains in Canada to feed a user population of about 30,000.

Vancouver, Montreal and Toronto are the principal areas of

heroin abuse and distribution in Canada. At the street level, the heroin is "stepped on" or diluted by dealers to about 5 to 6 per cent purity and sold for about $35 to $65 a capsule. A kilogram of 99 per cent pure number 4 heroin is sold by criminal syndicates in Canada for upwards of $200,000. The laboratory in the Golden Triangle sells it to the middleman in Chiang Mai or Bangkok for $5,000 or $6,000 a kilogram. He then turns around and sells it for between $8,000 and $10,000. On the streets in Canada, an ounce, or 28 grams, of pure smack sells for anywhere from $6,000 to $15,000, and a pure gram sells for $1,000.

According to a 1989 RCMP drug intelligence report, the Golden Triangle is the major supplier of heroin to Canada, controlling 63 per cent of the market, "and will continue to maintain its status as the principal exporter of opiates to Canada through 1990." The Golden Crescent area of South-west Asia – a crude swath of desolate and mountainous terrain cutting through Afghanistan, Pakistan and Iran – supplies the remaining 37 per cent. It is found mostly in the heroin shooting galleries of Montreal.

Meanwhile, international drug investigations in Southeast Asia have found that Canada is the major pipeline for China White heading for the American market, and the drug connections have been linked directly to Triad gangs and individual high-ranking members based in Hong Kong, Vancouver, San Francisco, Toronto and New York City.

According to the DEA, Chinese heroin traffickers have established themselves as the dominant force in the New York heroin marketplace and, since about 1984, Hong Kong has become a major trans-shipment centre for Southeast Asian heroin. The DEA reports that, in 1982, only 3 per cent of the heroin on the streets of New York came from the Golden Triangle. In 1988, that figure rose to 78 per cent. This development is directly linked to the prosecution in the United States of several major Mafia figures in the celebrated "Pizza Connection", in which heroin was sold to addicts from family pizza outlets in various cities in the eastern states. Scores of

Mafia dons and gangsters were eventually jailed both in the U.S. and in Italy. The Chinese gangs do very little retail distribution. Instead, they depend upon existing distribution networks developed by the Mafia and other groups.

Sergeant George Cowley, a member of the Asian Organized Crime Squad for the Metro Toronto Police force, noted that Canada is a popular trans-shipment route because Hong Kong residents do not need a visa to enter the country. He explained that the average shipment of heroin brought in by a syndicate is anywhere from 40 to 50 kilograms. "It will not be smuggled in one shot. The typical method is to send a few couriers per flight with 2 to 5 kilograms taped to their bodies or concealed in their luggage. An overseer is usually on the same flight, and they'll have dummy couriers who will act nervously when they get off the airplane. Their eyes will dart around furtively and they will have a bulge under their coat. It will be like waving a flag saying 'I've got drugs, come and search me.' So all the attention goes to the smokescreen and the real couriers slip by without any notice. Once outside, they will be met by a local connection and taken to a hotel. At that point, members from the New York gangs will be contacted and they will send their people to pick up the drugs and bring them back."

In late February, 1989, an international network of heroin traffickers with direct links to Khun Sa was smashed in New York City. For a year and a half, drug investigators with the FBI, the DEA, the New York City Police Department, the RCMP in Toronto, Vancouver and Calgary, and the Royal Hong Kong Police Department stalked gang members throughout the U.S., Canada and Southeast Asia. When police finally swooped in on the drug ring, the most they thought they would seize in the bust was about 25 kilograms of heroin. What they got was a staggering 386 kilograms – more than four times the amount seized when the notorious French Connection was smashed in the early 1970s. With an estimated street value of more than $1 billion, there was enough heroin to feed the habits of half of the 200,000 addicts in the Big Apple for an entire year. The drugs were concealed inside hollowed-out, solid rubber tires, like the kind used on golf carts. More than 100 FBI agents and New York City police took part in nighttime raids on three houses in Queens, N.Y. At two of the homes, they surprised workers using paint thinner to loosen the glue that held the tires to the rims. At the third location, they found $3 million in cash. In all, forty-two people, including the suspected kingpin, were arrested in connection with the operation, which was code-named White Mare – White because that is the color of China White heroin and Mare because heroin is often referred to by drug dealers as "horse".

White Mare was sparked in October, 1987, when an FBI informant fingered a respected businessman in New York City's Chinatown as a key player in the heroin trade. The man was identified as Kok-Leung Woo, better known as Peter Woo. Born in Canton, China, in 1918, Woo had come to the United States three decades earlier. He had no criminal record, no known vices besides gambling at casinos and the racetrack, and visiting Chinatown fortune tellers to see how his luck would be on that day. The owner of Tai Pei Liquors on Mott Street in New York City's Chinatown, he dabbled in local politics and claimed he was a founding member of the China- town Democratic Club. Police later learned Woo was con- nected to the notorious 14-K Triad in Hong Kong.

A preliminary investigation soon unearthed enough evi- dence for the FBI to target the man for a full-scale undercover operation. In December, a Chinese-American agent, posing as a high-rolling drug dealer, was sent in to infiltrate Woo's drug empire. He made a number of average buys involving several hundred grams and eventually got higher and higher into the syndicate. Then in March, 1988, the undercover agent was invited by members of Woo's gang to Hong Kong to meet some major heroin wholesalers. From a series of wire- taps, and the purchases already made by the agent, the FBI had enough evidence to move in on Woo. But after a high-level conference, they decided to stick with the operation to see how far Woo could take them into the netherworld of China White.

In wiretaps of phone conversations between Woo's syndicate and its Hong Kong suppliers, conducted almost exclusively in Cantonese, there were frequent references to "pieces" and "ginseng". It was a simple code to break. Ginseng referred to heroin and pieces were tightly packed 800-gram bags of China White. On one particular wiretap in early March, Woo was heard telling an associate that his suppliers were importing "fifty pieces" into Canada for trans-shipment into New York.

The RCMP were called in, and later that month undercover Mounties tailed Woo when he arrived in Vancouver on March 21. The following day, he flew to Calgary, where he met with a contact at the airport before leaving for Hong Kong. Another phone call was intercepted in which Woo was asked if he would front $30,000 for a ginseng shipment coming through Canada.

Sitting in the officers' lounge at the headquarters of the Royal Hong Kong Police Department, Chris Cantley, superintendent with the narcotics bureau, recounted some of the intriguing events on his side of operation White Mare. "When the agent arrived in June of 1988, we had his hotel room wired for sound and video. Over the period of a month, he met with one particular gang and all the meetings took place in his room. Then he went back to the U.S."

The scope of the operation began to widen. The agent returned in September and met with a second gang, who supplied him with 2.4 kilograms of China White. He purchased it with FBI front money to "improve his credentials", Cantley said. Leaders of the second gang told the agent that they had a Canadian route for heroin shipments into the U.S. They had an established network of mules or couriers who would enter Canada through the international airports in Vancouver and Toronto. Once they were through Canada

Customs, they would contact a connection in San Francisco or New York City to arrange a drug transfer.

Shipments were arranged, and the RCMP, who were working very closely with the FBI, got the green light from their American counterparts to intercept the couriers. They had concluded that their actions would not jeopardize the overall operation. On October 1, the RCMP drug squad in Toronto raided a hotel in a section of Agincourt known as the new Chinatown and arrested six people. The Mounties seized 2.6 kilograms of high-grade China White and $32,000 in cash. The heroin was still in the body-pack devices used to smuggle the drugs past Canada Customs at Pearson International Airport. At the time, Inspector Doug Ewing, head of the Toronto drug section for the RCMP, said the raid "neutralized" a major heroin-smuggling network that was shipping the drug into North America. Ewing noted that four of the suspects were Hong Kong residents carrying Hong Kong-British passports. Two other suspects were Hong Kong-born landed immigrants to Canada. In a related incident, two New York City residents who had picked up a packet of heroin from the Canadian connection earlier in the day were arrested by U.S. Customs agents when their car was stopped at the Rainbow Bridge in Niagara Falls.

In December, the FBI held a high-level conference in New York with all the White Mare participants. "At that stage, we could have indicted thirty people worldwide," Cantley recounted. "The operation had been going fifteen months. We had 200 people worldwide working on the operation and we were worried about a security breach. But we decided to give it a little longer."

The FBI undercover agent was called back to Hong Kong in January, 1989, for a meeting with a third gang. The agent met with Chan Hok Pang, the organizer of the 386-kilogram shipment. Pang had boasted that he was a friend of Khun Sa and that the opium king was his direct supplier. Cantley said the Hong Kong police dismissed his claim as grandstanding.

When the terms of the deal were agreed on, Pang travelled

to Chicago in late January to oversee the delivery of another heroin shipment. Early the next month, Woo phoned Pang at his hotel room instructing him to fly to New York for a meeting. Pang checked into a hotel in Manhattan. On February 20, through wiretaps and electronic bugs, the FBI determined the location of the heroin shipment and the net closed.

Cantley grinned. "When we raided Pang's apartment, we found out he hadn't been lying about his friendship with Khun Sa. We found pictures of him and the opium king in the mountains of Burma."

In a spinoff from the White Mare operation, a Brampton, Ontario, restaurant owner was arrested in New York City on May 6, 1989, as a principal conspirator in an international network involved in smuggling heroin from China into the U.S. New York City police seized 39 kilograms of heroin that had been concealed inside five of 300 boxes containing umbrellas. The drugs were discovered in an investigation by the Interpol Guangdong liaison office in the People's Republic of China on March 31 on a dock in the southern port city of Guangzhou. In a rare move, Communist Chinese authorities asked U.S. DEA investigators stationed in Hong Kong and members of the Royal Hong Kong Police to take up the investigation. Within days, the RCMP were also called in.

In late April, undercover investigators watched as the Brampton connection and his associates transferred the shipment, which originated in the Golden Triangle, to a ship in Hong Kong harbor which was about to leave for Vancouver. RCMP Staff Sergeant Don Kennedy of the heroin unit in Toronto said everything on the Canadian side was set for "a controlled delivery. We had an assistance role in the operation. We were to make sure everything went according to plan on this side without spooking anyone."

The umbrella shipment was routinely cleared by Canada Customs agents in Vancouver and placed aboard a CP freight train bound for Toronto. Under constant surveillance, it was retrieved and delivered to a house in Ajax, Ontario, and then flown to New York on May 5. A detective with the New York

City Police Department said undercover operators picked up
the trail after the plane landed with the heroin and arrested
three Chinese drug traffickers a day later. Two others were
picked up in Hong Kong. At the home of the Brampton man,
the Mounties found a small arsenal of weapons, including
several rifles, a shotgun, two pellet guns and a quantity of
ammunition.

Operation White Mare, as well as a series of arrests involving heroin couriers along the U.S.-Canada border throughout
1986, 1987 and 1988, has revealed a major Hong Kong-based
drug pipeline pumping millions of dollars of China White
into New York City and San Francisco via Toronto's and Vancouver's Chinese communities. In two cases, the RCMP and
Canada Customs officers arrested members of New York-
based Chinese gangs with connections to members of various
Hong Kong Triads as they were picking up shipments of
China White totalling about $20 million. The heroin had
been smuggled in body packs by couriers who had flown to
Toronto from the British colony via Western Europe. In both
instances, the couriers phoned Hong Kong on arrival in
Toronto and transmitted a code indicating they had passed
through Canada Customs safely. They then phoned the New
York syndicates and arranged to meet at a hotel in Toronto's
Chinatown for the pickup.

In one case, two members of a New York Triad arrived in
the city to make the pickup and were immediately arrested. In
the other, one of the couriers was found to be a member of the
New York Tung On street gang, which is connected to the Sun
Yee On Triad in Hong Kong. This Triad has established close
ties with the Mafia in the United States.

The Kung Lok, the largest Triad in Canada, is headquartered in Toronto. It was established in 1974 by Lau Wing Kui
shortly after he arrived in the city from Hong Kong, where he
was the "dragon head" of the Luen Kung Lok Triad. Lau, a
Hong Kong casino operator and drug dealer, fled the colony
to Canada on the heels of a criminal investigation. Within a
few years, under his stewardship, the Kung Lok expanded its

operations from Vancouver to Saint John, New Brunswick, and by 1980 had more than 150 core members. A confidential police report, prepared for the Metropolitan Toronto Police force in 1986, stated: "All evidence indicates the Kung Lok is the principal threat to law and order in the Chinese community in Toronto." In 1980, Lau was declared *persona non grata* in Canada, and a deportation order was made by the Immigration Department. However, he fled to the Dominican Republic before the order could be carried out and, a year later, returned home to Hong Kong.

In early January, 1983, working on a tip from Canadian police, Hong Kong police discovered that a half-dozen Triad dragon heads from Toronto, New York and San Francisco had checked into a hotel for what has been dubbed as the "Hong Kong Summit" with Lau. Two of the attendees were the leaders of the Toronto Wah Ching and Kung Lok Triad. Allegedly, Lau had convened the summit to examine ways of improving cooperation between syndicates in Hong Kong, Canada and the U.S. Hong Kong police missed the summit but later raided the hotel suites of several of the invited guests and, after brief questioning, let them go without laying any charges. The groups have held at least two more summits in Hong Kong since them.

While Canadian police have finally recognized the growing influence of Triads in Canada, they are just as concerned with the growth of Asian street gangs, many composed of immigrant and refugee youths from Vietnam, who are being recruited by Triad leaders in an anticipated struggle for control of Canadian Chinatowns as various Hong Kong-based Triad leaders move their operations into the country.

The most developed gang is the Wah Ching, which means Youth of China. Headquartered in San Francisco, it has branches in Los Angeles, Seattle, Vancouver, Toronto and New York. While the Wah Ching is uniquely North American, it operates like a Triad. And according to police intelligence, it is directly linked to leaders of the Sun Yee On and 14-K Triads in Hong Kong and the Kung Lok Triad in Toronto. The

Wah Ching is reported to have about 600 to 700 members and associates; about 200 are considered "hardcore" members by police. In New York City, the Ghost Shadows gang, with a total membership of about forty-five, are known to work as mid-level heroin couriers and, according to DEA intelligence, travel frequently to Toronto to make pickups of China White smuggled in from Hong Kong.

In just a few years, these street gangs and others have put a stranglehold on street activity in Vancouver's and Toronto's bustling Chinatowns, having instilled terror in those communities with their bent for physical violence and their use of weapons in settling disputes. The Vietnamese youth are the "untried soldiers", only too eager to commit vicious assault, woundings and murder for their chance to go up in the organization. Sergeant Cowley noted that while stiff jail sentences usually work as a deterrent to Chinese youths, they have little effect on the Vietnamese. "They laugh at jail, saying it's better than a refugee camp."

In 1986, Ontario Provincial Court Judge Robert Dnieper castigated a Vietnamese youth convicted of extortion for bringing shame onto Canada's refugee resettlement program. Judge Dnieper also lamented bitterly that no prison penalty imposed by him would rehabilitate the youth. "The only answer for him is deportation and the suggestion that he may try his gang activities in Ho Chi Minh City."

Police have found that as these gangs have moved to consolidate their influence in Vancouver and Toronto, there has been an emerging shift to firearms as their preferred weapon of choice. In Vancouver, street gangs of Asian extraction, such as the Big Circle, the Red Eagles and the Viet Ching, which is made up of ethnic-Chinese from Vietnam, have exchanged gunfire in restaurants and on the city streets. In the Prairie provinces, Triad activity concentrated in Calgary, Edmonton and Winnipeg has resulted in several violent encounters between various warring factions.

Today, there is a strong consensus among law-enforcement officials in Canada and the United States that Asian organized-crime gangs will become a major problem over the next decade, particularly with the approach of 1997. Yet while these criminal syndicates have been virtually impossible to penetrate in past years, the police now have several points working to their advantage. The first is that eventually, some-where toward the final few links of the China White chain, a Triad member has to surface to sell heroin to gangs outside his ethnic group. This opens up a possible vulnerability. The second is that the younger recruits are not interested in the traditions and initiation rites of the Triad. Their preoccupa-tion is money, and that has led to a serious breakdown in discipline in the ranks. Third, Triads are fighting among themselves for supremacy as they each try to gain a foothold in the lucrative Canadian and American market, and they will in turn find themselves squaring off against established crim-inal organizations who will not be willing to give up any turf without a fight.

"The next few years are going to prove very interesting," a Canadian drug investigator warned. "I just hope we're pre-pared to deal with what is coming."

4

No More Honor

Terry and Kirk Kirton had just put their two children to bed. There were lots of hugs and kisses, giggles and tickles. Five-year-old Sarah and 19-month-old Evan were bubbling with joyful anticipation. It was Christmas Eve, 1987. That afternoon, their parents had taken them to the St. Vital Shopping Mall to have their pictures taken with Santa Claus. They could hardly contain their excitement as their mother tucked them into bed. All the children could think of was that Santa Claus would soon be visiting their home and their Christmas wishes would be fulfilled.

With Sarah and Evan asleep in their beds, Terry and Kirk sat down on the couch in the living room of their modest two-storey Fort Garry townhouse at 31-1321 Beaumont Street, filled a syringe with heroin and injected into their veins.

Kirk and Terry were junkies with an addiction that cost thousands of dollars a month. Despite their habit they loved their children and were no different on the surface from most other working-class families. Kirk was a good mother, doting on her children, and Terry used to love to brag to neighbors about his wife's mouthwatering Roseannadanna Banana Cheesecake.

Kirk had long, flowing brown hair, warm dark eyes and a sad smile. Sarah and Evan were her life and she was very protective of them. The 35-year-old woman never left them with a babysitter because she feared for their safety, a fear that stemmed from her own background as a severely abused child. Through most of her young life, she had bounced in and out of a string of foster homes.

No stranger to the police, Kirk had an extensive rap sheet. In July, 1972, she was sentenced to fourteen months in jail for

90

possession of narcotics and, for a long time afterward, she was in and out of jail for escape attempts, car theft, drug possession and parole violation. She met Terry in 1980 while visiting a friend at a half-way house. Terry, a heroin addict and two-bit drug dealer with a long history of scrapes with the law, had just been released from prison.

A balding, bearded man, who looks much older than his 35 years, Terry was arrested on December 2, 1987, with Edward Speidel, a cocaine addict with a lengthy record of armed robberies and prison breaks. Earlier that day, Speidel had held up a branch of the Bank of Montreal in Winnipeg. He was later sentenced to a total of fifteen years for the bank job and a string of other robberies. Terry was charged with possession of stolen money after he was found holding $1,100 taken by Speidel in the bank robbery. He was released the following day on his own recognizance.

It was 9 p.m. when Terry and Kirk cranked up. They were just starting to feel the euphoric surge of the heroin when they were startled by loud hammering on the front door. Terry rushed to the window and peeked out. Because of the imposing size of the two silhouettes, he figured they were detectives and opened the door. But they weren't the police. It was Larry "the Captain" Fisher and Jon Waluk, and they were looking for some cocaine.

Kirk scurried nervously upstairs to stay with the children. She knew there was bad blood between her husband and the Captain. Terry didn't like the idea of Fisher, a former motorcycle gang enforcer, being in his house, but kept his mouth shut. He and Waluk, a long-time school chum, went upstairs for a chat, leaving Fisher in the hallway.

Waluk, a former kick boxer turned cokehead, boasted that he was armed with a .32-calibre revolver and that the Captain was carrying a 9-mm automatic pistol. Terry handed the blubbery rounder from Winnipeg's north end a small packet of cocaine. Waluk ambled into the toilet and mixed a little coke with water, drew the mixture into a syringe and jammed the needle into his arm.

Terry's mind was racing, wondering why Fisher had come to the house. He hated the man and he knew the feeling was mutual. He jumped when Sarah burst out of a nearby bedroom, screaming that she smelled smoke coming from downstairs. Waluk barrelled down the stairwell to investigate and Terry darted into the children's bedroom. He passed his wife $2,000 in cash for safekeeping and started hunting frantically for a weapon to protect himself and his family.

"Where's the hammer, where's the hammer?" he whispered urgently. He planned to bury it in Waluk's head and try to get his gun.

Waluk suddenly appeared at the bedroom door. "Come down to the basement," he ordered.

Terry pleaded with Waluk. "I've known you for thirty years. Just leave me alone." In a panic, he lunged for the gun in Waluk's grip but the struggle was shortlived. Fisher was on the landing in a flash. His eyes were cold steel.

"The time for talking is through. Let's go," the biker shouted.

Terry made a wild dash for the bathroom window and dove through it, landing on the frozen lawn a floor below. The last words he heard as he scrambled across the yard was Waluk yelling: "He's getting away!" and Fisher shouting: "Then I'll kill his family."

The terrified man ran to a neighbor's house screaming frantically: "My wife – my kids – gunmen – call the police."

In a fit of blind rage, Fisher kicked open the bedroom door where Kirk and her two children huddled together in a corner trembling with terror. They were crying and screaming. Ten gunshot blasts from a 9-mm pistol shattered the nighttime calm. Before she died, Kirk hastily scrawled a note in large black-ink letters in an address book. It said: "John and Captain did it, Dec. 24/87."

The two men bolted out of the townhouse and disappeared into the cold night. In minutes, police cars were swarming over the area. With revolvers drawn, Constables James Pelland and Weldon Peters and other officers carefully entered the house. Pelland heard the cries of a baby coming from the floor above and charged up the stairs with his partner. In the living room, two police officers extinguished a fire on the couch and snuffed out a smouldering cushion that had been tossed under the Christmas tree.

"The first thing I saw was a little girl," Constable Pelland recounted at the trial. Tears welled in the officer's eyes. "She was slumped in the corner and just covered in blood. When we first looked at her she appeared to have been shot in the face. We figured she was dead." Sarah had been shot in the face at point-blank range and in the thigh. "There was also a small child directly at the foot of the bed, face down on the floor. He was crying and trying to get up, sort of pushing with his hands," Pelland recounted.

Also fighting to hold back his emotions, Constable Peters told of finding Evan. "The young baby . . . was screaming off and on." Peters said when he scooped him up, he noticed a hole in the crotch of the diaper. It was a bullet hole. Evan had also been shot in the left arm and chest.

Kirk was barely alive. She had been shot between the eyes and twice in the chest. She died en route to hospital.

Evan was rushed to Victoria General Hospital where he was placed on a life-support system, and then taken to Children's Hospital where he was operated on. The doctors and nurses who were called in from their Christmas celebrations worked feverishly to save his life. Later, Dr. Cal Cameron, head of the hospital's intensive care unit, said Evan spent his last minutes on earth in the arms of hospital staff. "We prefer that children never die without being touched. We will act on behalf of the parents so that the child is not seen to be dying alone."

Evan died at 4:17 p.m. on Boxing Day.

Police questioned Terry into the morning hours in an attempt to piece together the grizzly events that had occurred at the house. A massive manhunt was immediately launched for the two prime suspects. Waluk was arrested without a struggle at his home on Christmas Day, and Fisher, on the advice of a lawyer, turned himself in to police on Boxing Day.

Terry told police that Fisher, a former member of the Silent Riders motorcycle gang, wanted to teach him a lesson for destroying his relationship with his girlfriend, Helen Laramee. Laramee, who happened to live two doors away from the Kirtons, was a close friend of Kirk's. They met each other in the hippie days of the 1960s when they partied, smoked pot and injected heroin together.

At the trial, Laramee testified that she met Fisher in 1984 and found herself inextricably trapped in a stormy and violent relationship. She described Fisher as an overly possessive, extremely jealous and obsessed man, who threatened to kill anyone she was friends with. She said he believed her friendship with the Kirtons, whom Fisher repeatedly referred to as "scum", was based solely on her heroin addiction. The blonde Laramee said her former boyfriend convinced himself into believing that the couple was deliberately trying to drive a wedge between them. She quoted Fisher as saying that the Kirtons were "a problem and he'd have to get rid of the problem."

The crushing blow for Fisher came Christmas Eve when he learned that Laramee had taken off to Jamaica to get away from him during the festive season. When he discovered she was gone, he flew into a violent rage. He sped around the city in his car looking for Waluk and finally found him partying at a bar at the Kildonan Motor Hotel. Fisher knew Terry and Waluk were long-time friends and that, he figured, would be his ticket into the Kirton home.

Waluk testified that Fisher had told him that evening he had patched up his differences with Terry and just wanted to go over to the house to buy some cocaine. Waluk, who was stinking drunk after polishing off two bottles of vodka, agreed to take him. "This was Christmas and I was happy," Waluk told the court.

His eyes downcast, Waluk said that, after arriving at the house, he remembered going upstairs with Terry and injecting cocaine into his veins, and then smelling smoke. "I went downstairs to put the fire out. Captain set the fire." His voice breaking, he then described the blood-curdling seconds after Terry crashed through the bathroom window. "I could hear screaming . . . kids crying."

Fisher, Waluk told a hushed and horrified courtroom, was in the bedroom pointing a gun at Kirk's head. "The Captain said, 'You fuckin' bitch, you're never going to stick your nose in my business again.' She was saying something and I just said, 'No.'" And the gun was going off all over the place. I grabbed his wrist. He had it bouncing. It was going off all over the place. He pushed me aside. I just stood there. I froze. All I know is everyone was just dropping. I've seen it so many times. I see bodies kneeling. I see bodies dropping."

Sobbing in the witness stand, Waluk moaned: "I'm at fault for not stopping [the massacre]. I didn't even budge and the gun kept going off. I just stood there in front of the bodies. I was shitting my pants. I didn't know what to do."

Waluk then motioned in exasperation at Fisher, who sat stone-faced and shackled in the prisoner's dock. "It's not a fuckin' joke, Captain! Don't keep looking at me."

Turning to Crown prosecutors George Dangerfield and Richard Saull, a desperate Waluk shouted: "He had it all set up. He had it in his head a long time ago. This guy hustled me. He buffaloed me into this thing. I want the truth out. I don't want him to get away with it."

But the story was different when Fisher took the witness stand. "I did not shoot anybody," he said in a quiet, husky voice. Wearing leg irons, a grey suit, and a red-and-grey-striped tie, Fisher calmly fingered Waluk as the trigger man and flatly denied ever threatening to kill Terry or Kirk. He also denied conning Waluk to get into the Kirtons' house, being armed with a 9-mm handgun, and starting a fire in the living room.

The 41-year-old former biker said he was downstairs in another part of the house when he heard Waluk and Terry scuffling, and then heard Waluk shout: "He's getting away!" Fisher said he ran outside looking for Terry and as he was heading back into the house, he heard gunshots. He said a

crazed-looking Waluk came down to the main floor carrying
an empty revolver.

"He looked really strange, like he was in a twilight zone or
something. He wasn't really there. He was just walking."
Moments before the shots rang out, Fisher said he heard Kirk
plead: "Not in front of the kids."

The 2-metre, 109-kilogram Fisher testified that he simply
tagged along with Waluk, who was going to the Kirton home
to buy some cocaine. Fisher also said he wanted to see what
Terry looked like because he had heard a rumor that the man
wanted to kill him. "I thought it was important that I knew
what he looked like," he said, explaining that he was afraid of
being shot or stabbed by Terry, who is 1.7 metres tall and
weighs 63.5 kilograms.

Fisher, who has a criminal record for a couple of drug
possession offences, added that he had found out that Terry
was selling heroin to his girlfriend and wanted to tell him
"that if he didn't knock it off I was going to beat the shit out of
him. I was deeply in love with Helen and I didn't want her to
do heroin. It affected her mood greatly." Under questioning,
he acknowledged that he once owned a 9-mm handgun, but
threw it away in 1986 because it didn't work. Instead, he said
he carried a replica of a Walther 9-mm automatic to ward off
death threats from the Hell's Angels and Los Bravos biker
gangs, and from Terry Kirton. The murder weapon and Fisher's car were never found. Fisher denied ditching the car,
saying it disappeared or was lost after he turned himself in to
police.

When Terry Kirton took the stand, he testified that he never
expected Fisher and Waluk would kill his family after he
jumped out the bathroom window. He thought the duo would
chase him. Struggling to find words to express his deep guilt
and shame at abandoning his wife and children, he said: "I
found it very hard to live with the decision I made. How could
I leave my family in a situation like that? I was ashamed of
myself. I still am ashamed of myself. I had no other way of
protecting them. These guys are 240 pounds apiece. They're

both armed. What am I going to do? Take a gun away from them? This was not a movie."

On June 24, after a tense and emotionally charged three-week trial and two days of deliberation, the six-man, six-woman jury convicted Fisher of first-degree murder in the premeditated killing of Kirk Kirton. He was also convicted of second-degree murder in the slayings of the two children. Fisher showed no reaction when the verdict was read out. Court of Queen's Bench Chief Justice Benjamin Hewak sentenced Fisher to life in prison with no possibility of parole for twenty-five years. Waluk was convicted on three counts of second-degree murder and sentenced to life with no chance for parole until he had served at least twenty years.

When Ken Ross first went undercover a dozen years ago for the RCMP to pose as a drug trafficker on the west coast, making dope deals was a laid-back, simple business transaction. There were no guns, no threats and no violence. There was honor among thieves in those days, he recalled. Years later, Ross flew east to Montreal for a drug deal and quickly got the feeling he was in Dodge City. "Everyone in Montreal carried guns. There were guns under their jackets and guns on the table. And they would want to take hostages before they would go through with a deal," the RCMP sergeant recounted.

Today, violence has permeated the drug world. Deals are struck between heavily armed gangs. The words "mother-fucker", "kill", "die" and "knife" punctuate discussions over tables cluttered with switchblades, revolvers, sawed-off shutguns and a variety of automatic weapons. No one feels safe. No one trusts anyone. Everyone glares and everyone expects a ripoff. Drug dealing has become a dangerous business and the life of a drug dealer is constantly on the firing line.

Police forces throughout Canada have become alarmed, and at times frightened and unnerved by the level of viciousness in the drug scene. Increasing incidents of intimidation, beating, kidnapping, wounding and murder linked to drug dealing have left few regions of Canada unscarred.

In Toronto, a young street drug dealer is shot in the head in an underground garage. His murder is a message to other would-be dealers who venture into another gang's turf to peddle drugs. In Calgary, a teenage boy ventures into a back alley with two drug dealers. He wants to score some LSD. Instead, he is ripped off and severely beaten. An Iranian heroin dealer in Montreal is clubbed over the head and knifed twenty-one times because his associates suspect he was a police snitch. His battered body is dumped in a laneway.

The number of armed attacks on police officers has also risen to unheard-of levels. Drug suspects no longer simply surrender when they are busted. They challenge the police and, often, they put up a good fight before finally being subdued and handcuffed. Some will even try to kill the arresting officers if they can.

"The average person on the street does not realize how dangerous and violent the drug scene has become," Metro Toronto Police Staff Sergeant Ernie Beale said. "I've had several of my men who were working undercover mugged, robbed and beaten up. A 17-year-old youth tried to kill one of my undercover officers with a knife. These drug dealers have a total lack of fear for the police, and I'm afraid that we're going to see more cops shot as the situation worsens."

While the murder of the Kirton family painfully illustrates the viciousness of petty dope dealers and addicts, the drug-dealing Quebec Hell's Angels are the embodiment of organized savagery, brutality and ruthlessness.

The Hell's Angels – with their chilling emblem of a winged, smirking skull – arrived in Quebec in 1977. Since that time, they have become somewhat of a permanent fixture in rural parts of the province. Dubbed *Les Hells* by the French-language newspapers, the three chapters – Sorel, Lennoxville and Laval on Montreal's south shore – ran their crime empire out of fortified clubhouses. Outside the sleepy college town of Lennoxville, 160 kilometres southeast of Montreal, the gang's hilltop clubhouse was a minefield of bear traps and sensor wires. It was equipped with floodlights, closed-circuit television cameras and burglar alarms. Guard dogs patrolled the perimeter, and the building's walls were reinforced with concrete and steel. Outside the Sorel clubhouse, 50 kilometres northeast of Montreal, signs in French warn intruders: "Enter at your own risk" and "No Bozos allowed."

Within a few short years, Les Hells managed to put together a powerful crime syndicate. Drug dealing was its foundation. They had waited patiently to make their move as Montreal's biggest bike gangs – the Popeyes, Satan's Choice and Devil's Disciples – fought a bloody war for control of the city's lucrative and booming drug market. When the smoke cleared and most members of rival gangs were either dead, in prison or otherwise out of circulation, the Hell's Angels took over the largely French-speaking Popeyes. The remaining gangs melted away or merged with the Chicago-based Outlaws, which in turn triggered an ongoing war between the two rival gangs that has left dozens of people dead.

Les Hells established a network of clandestine chemical drug labs, and they imported and trafficked in cocaine, hashish and marijuana. They owned a string of nude bars and cheap flea-bag motels and were heavily involved in prostitution, extortion, weapons trafficking, security and loansharking. They also ran their own version of Murder Inc., carrying out contract killings.

The most infamous member of the Quebec Hell's Angels is Yves "Apache" Trudeau. A cold-blooded killer and hired assassin, Trudeau holds the distinction of being the most prolific murderer in Canadian history, having confessed to forty-three slayings. Throughout the Montreal criminal underworld, Trudeau, whose killing spree spanned sixteen years, is known in both English and French as "the Mad Bumper". He was nicknamed Apache by fellow bikers after he cut off a rival gang member's ear with a hatchet.

Upwards of thirty-five of Trudeau's targets were members or associates of rival motorcycle gangs. Ten of his victims were blown apart by bombs. Another twenty-nine were shot by an array of handguns, automatic weapons, rifles and shotguns. Three, including a grandmother who was defending her grandson, were beaten to death by blunt instruments, and one was strangled. Two of his victims were cases of mistaken identity; one was blown up inside a van, the other shot outside his home.

Trudeau was convicted of manslaughter in March, 1986, and sentenced to life in prison, but he will never serve the full prison term. The 40-year-old founding member of Les Hells struck a deal with the Quebec Justice Department to have the first-degree murder charges reduced to manslaughter. The agreement was reached in exchange for turning police informer against the gang's network in Quebec. He will be eligible for parole in seven years and, upon his release, will be given a new identity and relocated somewhere in Canada.

Trudeau turned on his brothers after the Hell's Angels' Sorel, Lennoxville and Halifax chapters held an urgent, secret summit in mid-March, 1985, and voted to eliminate the troublesome "sex, drugs and rock and roll" Laval chapter. About forty members of the other three chapters met at the Lennoxville clubhouse to discuss the rampant drug abuse of the Laval gang. A decision was reached to "retire" the chapter. All the Laval members were invited to a party on March 23. They were informed that, prior to the festivities, there would be a discussion on problems with the rival Outlaws biker gang. Although a call for such meets is mandatory under the Hell's Angels' charter, only three Laval chapter members bothered to show up. The execution was put off and phone calls went out ordering other Laval members to get to the Lennoxville clubhouse.

The following day, with five key Laval members at the party, the signal was given and the shooting began. The bullet-riddled bodies of Guy-Louis (Chop) Adams, 31, Michel (Willie) Mayrand, Guy (Brutus) Geoffrion, 40, Jean-Pierre (Matt Le Crosseur) Mathieu, 35, and Louis (l'Anglais) Viau, 33, were stuffed into sleeping bags, anchored with cement blocks and body-building weights, and dumped into the St. Lawrence River. On Easter weekend, about two weeks after the party, the gang caught up with another member of the Laval chapter, Claude (Coco) Roy, who was hiding out in a sleazy motel on Montreal's South Shore. The 31-year-old was brutally beaten to death. His battered body, clad only in undershorts, was dumped with the others. When the corpse was retrieved three months later from the watery grave, the pathologist found five packets of cocaine tucked in the victim's underwear. A seventh member, Regis (Lucky) Asselin, was tracked down near the Laurentian foothills town of St- Jérôme on May 2. While driving his van, the 28-year-old biker was hit seven times by fire from automatic weapons. He managed to drive himself to hospital and survived. He was later convicted on two counts of first-degree murder on information supplied by Trudeau and sentenced to life with no chance for parole for twenty-five years.

But the man Les Hells really wanted to put out of commission was Trudeau. He had escaped the execution plot only because he happened to be in a drug detoxification program in Oka, Quebec, at the time. Members of the Sorel, Lennoxville and Halifax chapters were terrified of Trudeau. To them, he was a maniac, a loose cannon, totally out of control and extremely dangerous.

Trudeau was a member of an exclusive fraternity within the Hell's Angels known as the Filthy Few – a band of assassins designated to kill for the gang. While most of his killings were gang-related, the Mad Bumper also undertook contract hits for other crime syndicates. His most spectacular job came when west-end mobsters paid him $200,000 in November, 1984, to kill Paul April, a former Murder Inc. accomplice of Trudeau's. April, 42, had been fingered in the shooting death a year earlier of Montreal underworld figure Peter Frank Ryan, a suspected major cocaine dealer. Trudeau rigged a bomb in a color television set and had it delivered to April's apartment in a downtown Montreal highrise building. It was a gift to an old friend. April and three other men were watching an NHL game when it exploded. The force of the blast blew down the walls of eight apartments on that floor, sent the elevators plummeting to the basement and shattered windows in nearby buildings. All four men in the apartment were killed.

One of his last contract killings involved Jean-Marc "La Grande Gueule" (Big Mouth) Deniger, an Angel who had fallen from grace with Les Hells. At a gang summit, it was decided that the biker be retired and a beaming Trudeau, who coveted Deniger's Harley-Davidson motorcycle, got the contract. His fee would be the victim's bike.

Trudeau's trigger-happy ways eventually became a problem for the gang because he began taking matters into his own hands rather than having disputes settled by gang members in a democratic vote. If the Mad Bumper felt someone should be eliminated, he simply went out and did the job whether the gang agreed or not.

The Mad Bumper's switch to police informer came about in early June. He was in jail for drug possession and slated to be released at the end of the month. While browsing through a steamy Montreal French-language crime and sex tabloid, his attention was seized by a bold black headline that said Les Hells had put out a $50,000 contract on his life. Trudeau saw red and decided to call the Quebec Provincial Police. He knew his options were limited, but he wanted to get even. While Crown prosecutor René Dominque worked out the legal details with his superiors in the Quebec Justice Department, Trudeau was secretly moved to a special holding unit on the fourth floor of the Parthenais jail in east-end Montreal. He began singing and proved to be a geyser of information, giving the police an insider's view of the Hell's Angels' criminal operations throughout the province and in other parts of

Canada. And because of his close association with other mobsters in Montreal, he supplied police with information on
other criminal enterprises, including drug dealers and their
trafficking networks in cocaine, hashish and marijuana; the
locations of chemical drug laboratories; prostitution rings;
loan-sharking rackets; and car and motorcycle theft rings. He
also recounted the details of the killings he was involved in,
supplying the motives behind each slaying, and fingering his
accomplices. His information, and that of three other Hell's
Angels-turned-informers, shattered the gang's organization
in Quebec and Halifax. For his efforts, Trudeau was paid a
stipend rumored to be around $10,000 a year that is being
banked in trust for his eventual release, and a $35 weekly
allowance to purchase various sundries during his stint in jail.
While he isn't living a life of opulence in prison, he isn't
suffering. He is given amenities, such as a color television in
his cell and a diet that consists of all the steaks, hamburgers,
french fries and soft drinks his heart desires. Every fifteen
days or so, under a veil of heavy security and secrecy, the Mad
Bumper is taken out of his cell, sandwiched between two
burly detectives in the back seat of an unmarked police car,
with another two detectives in the front, for a clandestine
conjugal visit with his common-law wife and two children.

Homicide detectives with the Sûreté du Québec provincial
police came up against a brick wall in trying to find out what
had happened to the six missing members of the Laval chapter. Through a seedy coterie of snitches, they had concluded
that the bikers had met with foul play. The problem was they
had no cadavers to support their thesis. In an unprecedented
move, the detectives decided to release to the news media the
names and photographs of the six alleged to have been murdered. "We have information which banishes any doubt that
there are corpses somewhere," Sûreté du Québec spokesman
André Blanchette told reporters. "Let's be logical. Do you
think that we would have given names, published photographs, of fictitious alleged corpses? This is the first time in
our force's 178-year-old history that we have done that. Rest

assured that the reason for it is the total certainty that murder has been committed."

Rumors were flying that the dead bikers were buried in a shallow grave behind the Lennoxville clubhouse. So, in the early morning hours of April 10, 1985, more than 400 provincial police officers conducted a massive raid on known Hell's Angels' hangouts throughout the province. They were looking for clues to the mystery of the missing bikers. Heavily armed tactical teams swooped down on the Sorel and Lennoxville clubhouses, using front-end loaders to smash through reinforced steel doors. They even brought in Humane Society personnel, armed with tranquillizer guns to disable the vicious German shepherd and Doberman pinscher guard dogs. Police found no sign of the missing six. Instead, they netted more than 200 weapons, ammunition, police radio scanners, $150,000 in cash, a small quantity of drugs and enough baseball bats to equip several little league teams. Meanwhile, in a simultaneous raid on the Hell's Angels' clubhouse in Halifax, the RCMP found the motorcycles belonging to four of the missing bikers.

Then, in a bizarre twist, the Lennoxville chapter decided to launch a lawsuit against the Sûreté du Québec for raiding its clubhouse. The gang cited damages "to its reputation" and demanded $10,000 in compensation as a result of the bad publicity emanating from the raid.

The hunt for the corpses continued, and on June 6, working on information gleaned from wiretaps, the police began dragging the bottom of the St. Lawrence River at Berthierville, about 40 kilometres downstream from Montreal. They snagged the bloated bodies of five of the bikers. The body of the sixth was found washed ashore a few kilometres down river.

Homicide detectives began questioning suspects in earnest but found they were getting nowhere fast. Then came an unexpected break. The police officers noticed that Jerry (Le Chat) Coulombe, a striker (recruit) in the Hell's Angels, appeared extremely tense and nervous when they arrived at his home. At first, the 29-year-old biker had nothing to say, shrugging his shoulders to every question. But as the frustrated detectives got up to leave, Coulombe suddenly began to blurt out the macabre details of what has become known as the "Lennoxville massacre". Coulombe was desperate to strike a deal. It seemed that he too had been marked for early retirement. Earlier in the day, he had been invited to the Sorel clubhouse for his full initiation into the gang that weekend, but when he called around to his friends to find out who else was invited, he learned he was the only guest.

Coulombe, a stocky man who wears wire-rimmed glasses, confessed to the detectives that he had been posted to lookout duty on a hilltop outside the Lennoxville clubhouse when the executions took place. He said that the powerful Sorel chapter, which prohibited its members from using cocaine. had issued an edict that the other Quebec chapters, especially Laval, obey the rule. "They wanted to prevent others from sniffing then though it wasn't an international rule. I've seen Hell's Angels in British Columbia and Europe sniffing," Coulombe said.

The gang was to be eliminated for "rowdyism", but Coulombe said he was later told by Rejean Lessard, the president of the Sorel chapter, that the Laval gang had "burned" the Halifax chapter for $200,000 in a botched cocaine deal involving Peter Frank Ryan. "Lessard told me that the North [Laval] chapter stole money from Halifax. He said it was a burn, and that was the reason why several members of the Halifax chapter were invited to the fateful party at the Lennoxville clubhouse."

On the morning of March 23, Coulombe said he was ordered by Boule Tremblay at the Sorel club to pick up a truck from a nearby rental company. The manager was expecting him and he wouldn't have to sign anything. The biker was instructed to wear gloves while inside the vehicle and was given a bottle of Javex and of Mr. Clean, a jacket and a large knife that he was to leave in the truck. After delivering the vehicle to Tremblay, he was given two packages containing three revolvers and he placed them under the seat of his car before driving off to Lennoxville. He brought the weapons into the clubhouse and gave them to Jacques Pelletier, and was then told to go outside and stand guard. He noticed members of the Sorel, Halifax, Lennoxville and Laval chapters in the clubhouse.

The following day, Coulombe was sitting in his car along the road leading to the clubhouse keeping lookout when he heard shots. He turned and saw Guy-Louis Adams tearing out of the clubhouse. A gun-toting biker was in hot pursuit. "Somebody followed him and shot at him five or six times. It was Robert (Snake) Tremblay. The last shot was fired fifteen to twenty feet from where I was."

Coulombe recalled that when Adams fell, Charles Filteau, Guy and Yvon Rodrigue and Richard Rousseau ran out of the clubhouse to retrieve the body. The garage door flew open, and the striker saw four more bullet-riddled bodies on the cement floor. Later, Coulombe said, he acted as an armed escort when the van carrying the bodies was driven to a ferry dock near Berthierville. His instructions were to ram any police car that attempted to stop the van. He heard splashes as gang members emptied the truck's contents into the river.

Investigators got a second break when another Hell's Angel, Gilles (Le Nez) Lachance, decided to turn informer. The 38-year-old biker told homicide detectives that he was sitting at the Lennoxville clubhouse bar drinking a beer when the shooting spree started. "I saw [Louis] Viau trying to protect himself, waving his fist in front of his face, and then he was on his back on the ground. Someone was standing over Viau pumping bullets into him." When the shooting was over, Lachance said, the bodies were dragged from the clubhouse and put into a truck. Other gang members grabbed mops and pails and began cleaning up the blood.

Both Lachance and Coulombe were given police protection and new identities in exchange for their co-operation. Based on their statements, the Sûreté du Québec launched a roundup of the forty gang members that were in the clubhouse at the time of the killings, charging most with first-degree murder.

Three separate trials were held: one in Montreal and two in Sherbrooke, 160 kilometres southeast of Montreal. At the Montreal courthouse, security was especially tight. A special prisoners' box with bullet-proof glass had been constructed in the largest courtroom at a cost of $40,000. The box, which had room for thirty people, was equipped with a sound system so the accused could hear the proceedings. The gang members were brought in manacled hand and foot and accompanied by machine-gun-toting members of the Sûreté du Québec tactical squad.

During the trials, Yves Trudeau was brought in for a brief court appearance. He had undergone a remarkable transformation, forsaking his sinister Hell's Angels' look for a conservative businessman's attire. Gone were his long black locks, the motorcycle boots, jeans and leather jacket. He was clean-shaven and was wearing a grey tweed sports jacket, a white shirt and blue tie, navy blue slacks and Gucci-type loafers. On his left wrist, he was sporting an expensive watch and on the pinky finger of each hand he wore a gold ring.

His former "brothers" shifted uneasily in their seats when Trudeau entered the courtroom. The Mad Bumper stopped within a few yards of the prisoners' box and stared coldly into each of the biker's faces. Then he grinned mischievously, lifted up his arms and mimicked holding a machine gun. He fired an imaginary round at each of them and laughed.

On December 4, 1986, verdicts were reached in the first trial of three members of the Hell's Angels. Jacques Pelletier, Luc Michaud and Rejean (Zig Zag) Lessard, who acted as the "master of ceremonies" at the massacre, were found guilty of first-degree murder. They showed no emotion when the jury of five men and six women read the verdicts after deliberating for sixteen days. Mr. Justice Jean-Guy Boilard, the trial judge, sentenced each of the men to life in prison without parole for at least twenty-five years. A fourth gang member,

Robert Richard, was found not guilty. Stunned that he had been cleared, he turned and grinned at his wife.

On June 17, 1987, four Halifax Hell's Angels were found not guilty by a Quebec jury on charges of first-degree murder. Three were released immediately. They gave police the finger as they drove off in a luxurious Jaguar. The fourth remained in custody serving time on an unrelated charge.

Three months later, on September 9, 1987, nine members of the Hell's Angels' gang were jailed for terms ranging from two to nine years for their part in the Lennoxville massacre. Crown prosecutor René Dominque withdrew the first-degree murder charges because of insufficient evidence, and charged the bikers instead with being accessories after the fact.

Over that year, police rounded up several other gang members suspected of being involved in the massacre who had gone into hiding when the raids were staged. Robert (Snake) Tremblay was extradited from England in the summer and charged with murder, and Gaetan Proulx was picked up in a police raid. Both men were sentenced to life on December 13, 1987. On March 22, 1988, Georges "Bo-Boy" Beaulieu, leader of the Lennoxville chapter, was arrested in Amsterdam and extradited to Canada on April 8, 1988. A week later, three more wanted gang members walked into the Sûreté du Québec's Sherbrooke headquarters with their lawyers in tow and surrendered to police. They were later convicted of being accessories after the fact and sentenced to two years each. A Halifax Angel received five years on the same charge.

On April 15, 1988, Beaulieu pleaded guilty to a reduced charge of being an accessory after the fact and was sentenced to nine years. At the first of the murder trials in October, 1986, Coulombe testified that he saw Beaulieu at the Lennoxville clubhouse on the day of the bloody purge, and a Sherbrooke merchant told the court that the biker had purchased three sleeping bags from his sporting goods store shortly before the Laval men disappeared. The store owner said he remembered that Beaulieu specified that he wanted cheap sleeping bags and refused to accept a receipt.

Then on Monday, August 22, 1988, one of the last Hell's Angels wanted in connection with the Lennoxville massacre gave himself up to police. Richard Rousseau, 38, strolled into the Sûreté du Québec police headquarters in Sherbrooke at 9:30 a.m. with his lawyer. He was taken immediately to court where he pleaded guilty to being an accessory after the fact and to cocaine trafficking. Rousseau's role in the killings was to remove all traces of bullet marks from the clubhouse and mop up the blood from the floor. He was sentenced to nine years.

Only two bikers, Denis Houle and Jean-Yves (Bull) Tremblay, are still being sought in connection with the killings.

According to police intelligence, Les Hells are in the throes of rebuilding their depleted organization in Quebec. Money from international chapters has been sent to the province to help with the rebuilding effort and recruitment drive. The Quebec drug market, police say, is simply too lucrative for the Hell's Angels' international crime network to forget about.

"The Angels are reorganizing," an anti-gang squad member with the Sûreté du Québec said. "And we know that the Outlaws are trying to move in and take over some territory. We can see a serious confrontation between the two gangs somewhere down the road soon. There is too much money to be made here with drugs. It's a multi-million-dollar enterprise and just because we hit one gang a good blow, it doesn't mean they are finished. It just means they are out of action for a little while."

5

Cocaine:
The Snowman Cometh

I ventured into Blondies, a disco bar on Dovercourt Road in Toronto's west end, at the suggestion of Steve Peconi, an undercover drug investigator with the Metro Toronto Police. First, I parked a half-block away from the entrance and sat there for about an hour observing the street activity outside the club. Within seconds, a taxi pulled up in front of Blondies and disgorged a lone woman passenger. While the cab driver waited, she darted into the bar. A moment later, she reappeared, jumped back into the taxi and disappeared into the night. Another cab pulled up almost immediately, and then another. Within an hour, the scene was repeated at least forty times. Car doors slammed. High-heel shoes ricocheted off the cement sidewalk. Engines idled and sputtered. And the night had only just begun.

The cover charge to get into Blondies was five dollars. At the doorway, a beefy, beer-bellied bouncer gave me a once-over, trying to figure out if I was trouble or even worse, an undercover cop. He nudged my chest as I walked by in a patently obvious move to find out if I was carrying a concealed weapon under my jacket. Once I was seated, he dispatched an overly inquisitive waitress to the table.

"Hi! I haven't seen you here before," she shouted over the deafening blare of the disco beat.

"I haven't been here before," I yelled back.

"You from around here?"

"No. Montreal. I heard this place was a lot of fun. Good music. Good dancing."

On her way back to the bar, she nodded at the bouncer. He turned and gestured to a couple of characters sitting at a table

110

near a doorway leading to the washrooms. They resumed their conversation.

Except for a half-dozen tables, Blondies was almost deserted. In a darkened alcove at the back end of the cavernous club, several Spanish-speaking men played pool and, on the dance floor, two young, slinkily dressed women bounced to the repetitious thumping. They were totally absorbed in their reflections in a bank of mirrors against the far wall of the dance floor.

Throughout the evening, a steady parade of lone women and men trooped into the bar. Some ventured into the pool-playing area. Others sought out tables occupied by seedy-looking patrons. There were a lot of handshakes that had more to do with discreet transfers of cash and tiny plastic baggies filled with white powder than with cordiality. At one point, three men got up and headed toward the stairwell leading to the toilets in the basement. I waited a moment and decided to go down. The bouncer intercepted me.

"Where are you going?" he demanded, blocking the narrow staircase with his linebacker girth.

"To the john to take a leak."

"You just wait right here a minute." He jammed his index finger into my chest to demonstrate the ease with which he could stop my forward progress.

I stood there until the threesome reappeared. They were grinning broadly, sniffling and rubbing their noses. One man held a handkerchief to his nose. It was bleeding.

"You can go now," the bouncer growled, taking his finger out of my chest.

In the washroom, I ran my hand over the top of the ceramic water closet in the first cubicle. It was covered by a thin film of crystalline white powder.

"What the fuck are you doing?" the bouncer bellowed. He'd followed me into the washroom.

I jumped back with a start. "Take a hike. I'm going to the toilet."

Glaring into my face, he clenched his ham-like fists, and his left leg was shaking.

When I got back to my table, the bouncer was talking animatedly to a tall, casually dressed man. I assumed he was the manager or the owner. Their discussion was interrupted by the arrival of a rotund man sporting a stencilled beard. The bouncer and his boss greeted him with a warm bear hug and several slaps on the back. After a few words, the man strolled confidently through the club, nodding greetings to some of the patrons and saluting others as he headed for the back pool room.

My attention was captured by a short South American who was bopping by himself on the dance floor. It struck me that he had come and gone on several occasions in the three hours we were at the club. On his returns, he would make a beeline for the pool area. I concluded he was a courier. Coke dealers never keep a large supply of cocaine on hand. Better to dump a few grams on the floor in the event of a police raid than be forced to get rid of a costly large quantity. When existing stock is almost sold out, a runner is dispatched to a nearby stash to pick up a new supply.

I had seen enough and decided to leave. As I got to the door, the bouncer stepped in front of me and stared menacingly into my face, trying to see if he could extract something. I pushed by him.

A fine drizzle was falling outside. Two taxis pulled up and two hookers darted into the club, paid the cover charge and disappeared into the dark cavern. The bearded patron emerged and was shaking hands with the bouncer when a dark form appeared out of the shadows, jammed his hand into the man's pocket and retrieved a tightly packed, round ball wrapped in plastic.

"What the — "

"Ah! And what have we here? An eight-ball! By the way, I'm a cop and you're under arrest. You have the right to remain silent — "

"Someone planted that on me. It's not mine," the man protested.

"They all say that. Up against the wall and spread them."

"That's not mine. I swear. Someone planted it on me," he insisted.

An unmarked police cruiser screeched to a sudden stop outside the club.

"I guess this just isn't your lucky night, pal. You're out $300 worth of coke and you get to spend the night in one of our finer jail cells," the undercover officer said as he yanked a pair of handcuffs out of his jacket pocket.

Clutching a portable cellular telephone, the enraged manager charged out of the club screaming choice epithets at the police officer. "I'm calling your superiors. I'm going to get you for harassment. I'm fed up with this constant harassment of my establishment. I'm trying to run an honest business here. I'm calling my lawyer. I'm going to sue the police department and the city."

"Yeah, yeah, yeah. You do that," the officer said as he got into the police car with his suspect.

According to a detailed national drug intelligence report released by the Royal Canadian Mounted Police in June, 1989, cocaine abuse has become the nation's fastest-growing drug habit. It now rivals marijuana and hashish as the drug of choice. In just a few years, cocaine has moved out of the posh stretch limousines and high-priced European sedans and into the Fords, Chevrolets and GM vans. Once the drug of choice of the beautiful people – actors, baseball players, high rollers and fast-lane professionals – cocaine has descended to the ranks of the middle and working classes. "High purity levels and increased availability combined with decreased prices made cocaine more accessible to all socio-economic groups in Canada," the report states.

Rod Stamler, assistant commissioner for the RCMP, noted that the shift to cocaine "is so dramatic it overshadows everything else. . . . Because of the increase in cocaine use, Canadians are buying more drugs than ever."

The riveting 110-page account of international drug trafficking networks, arrests and seizures notes that while
cocaine has been in abundant supply in Canada's metropolitan centres, it is now increasingly available in rural and
remote areas throughout the country. Cocaine use, it said,
increased noticeably in Nova Scotia, Yukon and the North-
west Territories. And the future outlook, according to the
document, is grim. "There are no signs of this trend diminishing in the foreseeable future."

Intelligence gathered by the RCMP indicates that the price
of cocaine is dropping sharply because Colombian crime
families have succeeded in flooding the Canadian market
with the drug, "making it more accessible to middle and
lower socio-economic groups and the secondary school age
market, who were often unable to buy the drug in the past
because of its high price."

A profile of cocaine users shows that the majority are in
those groups. But the report points out that the "significant
percentage of the user population comprises upper middle
class professionals or double income earners. Typically, the
cocaine user is a professional male between the ages of 19 and
35, although this profile is shifting to include all socio-
economic levels, particularly with the emergence of more
affordable crack [a cocaine derivative]."

The RCMP document also notes that the incidence of
cocaine use among young people is rising. "In some parts of
British Columbia's Lower Mainland area, cocaine use is
reported to have spread to the elementary school level."

One alarming indicator is the amount of cocaine seized by
the RCMP in busts, and the number of people charged with
cocaine-related offences. In 1987, the RCMP recorded more
than 1,443 cocaine seizures totalling more than 145 kilograms, a 41 per cent increase over the 102.6 kilograms seized
in 1986. The Mounties also charged 1,618 people with
cocaine-related offences in 1987, an increase of 222 over the
previous year. And although official statistics were not yet
available, press reports on cocaine busts in Canada through-

out 1988 indicated that seizures and arrests far outpaced those of previous years.

On Thursday, April 3, 1989, the RCMP made its biggest cocaine bust to date when undercover officers seized 500 kilograms in a downtown Montreal townhouse. The total street value was conservatively estimated at more than $25 million. The cocaine, which was delivered to Montreal under what the RCMP describes as a "controlled delivery", consisted of individually wrapped one-kilogram packets. It was smuggled into the country aboard a twin-engine Aero Commander 1000 that landed at an isolated airstrip about 20 kilometres from Fredericton, New Brunswick.

Superintendent Neil Pouliot, who heads the RCMP drug squad in Ottawa, confirmed that a major Colombian drug trafficking ring had been infiltrated by undercover RCMP officers posing as dope dealers. "We knew the plane was coming and we were waiting for it," Pouliot said.

But the operation, code-named Overstep, almost came to an abrupt and disastrous finale when the aircraft, piloted by two weary Colombians, crash-landed after a wing hit a tree as it was approaching the gravel runway. The plane was severely damaged but no one was injured. In a panic, the pilots jumped out of the aircraft and charged off into the nearby woods. They were located by undercover agents, posing as drug-dealers, and whisked off to Fredericton, where they were placed on an Air Canada flight to Toronto. There, the jittery pilots were led to believe that arrangements were being made to put them on the earliest possible commercial flight back to Colombia.

Pouliot said the aircraft, with the name Worldwide Courier stencilled on its sides and a hand-painted Canadian flag on its tail, travelled along the northeast coast of the United States. "It was picked off on radar and followed by the U.S. Customs Airwing Service. We tracked it once it entered Canada and followed it into New Brunswick," he said.

The undercover agents, who were posing as middlemen in the smuggling operation, delivered the shipment to three

Colombians who were staying at the Montreal townhouse. On Thursday, April 6, police in Montreal and Toronto moved in on the drug syndicate and arrested fourteen individuals, including the two pilots who were holed up in a hotel. According to police, at least 25 kilograms of the shipment had been earmarked for delivery to a Colombian organized crime syndicate in Toronto, and another 25 kilograms were slated for distribution in Montreal by another Colombian gang. The rest was destined for the U.S. market.

Pouliot also confirmed the "possibility of a connection" to the arrival of a twin-engine Rockwell Turboprop Commander 980 that landed in Sorel, Quebec, on March 12. Investigators believe that that aircraft, which had been stolen and bore false Canadian identity numbers, was also involved in a cocaine-smuggling operation. The flight originated in Colombia and was picked up by U.S. Customs over the northeast coast and followed into Canada. However, when the armed American Customs agents landed in Sorel and arrested the pilots, they learned that the cargo, thought to be at least 400 kilograms of cocaine, had already been loaded on a truck and had disappeared into the night before it could be seized.

Peter Taylor (not his real name) had it all. An adoring wife, two cute pre-schoolers, a modest split-level home and a career in advertising that was spiralling upwards. His job paid $65,000 a year not including perks, such as a company car and bonuses for exceeding sales quotas. It took him to a whirl of cocktail parties with business associates and clients. It was at one of these get-togethers two years earlier that Taylor first tried cocaine.

"I was loaded. Bombed out of my tree," he recalled. "This chick that I worked with called me into a bedroom and asked me if I wanted to do some blow. She put a little powder on a tiny silver coke spoon she wore around her neck and snorted it. I figured what the heck. So I snorted a hit in each nostril and within a few minutes I was straight. Everything felt great. I wasn't stoned or anything like when I smoke weed or hash. I just felt great, like I owned the place, like I was in total control. I must have tooted up a half-dozen times that night." The following Friday, Taylor purchased his first gram of cocaine from a respectably dressed dealer who hung out in an upscale bar in midtown Toronto. It cost him $160. Since that day, he has squandered a small fortune on coke. He has also lost his family, his home and his job.

Taylor has dropped 14.5 kilograms. His skin is inelastic and grey. His hair is matted and his eyes are blank. He twitches and, in his less lucid moments, thinks his family and friends are plotting against him. He last saw his wife and children six months ago.

"My so-called wife threw me out. So much for better and for worse," he said bitterly. "I promised her I would get off the blow but she didn't believe me. She wouldn't give me a chance. I could get off it. I'm not hooked or anything like that," he insisted, snapping his fingers.

Taylor now sells coke to a steady stream of clients – all young professionals who, like himself, claim that they are in control and that they only use cocaine recreationally. "You know, if ever there was a drug for the 1980s, it is cocaine. This is the success drug. It gives you a quick lift. It enhances your mental alertness. It gets rid of fatigue and lets you stay up longer. And it's great for weight loss," he said sardonically. "But it's terrible for your sex drive and, in the end, it really, really fucks you up."

He stared blankly at a picture of his children on an Arborite coffee table in his sparsely furnished studio apartment. "Did you know the expression 'dope fiend' was coined for cocaine users, and that Sigmund Freud used cocaine?"

Throughout the evening, Taylor's mood and conversation swung like a pendulum that was out of sync with its gear box. One minute he was jovial, chattering frivolously and cracking jokes. "Did you know that cocaine is God's way of telling people they have too much money!" he laughed. Then he would shift into a darkly philosophical mode, followed either by intense silence or by loud, threatening tirades.

"You know, it's kind of funny in a weird sort of way. I make more bread selling blow than I did when I was working. The trouble is I blow it all on coke," he said, rubbing his nose. "Fact is, I don't snort it anymore. The lining in my nose is gone, burned out. I shoot up. But I never share a needle. Heroin addicts share needles. I'm not into AIDs. Occasionally, I freebase," he added matter-of-factly.

Taylor paused and stared up at the ceiling. His legs started to twitch. Tears welled in his eyes. "I can't believe how I screwed up my life. This all started with some bitch from the office offering me a line. Now my career is shot and my life is fucked. I must have blown over 200,000 bucks in the last couple of years on coke. I know guys who've lost everything because of cocaine. This shit just takes over your life. It's hard to get off after you've gotten into it the way I have. I don't do it all the time. I do it in binges. Three, four days. I toot till I drop and then I sleep for two days straight. Then I swear to myself I'll get off the stuff. But you get these cravings. You start getting edgy and depressed. Your nerves have jagged ends. You get pissed off real fast. I've been off it for a couple of weeks straight so many times, and I think to myself I've got it licked. Then, I go out for a walk and before you know it I find myself heading for the bar to get more blow. In my mind I convince myself that I'm just going in for a beer but unconsciously I know the real reason I'm going there."

Later that evening, on a stool at the far end of Taylor's favorite coke bar, a dark-haired man in a black leather bomber jacket sat chatting amicably with the bartender. Every so often, someone passed by, tapping him discreetly on the shoulder. He would look around and then head off to the toilet. He was the local "snow man".

"That guy has made a pile of bucks selling blow," Taylor said. "He's messed up a lot of people's lives in the process. But he doesn't give a shit. It's got him a house with no mortgage. He's got a Corvette and he bought his wife a BMW and his son a Jeep. He's smart. He doesn't do coke at all. He's seen what coke does to people. He just drinks. I hope someone fixes his ass one day."

Sniffling as if he had a cold, Taylor slumped over the bar like a defeated boxer. After another long silence, he began again to wax philosophical: "I really screwed up but I'm going to beat this thing. I know I can and this time I will. Yvonne and I will get back together. I'll make it up to her and the kids. You just wait and see."

At first, Taylor's wife didn't want to discuss her husband's drug problem. He was out of her life and she wasn't going to allow him back in, ever. But with a little persuasion and a promise not to reveal her identity, she gave in to a powerful urge to talk to someone about her torment, preferably a stranger.

The past two years have etched their toll on the petite 32-year-old high-school teacher's face. "I don't hate Peter anymore," she said sadly. "I feel sorry for him. But I don't want him around. It's better for everyone, for me and the children, if he just stays away. Sometimes he calls and starts crying and promising all over again that he'll change and get help. I just hang up. I don't want him back. I don't ever want him back. He's done enough damage.

"He used to be such a good guy. Fun-loving. Full of surprises. He really loved the children and he really loved his job. He was always very sociable. He was never a bore or obnoxious or anything like that. Everybody liked him. He drank and occasionally got drunk. But that would only make him silly and amorous. I didn't mind that. I simply cannot understand why he let himself get dragged down like he did. He had everything going for him."

When Yvonne first discovered that her husband had been using cocaine for more than a year, she was horrified. "He told me at first he had played around with it. He said it kept him alert. But I knew there was more to this. I pressed him and found out his so-called playing around had cost us all our savings." Taylor had by then run through cash, bonds, regis-

tered retirement savings plans and guaranteed income certif-
icates totalling $142,000.

Yvonne collapsed when she was confronted with the scope
of her husband's addiction. "I wanted him out of my life then
and there. I told him to get out. I never wanted to see him
again. Then he began to cry. He begged me for my forgiveness
and pleaded with me to let him stay. And he swore he would
go for treatment. I didn't know what to do. I didn't know
anything about cocaine.

"The next day, I began looking for help. It was impossible. I
found one treatment centre and it was booked solid with an
eight-month waiting list. I never realized so many people were
taking cocaine. Peter told me about Cocaine Anonymous so
we went there together. It was filled with so many shattered
individuals. Pathetic young professionals who were going
places. They had good careers but couldn't keep their noses
out of that pile of white powder. After sitting there for an hour,
I realized it wasn't going to help Peter. It wasn't structured.
Attendance wasn't mandatory. Some guy would ask a few questions, make a few comments, and then leave the floor for these
pathetic jerks to get up and deliver empty testimonials.

"That night, after we got home from the session, we talked
and talked and talked. Peter promised he was going to get off
cocaine for my sake and for the sake of the children. He was
really depressed and I believed him. I wanted to believe him.
Then after work the following Friday, he didn't come home.
No phone call. Nothing. I was frantic. I thought something
terrible had happened to him. He finally showed up Sunday
afternoon with this goofy smile on his face. I knew he was
high. He was just full of himself. He was rude and foul-
mouthed. Then he started physically pushing me around.
Later, when he started to come down, he started to cry and
beg my forgiveness.

"This going up and down like a yo-yo went on for four
months. It was agonizing. One confrontation after another.
Then more promises and reconciliation. I was scared for the
children. They were afraid of him. They kept crying to me

that he was always acting so strange. One minute he was so friendly and loving, the next he would fly off into a rage, throwing things and swearing, and then he would get depressed and start to cry."

The last straw came when Yvonne found out by accident that her husband had lost his job. "He hadn't worked for an entire month and he never told me. It was just one lie after another. If there is one thing I've learned about cocaine addicts from this experience, it's they are the biggest liars in the world. Peter was leaving every morning for work, and he would come home after work and tell me about his day. I never imagined he had been fired. I happened to be downtown one afternoon for a meeting when I ran into one of his associates. He seemed a bit awkward and finally he says, 'Too bad about Peter losing his job.' I was dumbfounded."

When her husband got home from "work" that evening, he found two suitcases packed with his belongings sitting on the front porch outside the house.

Robert and I first met as youngsters in Weredale House, a home for boys from broken families in Montreal. Now forty, Robert considers himself a success. He is a coke dealer and has amassed a small fortune selling the drug in bars and taverns in the west end of the city.

"It's okay to sell blow. But don't do it. Once you do it, you'll never get rich. You'll just make enough money to supply your own habit and I've seen what this shit can do to people. It's poison, man," he offered from behind the wheel of his red Corvette.

A wiry, affable character, Robert said he feels no guilt selling cocaine." I don't sell to kids. Anyway, most of them can't afford it. I sell to people with money and, man, there's a lot of people with a lot of money to blow shoving this stuff up their noses. If they want to toot that's their business. I'm here to supply a demand. I don't twist anyone's arm. They come to me for a product and I sell it to them for a profit. That's the enterprise system. If I didn't do it, someone else would.

"But I'm always amazed at how much money these idiots blow on coke, man. I've seen people lose their entire inheritance. Their homes, their cars, all the money they had saved in the bank on blow. They start with everything and end up without a pot to piss in. Rich people with brains in their heads. Not these dummies on the streets. And no way do I feel sorry for them. They're big enough to make decisions about their own lives. Anyway, no one ever gave a shit about me when things were tough. Now, I've got it made and they don't."

Robert pulled up in front of a bar on Bishop Street. The club-lined street was packed with bar hoppers. "This is my office. It's where I do my best business," he said with an indifferent laugh. As we passed by one bar after another, doormen, waiters, waitresses and patrons waved or nodded at Robert. He strutted into his favorite watering hole and greeted the bartender with a warm handshake.

"Still a little early. The place should pick up in an hour," Robert said. "Hey, you remember Phillips? He used to be in the home with us."

"Yeah. I haven't seen him in years. Someone told me he was dealing in Park Extension," I replied.

"He's dead. Broke the main rule, man. *Deal but don't use.* That guy had everything, money and broads. He started doing blow a year ago. He was snorting and freebasing, and then he started cranking up. He lost it all. His buddies told me he blew 250 grand on blow. His wife took off with his two kids last year. That really fucked up his mind. He couldn't find her. A month ago, the cops broke into his apartment after the neighbors complained of a funny smell coming from it. He was dead in his washroom with a needle stuck in his arm. His heart blew up. Judging by the way he died, I'm sure he killed himself. He just gave up and hot-wired himself."

Gazing around the bar, Robert spied a former Weredale alumnus sitting by himself at a table in a secluded corner. "Remember Foster? That's him over there. A real cokehead. You want to talk to a cocaine addict, talk to him. He'll tell you

what it's all about. The true confessions of a cokehead!"
Robert joked.

Foster was overjoyed at having company for a drink. He was
still buzzing on cocaine and only too eager to talk to someone,
anyone. His first confession was that he was unemployed. In
fact, he hadn't worked in years. He was on welfare. That paid
for the rent and food. He got his drug money from "boosting"
televisions, VCRs, car stereo systems and cameras, and spent
most of it on cocaine.

Tall, thin and never married, Foster had always been a shy
person who didn't talk much. But fortified by high-octane
cocaine, he wouldn't shut up. "I started doing coke about
three years ago. I tried everything. Pot, chemicals, even a little
smack. But this stuff, man, this stuff made me feel incredible.
What a rush! I felt so fantastic inside and outside. I would walk
on the street and feel real cool.

"But the trouble with coke, man, is once you get into it, it
takes over your existence. I live for this shit. I crank it. It gives
me a super rush. I used to toot but the lining in my nose is
burned out. You know a lot of people tell me they toot and
they freebase and look down at anyone who cranks. They say
cranking is for junkies. I say, what's the difference. Snort,
freebase or crank, they're just as hooked on blow as I am. They
do it their way and I crank. It's a bullshit technical argument.
Right, Rob? You got a QT you can lay on me?"

Robert shook hands with Foster and discreetly passed him
a quarter-gram baggie for old times' sake.

Later, over a drink at his sharply decorated two-bedroom
condominium apartment, Robert boasted about the dope
deals he has been involved in. "I've seen kilos of the stuff. One
hundred per cent pure powder glistening on a kitchen table.
The main importers are Colombians. You don't want to mess
with them. They'll kill you if you twitch the wrong way. They
deal only in keys [kilograms] and only to people they know. I
used to work for a guy who bought heavy weight. I was a cutter.
I'd cut the coke for street dealing. They knew they could trust

me because I won't do coke. I'd cut it, step on it with baking soda or this Italian powdered laxative. I preferred the laxative. I like to keep my customers regular," Robert laughed.

"You know, between you and me, if this stuff was ever legalized you might as well open up a bunch of new cemeteries and funeral parlors because you'll have a lot of bodies dropping all over the place, especially young bodies. This stuff is bad. It robs you of your money, drains your emotions and eventually it kills you. It causes all kinds of problems with your central nervous system and it causes cardiac arrest. Your heart is a piece of meat and it can only take so much snorting and cranking up before it cuts out on you. I can't understand why people do this shit. Me, I'd rather sip on a glass of twenty-one-year-old Scotch on the rocks."

To people looking in from the outside, Carlos lives what appears to be a quiet, hard-working, honest life. A recent immigrant to Canada from Medellin, Colombia, he shares a house with his father and mother in a struggling working-class area of west-end Toronto known as the Junction. His lifestyle is simple. He has a decent roof over his head, doesn't wear flashy clothes, and drives around in a Mercury Sabre or, more precisely, he is chauffeured around-the-clock by two bodyguards. And that is where the outward display of ordinariness ends.

Carlos is one of five heads in southern Ontario connected to the notorious Medellin cartel, the vicious Colombian gang that dominates the world's cocaine trade. He owns two restaurants, and has at least six other businesses and more than two dozen properties throughout the city registered in the names of family members.

For more than a year, William Blair, a staff sergeant with the Metropolitan Toronto Police drug squad, worked almost exclusively on a major joint project with the Ontario Provincial Police trying to catch Carlos and other top Colombian drug barons in Toronto who run a major cocaine distribution network in southern Ontario. Again and again, Blair, a meticulous cop with a sharp mind for detail, slammed into a seemingly impenetrable wall surrounding the drug kingpins. He tried the usual bait of money to get close to them, but it just wouldn't work. He couldn't even get a nibble. But through dogged persistence he finally got lucky.

On agreement that no names would be mentioned in order not to jeopardize the undercover operation – dubbed Amigo – or subsequent court cases, Blair talked about the investigation and what he had learned about the inner workings of the Colombian cocaine syndicate operating in Ontario. It is headed by one man, known as the general, with close family ties to the top echelons of the Medellin cartel in Colombia. The general also has direct links to other Colombian syndicates operating in Montreal, New York City and Miami.

"He's the palm," Blair said, laying his right hand open on his desk. "He is the one man who is responsible for the organizations operating in southern Ontario. His five fingers are the cells or franchises operating here. Each of the organizations is not as structured as the Mafia but they are organized along family lines, and they are linked to the Medellin cartel.

"These people are better organized than we had first thought," Blair continued. "We used to think that four or five people were distributing cocaine in Toronto at the wholesale level. Now we find a detailed organizational structure tying them all together."

RCMP drug intelligence has discovered that Colombian crime organizations, which provide 80 per cent of the cocaine consumed in North America, assign members to various key cities in Canada and the United States on a rotational basis to oversee drug distribution networks. "The Colombian crime organizations have related groups operating in the Caribbean and in major metropolitan areas in the United States and Canada," a 1989 drug intelligence report by the RCMP states. "Members of these affiliate organizations, who operate at the middle level of the Colombian trafficking groups, are

assigned to foreign illicit distribution networks on a rotational basis. These members, who are most often Colombian
citizens, will move into a Canadian city for a period of up to
six months and then return to Colombia and be replaced by
other members, making identification of their activities
extremely difficult." The report also notes that "their propen-
sity to be highly organized and, at the same time, commit
vicious crimes such as serious assaults and homicide in an
effort to acquire new territory has made them potentially the
most dangerous crime groups in the world."

Intimidation and violence are the trademarks of the
Medellin cartel. Its reputation for brutality is feared even in
the drug-dealing dens of Toronto, Montreal and Vancouver.
In Colombia, the wealthy and powerful cocaine drug barons
have neutralized the very weapons needed to fight the war
against drugs by their use of murder, assault and bribery.
Dozens of judges, government officials and journalists who
dared to take on the Medellin cartel have been silenced.

Blair said that about twenty people, all from South
America, are at the top level of the Colombian drug-dealing
network in southern Ontario, with most living in the Toronto
area. Because of the tight-knit structure and operating procedures of the gangs, they are considered "untouchable" by law
enforcement agencies. For years, drug investigators across
Canada have made little progress in identifying or getting
close to the syndicate commanders.

"They are so well insulated and it's hard to get near them
because they trust only family," Blair said. "They know you
don't rat on family. And you just can't impress these guys by
buying a kilogram of cocaine. They won't deal with you if
you're not one of them. They supply only the people they
know and trust. They really check you out. And they only deal
in weight."

The principal rule of business of these cocaine barons is
that the drugs and the money never come together at the
same time. If a buyer places an order for several kilograms of
cocaine, the Colombian dealers first take the money, sit on it

for a day or two, and then instruct the purchaser on how and where he can pick up his merchandise. This simple practice provides the kingpin dealers with a great measure of protection because they know that undercover drug cops would never be cleared by the top brass in any metropolitan police force to part with the kind of money required for a major cocaine deal. The rule of thumb for undercover cops is that large sums of money are to be used only for "flash" purposes, to entice drug dealers by showing them the cash. The cash changes hands only when the drugs are handed over, and then the bust is made.

Blair bamboozled the Colombian bad guys by changing the rules of the game. He managed to convince his bosses to approve a plan to nail the key players in the city's cocaine trade by using their own rules against them. "They knew too much about our limitations. The big guys never handled the dope. That end of it was handled by their runners, and they're very good at counter-surveillance, using two or three cars at a time to do heat runs to see if they can draw any heat. But the big guys didn't mind coming to get the money. And that would prove to be their downfall."

In 1988, a kilogram of pure cocaine in Colombia cost the Toronto organization about $6,000. After paying various bribes and couriers, the final cost on arrival in Canada was about $20,000. That kilogram was then sold in bulk deals for a minimum $15,000 profit. Bulk sales are handled only by a small and trusted contingent of managers who distribute the cocaine to large criminal syndicates and independent street dealers.

The Colombian syndicates also import South American labor to deal drugs at the more risky but profitable street level. Often, they employ women with small children or young men who have claimed refugee status as a means of buying time in Canada. These dealers are set up in apartments and warned never to talk to the police. They are told in graphic detail what will happen to them and to their families both here and back home if the police are given an iota of information on any gang member or drug-dealing activity. They are also assured that bail will be posted within hours should they get busted and, that within a couple of days, they would be on an airplane bound for their homeland. Against these sorts of intimidation levers, threats of imprisonment by Canadian police and offers for protection and entrance to witness relocation programs have little or no effect on South Americans caught dealing cocaine. They will simply not "roll over" and give information to police on a promise of no prosecution.

In 1987, five mid-level Colombian coke traffickers were arrested in Toronto after a drug deal had gone sour. Two of the five were arrested after having sold a kilogram of cocaine to an undercover drug cop in Toronto. The sister of one of the arrested dealers telephoned a colleague in a panic to warn him the heat was on. He just happened to have 5 kilograms of cocaine stashed in his apartment. He quickly transferred the drugs to the trunk of a rental car parked in the basement of the building. But in a bizarre twist of fate, he had not paid his rental bill in months and the leasing company decided the following morning to repossess the car without notifying him. At the leasing outlet, the manager opened the trunk and found five 1-kilogram blocks wrapped in heavy-duty masking tape. He immediately phoned the police. Drug squad officers removed the tape and plastic covering and found almost pure cocaine wrapped in a Colombian newspaper from the city of Medellin.

Finding the car missing later that day, the frantic Colombian dealer phoned the leasing company manager to ask if he had repossessed the vehicle. Calmly, he informed the manager that he had left some important papers in the trunk and would come down to pick them up. Within minutes, a police officer phoned back posing as a car jockey at the leasing company. He informed the dealer that he had found the missing papers while cleaning out the trunk and advised him that if he wanted his merchandise it would cost him $1,500. A rendezvous was set up at the Inn on the Park hotel where the dealer arrived with two Colombian associates to make the payment. They were promptly arrested and charged. Only the dealer, James Cavouti, was eventually convicted and sent to jail. The other four Colombians managed to get bail and headed straight for home.

Like every other crime syndicate, Medellin gangs are drawing on high technology and boardroom expertise to transfer their profits into legitimate enterprises. They have hired experts in law, international banking, business and computer technology. But the emphasis is on keeping a low profile outside Colombia. In Toronto, Montreal and Vancouver, high-ranking Colombian drug barons live modest lifestyles. They own average houses that are mortgaged to the hilt and drive mid-size American cars. Nothing flashy, they do not want to draw attention to themselves. Each owns a number of legitimate businesses or front operations which they use to launder cash, and even those businesses are low-profile – convenience stores, video arcades, bookstores and restaurants. Often they buy into the business as silent partners.

The amount of cocaine money trading hands in one day is remarkable. While Toronto drug squad officers were on a stakeout in an unrelated case, they saw a car stop in a parking lot. A man got out, dashed to a nearby car and handed the driver a shopping bag. The police chased the second car and pulled over a Colombian national. Inside the shopping bag was $71,000 in small U.S. bills. The driver denied ownership of the money or any knowledge of where it came from, and no one showed up at police headquarters to claim it.

In late March, 1988, a Loomis armoured truck lost more than $300,000 in cash when the rear door flew open on the Gardiner Expressway in Toronto. Traffic came to a virtual standstill as excited drivers rushed to scoop up the windfall. The next day, Metro police asked local banks to be on the alert for anyone making rather large, unexplained deposits of cash. Three banks reported questionable cash deposits of $40,000 each in one day. They just happened to be made by Colombians.

Blair warned that the volume of cocaine destined for consumption in southern Ontario is constantly increasing. "The amounts out there will blow you away. The five organizations operating in the Toronto area deal about 400 kilograms of cocaine a month each," conservatively worth $40 million on the street. "They are flying in so much I expect it to start falling out of the sky any minute. Things are so hot in South Florida that much more is coming here and then they're shipping it south."

Until the heat was turned up south of the border, much of the cocaine destined for southern Ontario came from New York City, and, through wiretaps and surveillance, police uncovered strong ties between Medellin families in Toronto and New York. Blair noted that a large portion of a massive 2700-kilogram cocaine shipment seized in Hicksville, New York, in late June, 1988, was earmarked for the Toronto Colombian gangs. He noted that the Toronto cocaine "general" was placed within three kilometres of each of the seven stops the ship made en route from Equador to New York State. Ironically, the drugs, which were concealed inside blocks of chocolate, were destined for a company in Port Newark, New Jersey, called Toronto Import Company, a fake business.

On May 17, 1989, Blair got orders to take down the Colombian gangs. In the sweep, police made twenty-six arrests and seized an estimated $40 million worth of cocaine and $135,000 in cash in what was described as the largest drug investigation in the city's history. At a press conference, Blair said he expected cocaine prices would probably go up over the next few weeks, but added that there was still a lot of dope stashed around the province. "The arrests will slow things down a bit but they won't stop drug organizations from importing cocaine. It's like a salamander. You cut off an arm and it grows back. It's going to continue."

While Operation Amigo was chugging along, undercover operators learned that the Colombian cocaine barons in Toronto had become worried about the number of drug busts

in the trouble-plagued Ontario and Metro Toronto subsidized housing projects where crack dealing was running
rampant. Several trusted soldiers were called in by the general and asked if there was any chance they could be linked to
the Jamaican gangs that were dealing in crack cocaine. They
were sternly warned to tread carefully. One slip, they were
told, would give the police a step up the drug chain, leading
them closer to the major suppliers. Crack could cause the
Colombian syndicates irreparable harm, the general said.

6

Crackdown

Eric was twelve when he started running errands for drug dealers operating out of a subsidized housing project in Toronto's infamous Jane-Finch corridor. By fifteen, he was making up to $600 a week selling crack cocaine to high-school kids. Late last fall, his enterprising career was interrupted after he made a sale to an undercover cop.

Sitting in an interview room in a bleak Toronto youth detention centre, Eric puts on a transparent show of bravado in an attempt to pass himself off as a big-time drug dealer when in fact he was nothing more than an insignificant cog in the city's multi-million-dollar illegal drug network. He is a short, wiry kid with a mouth full of tangled yellow teeth and a tongue that spits out a steady stream of obscenities. His eyes are dark, cold and uncaring, and his attitude – "No one is going to tell me what to do or how to live my life" – is typical of many teenagers. In spite of being in a lockup, he believes he is in total control of his destiny.

Dressed in expensive designer running shoes, jeans and a sweater, the tough-talking teenager, known to his customers as Rock, brags incessantly about the money he made selling crack. "How do you think I can afford these clothes?" he asks, tugging at his sweater. He also boasts about his streetwise ability to outwit the cops and becomes visibly irritated when reminded that he is in detention because he got caught.

Eric's mother has lived on welfare for as long as he can remember. His father is dead. An alcoholic, he died from cirrhosis when the boy was seven. "I don't get along with my mother. She does her thing and I do mine. No questions asked. She has a boyfriend and takes off with him to Florida in the winter. She went to France for a month last summer and didn't leave me any money for food or anything."

At fourteen, he was recruited by a gang of crack dealers who controlled a parking lot outside the highrise public housing project where he lives. He was taken on as a "whistler" or lookout for what he calls "chump change". His job was to keep watch from a nearby balcony and whistle if he spotted a suspicious car that screamed cops. Within weeks, he took a step up the drug-dealing ladder to steerer, directing customers to specific dealers, and a couple of months later, he graduated to hustling customers.

"We call hustlers Joneses. We'd make a deal and go to the dealer and get whatever the customer wanted and skim a bit for ourselves. One time when I was hustling, I lost a 40 piece [a $40 mothball-sized chunk of crack] that a dealer fronted me and I almost got a bullet. He beat the crap out of me for $40 and I still had to make good on the debt."

After almost a year of hustling, Eric had amassed enough regular customers to go independent. So with $400 in savings, the cocky little street prince bought 3 grams of high-grade cocaine and, using a simple cooking technique, turned it into a small mound of crack worth double his initial investment on the streets. "I watched all these guys selling and making $500 profit a day and $1,000 on a good day," Eric recalls. "I know this one guy who is selling. He's a high-school graduate. Very intelligent and he makes a lot of money."

Eric reached a payoff agreement with certain gang leaders in the area and staked out his turf, a patch of asphalt outside the highrise where he lives. He was warned not to sell anywhere else and assured that no one would deal in his area. "The whole area is controlled and if you try selling on someone else's turf, you're as good as dead."

That first week, Eric made about $900. "I sold to everyone, as long as I knew them. It didn't matter how old or how young.

But most of my customers are high-school kids from the neighborhood. Most of the kids around here do crack. What else do they have to do?"

Eric gave no credit. "Money talks. Bullshit walks. I don't care where the money comes from as long as they pay me. I know some came from purse snatches. These rockheads would offer me stuff they boosted or stole from break-ins, like jewellery, watches, cameras, VCRs and car radios. One guy came with an air conditioner. Can you believe it? I even got chicks to give me a blow job for a piece of rock. Now that's sick." Smacking his bony fist against the cement wall, he blustered: "I never go ripped off. If anybody ever tries to rip me off, they know I'll pay someone to blow them away."

In his first heady weeks as an independent dealer, Eric spent most of his profits on clothes and toys – an expensive stereo system, a Sony Walkman, a compact disc player and a color television set for his room. "My mother asked me where I got this stuff. I told her to fuck off and mind her own business. All of a sudden she's interested in what I'm doing."

But the late hours began to take their toll on the teenage pusher, so to stay awake and alert while doing business, especially on weekends, he started smoking a little crack for a "pick-me-up". Before long, his profits were being squandered almost entirely on crack for himself. "I used to do some hash and weed. I like to drink. I even tried these purple microdots [LSD] at a rock concert at Canada's Wonderland. But I never wanted to do crack. I saw what it did to people. It's dangerous shit. It makes you weird. I did it at first just to stay awake. I figured I could control it. I wasn't like those kids who would do anything for a piece of crack.

"I've done a lot of crack since then. I probably smoked $600 a week. Man, once you start doing it, it becomes the most important thing to you. You get a buzz that lasts about ten to fifteen minutes. Then you want more and more. That's when it becomes an expensive habit.

"I know this guy. He used to be really okay. Healthy, into sports and chicks. Pretty smart in school. He graduated from high school. He wasn't from around here. His parents were rich. I don't know why he got into crack. I mean, he had everything. A car, money, clothes. He lived in a really neat house in Etobicoke. Anyway, he came to me one night for some rock. At first I didn't know who he was. Then I recognized him. He was walking on bones covered with a layer of grey skin. He couldn't even speak right. He was stuttering. He looked retarded. I got really scared and told him I had nothing left to sell. I heard he died a couple of months later. The guy was only nineteen."

Eric admits that his stint in detention is the antidote he needs to cleanse his system of its powerful cravings for crack. "I won't do it again. My main thing is to get out of here. I've got a few people who owe me money. I think I'm going to cool down. But I don't know yet if I'm going to give up selling drugs. I worked at a few jobs but why should I work for $5 an hour when I could get $600 or more in a week tax free? My main aim is to get out of the welfare ghetto I live in. I have to get out of there. I hate the fucking place. I hate everything about it. It drags you down, man. It drags everybody down.

"You know, just a couple of years ago there wasn't any crack around. Nobody in Jane-Finch could afford coke. Too expensive. Too upper class. The drug of choice of the rich and beautiful and famous. We had weed, hash and some chemicals. Then the crack came. It's really frightening how much of it there is around today. The cops could come around and bust dealers every day of the week and there will always be someone else ready to take their place. In no time, there wouldn't be enough room in the jails. Selling crack is a way to make money and get out of that place if you're smart."

Eric pauses and ponders his last comment. "I guess smoking crack is another way to escape that place," he mumbles.

"I really think there is a serious crack problem in Toronto. I really do. I see quite a bit of kids getting into it. And it's spreading all over to other parts of the city. My advice to kids would be not to get involved with drugs. I'd tell them that if they do get into drugs, make sure it's only weed. It won't kill you like crack. This stuff burns a hole right through your lungs and you lose twenty-four hours of your life everytime you do crack."

At the Metro police drug squad office in downtown Toronto, Staff Sergeant Ernie Beale looked down at a stack of arrest sheets and shook his head. He cannot believe how swiftly crack has entrenched itself in the government-subsidized housing projects throughout Metro since the start of 1988.

"It's in every Metro and Ontario housing project," he said. "And it has spread to all of the poorer neighborhoods in Metro. In 1986, crack was virtually unknown. I don't think we made any crack seizures. The following year, we made 177 and most of that came in the latter half of the year. In 1988, we made 789 crack seizures and we expect to double or triple that in 1989. And I would estimate that there are at least a couple of hundred crack houses operating today in the city."

In the summer of 1988, Beale's undercover drug teams carried out a major drug bust in the Regent Park housing project, arresting dozens of crack dealers, seizing large quantities of the drug and shutting down a couple of crack houses. "The day after we busted the place, it was business as usual. The dealers set up shop and the crack houses reopened," the staff sergeant recounted.

But on this hot, hazy summer morning in early August, his preoccupation was the rampant and brazenly open crack dealing in the Jane-Finch corridor. For weeks, Mel Lastman, the gregarious mayor of North York, had been clamoring for a drug crackdown, and Beale's undercover unit was about to blanket the area on a buying binge from local street dealers. It would be the second time the squad swept the area. In the spring, undercover officers launched "Operation Mellow" in response to earlier public protests from Lastman and arrested scores of crack dealers. This latest drug sweep was code-named "Operation Return", and this time the squad made more than 180 buys, identified more than 100 drug dealers and uncovered a couple of crack houses. The round-up of street-level dealers began in early November with six to a dozen suspects being picked up every other evening. But less than a week after everyone was finally herded in, fingerprinted, photographed, charged and arraigned, the Jane-Finch area was a rekindled beehive of drug activity.

Beale has seen the devastation the drug has wreaked on the fragile ghettos of major urban centres in the United States. Since it hit the U.S. in the mid-1980s, crack has spawned vicious drug wars, leaving the bodies of thousands of victims – many innocent bystanders – in its destructive path. American television networks have broadcast blood-curdling documentaries about the crack epidemic in the U.S. with footage of murder victims being carted off in body bags; of grieving families; of open-air crack deals being struck on street corners; of platoons of cops dressed in commando fatigues battering down reinforced steel doors in dilapidated apartment buildings; of burned-out crack houses; of heavily armed thugs swaggering through schoolyards and parks; and of wounded children who got caught in the crossfire. Large urban areas are war zones where drug dealers shoot it out for control of a street corner.

For a time, it appeared that Canada would be spared. Even up to the summer of 1987, crack could not be found in the many drug bazaars that infect Canadian cities. Then it slammed into Toronto with a vengeance. By early 1989, "Toronto the Good" became the first Canadian city where crack had managed to gain a deadly foothold.

A drug intelligence report released by the RCMP in June, 1989, states: "The widespread inner city use of crack found in the United States is spreading to Metropolitan Toronto, where crack houses are appearing and crime rates linked to crack use are climbing."

Toronto has not yet fallen into the sheer barbarism of New York, Miami, Detroit, Washington, Dallas or Los Angeles. "We're still a civilized society," Beale explained. "People are a lot saner in Toronto. The thing about Toronto is that people here still get shocked when someone dies on drugs. Toronto still has the ability to get pissed off and that's what saves our ass, that conservative composition of our population. It's eroding but it's still there. But this town is getting more and more like New York every year. It's getting so large that it's fragmenting communities that no longer respond to issues that affect them," he warned.

Beale cited the sharp increase in crime rates in areas where crack has hit to illustrate the point. "The most frightening thing about crack is that it sponsors street crime; immediate, unsophisticated crimes that don't require any planning or skill." Especially assaults, purse snatchings, muggings, break and enters, and prostitution.

There have even been a few killings and woundings tied to crack dealing. But the crime most directly linked to crack, the police officer noted, is purse snatching. There were more than 750 purse snatchings in 1988 compared with about 500 the previous year. It was the biggest jump in any single category of crime, and the victims were largely senior citizens, easy prey for strung-out crack addicts. Most victims walked away with only scratches. A few were taken by ambulance to hospital with broken arms and legs. All have suffered psychological trauma and are afraid to go out even for a pleasant stroll on a warm summer day.

One victim was 66-year-old Blanche Barnett, who was attacked by a pipe-wielding youth outside her east-end bungalow on December 9, 1988, as she returned home from playing bingo. She was robbed of $18. Another victim, Wilhelmine Niebuhr, a 78-year-old resident of a Toronto senior citizens' home, was knocked to the cement sidewalk when two youths tried to grab her purse to which she clung tightly. The link between crack and purse snatching is simple, Beale explained. First, crack is relatively cheap. A "rock" sells for $20. So any person with just a few dollars – especially a woman carrying a purse – becomes a potential target. Secondly, purse snatching is an easy crime to commit. "It takes a certain amount of nerve to stick up a convenience store. What does it take to rip off an old lady and run?" Beale asked rhetorically.

It is the frightening violence associated with the drug that has so many residents of crack-infested neighborhoods scared to leave their homes. At dusk, they retreat behind the bolted doors of their apartments and townhouses until dawn. They live under constant siege, afraid of reprisals from armed drug pushers if they dare to speak out. Intimidation has become a way of life in most Metro Toronto and Ontario housing projects.

"People have become hostages in their own apartments. Throughout the night they hear banging on doors in the hallways and when they come out in the morning they see crack vials and tinfoil littering the place," Beale said.

The level of violence tied to crack scares even seasoned pushers who deal in a vast array of other drugs. "I never go near crack dealers," a convicted marijuana dealer commented from his prison cell. "They're crazy. You can't trust them and you can't trust their customers. They're vicious and sick people. You know when you're dealing with them, they're packing heat. They're so paranoid that they'll start shooting if you just happen to blink the wrong way."

For the paltry numbers of front-line community workers assigned to give assistance to people living in government-subsidized, low-income housing, the most worrisome aspect of the crack plague is the toll it is taking on the youngsters. More and more kids are being sucked in by the almost irresistible lure to peddle crack. Police and community workers are seeing kids getting into crack dealing at younger and younger ages, and they warn that if something is not done soon, an entire generation will be inextricably trapped in a violent lifestyle where the average lifespan is about twenty-seven years.

Community workers lament that so many of these kids are prime, easy pickings for adults who prey on the weak and susceptible. Their educational levels are as low as their self-esteem. After they leave high school, or more likely drop out, they go directly into the lowest-paying, menial jobs, or no jobs at all. Many simply give up, seeing only a life of despair and boredom before them. The only light at the end of the long, dark tunnel comes from the distorted images of reality on the television screen. Night after night, they are subjected to scenes depicting one-time ghetto losers living in luxurious homes, driving fancy cars and wearing high-fashion clothes and jewellery. Sure, they see some die in shootouts and others go to jail, but the image that remains most vivid in their impressionable young minds is that a lot of dope dealers make it big. If the opportunity presents itself, many of these young-sters will jump at the chance to make a few hundred dollars a day dealing drugs. These kids no longer look for role models in mainstream society. Instead, they focus in awe and envy on the drug dealers, who become folk heroes of sorts. The violence and threat of arrest and imprisonment that go with the lifestyle have little deterrent effect on these youngsters.

Drug dealers are attracted to crack because it yields more than double the profits made by trafficking cocaine.

"Crack is the classic entrepreneurial drug," Beale explained. "It's a mass-marketing success story. It's easy to prepare, easy to use, easy to hide, and a single dose sells for as little as $10. And in just a few hits, it can turn the user into a repeat customer. A dealer can buy an ounce of cocaine for as little as $1,400 – almost twice the price of an ounce of pure gold on the stockmarket – and more than double his money almost instantly by converting over a kitchen stove into 190 vials of crack at $20 apiece.

"Anyone who can afford a few grams of cocaine and can mix it with baking soda and water over a stove can start dealing crack off a street corner," the drug investigator con-tinued. "Crack has become a cottage industry. It's free enter-prise gone mad. And the common denominator is money. I don't know of any other product that you can sell and make so much profit as in this drug.

"But the scary thing about crack," Beale said, "is that it is a central-nervous-system stimulant similar in virtually every way to methamphetamine or speed. People who use crack become very weird very quickly. You're talking a very paranoid, psychotic group. You just can't ingest crack and function in a normal day-to-day situation. You have to turn to crime to survive and that's what alarms me about crack."

Another worrisome aspect of crack is that most of the customers are disillusioned teenagers. Crack is the poor man's cocaine, an equal-opportunity drug. It is cheap, plentiful and intensely addictive. Once it grips you, it is deadly. Users can become addicted after only a few days of their first hit on a pipe. But the dark and deadly side of crack is that the intense euphoria it produces fades very quickly. Within fifteen minutes, the user begins to come down, and is left feeling profoundly depressed, anxious and desperate for another hit.

Stella, a 17-year-old, bleached-blonde hooker, recounted that when she first smoked crack she fell in love with it. At a drug treatment centre, she talked about her six-month obsession with the drug. "I was sixteen. I was in grade 12 but I wasn't doing too well. Just getting by. I had done a little marijuana. No big thing. Then I went to this party with this guy and we smoked some rock. Man, did it ever take hold of me. What a rush! It was better than an orgasm. I just wanted more and more, and I would do anything to get it. At first, I stole from my mother and my older brother, and when I got caught, my mother and I had a big fight and she threw me out of the apartment. I didn't care. I just wanted to get some money to buy some rock. So I sold my body. I didn't care about anything. I wasn't scared or anything like that because that hit off the pipe made everything so absolutely supreme."

Sullen and somewhat remorseful, Stella talked about her struggle to rid her body of its cravings for crack. "I'll beat it. I know it's bad for me. It destroyed my life but now I'm working hard rebuilding it. I'll beat it." Three weeks later, Stella went AWOL from the treatment program. The craving for just another hit off the pipe was too much for her to battle.

The sky-blue 1987 Ford Mustang manoeuvred cautiously through the parking lot of a three-tower Ontario Housing Corporation highrise complex in the Jane-Finch corridor. Ted Payne, a black, bearded undercover drug cop, cautiously surveyed the asphalt jungle.

"No matter how many times you do this, you're always nervous. You never know what might go down," Payne said, drumming on the steering-wheel to a tune bopping in his head. "The adrenalin really starts to flow. I get so excited, I put myself into high gear and switch to the lingo. Look over there. They're coming over."

Two young black teenagers appeared out of the darkness and stood about 18 metres away staring in the direction of the car. Payne rolled down the window and waved them over.

"You looking?" the smaller of the two asked curtly.

"You got good rock, mon?" Payne asked.

"I got 20 and 40 piece. What you want, mon?"

"I want a 40 piece. You get me a 40 piece. And I don't want no shit, mon. I want the yella not the white." Born in the Bahamas, Payne affected a convincing Jamaican accent.

The two hustlers told us to wait and disappeared behind one of the buildings.

"You flash this money. That'll drive them crazy to deal. But hold onto it tight," Payne whispered, handing over a small wad of tens and twenties. "A 40 piece costs $40 but I'm not going to make any buys tonight. I don't have any backup. There could be trouble."

A moment later, the twosome reappeared. The heavyset kid stuck his hand through the window inches from Payne's face. He was holding two pieces of crack the size of two pearls in his palm.

"No, mon. You tryin' to rip me off. This no 40 piece. I go elsewhere," Payne bellowed.

"No. I swear. They two 20 pieces. You wait, mon. I go back and get you another 40 piece."

"Forget it, mon. I go elsewhere." Payne was weaving out of

the parking lot when the headlights on a gleaming red 1988 Toyota Celica flashed twice in our direction.

"They want to deal. To hell with them. We'll go to another building," he said.

As we passed the Celica, a head popped out of the window on the passenger's side. "Come here, mon. We deal. I got what you want. I got the good stuff."

Payne ignored the pleading sales pitch. Within minutes, we were cruising through the parking lot of another three-tower highrise complex. A big-shouldered Jamaican wearing a light blue nylon track suit made an almost imperceptible hand gesture and Payne stopped. The man ambled over to the car. He was suspicious, not of Payne but of me. He stared menacingly into my eyes. I calmly stared back.

"Who this guy? He don't talk? You say something, mon." The man stepped back and clenched his fists.

Payne shot back: "He's French, mon. From Quebec. He don't understand you."

"You tell him don't look at me or I break his face. You lookin', mon? What you want?"

Payne asked for a 40 piece and the man retreated into the building. Minutes later, a skinny teenager showed up with a marble-sized chunk that looked like a piece of weathered plaster. Payne quizzed him about the quality, then refused to buy it. The kid stormed away in a huff. As he reached the building, he turned and offered us a one-arm salute and a few well-chosen parting salvos.

Throughout the evening and into the early morning hours, Payne drove from one government-subsidized apartment complex to another. The scene was the same, a non-stop choreography of dealing, desire and despair being played out in glassed-in foyers, dimly lit parking lots, deserted asphalt basketball courts and forbidding underground garages. It was a wide-open, brazen hustle.

At one townhouse complex, we were instructed by a steerer who looked no older than fourteen to go to the basketball court at the back of the buildings to make a buy. Just as we were about to get out of the car, Payne spotted a dealer who was sporting a goatee and army fatigues. "We're out of here," he said anxiously. "I know him and he knows me. I busted him a few weeks ago for dealing. He must have just got out of jail."

As he passed a nearby lowrise apartment complex, Payne spied a lone crack addict lurking in the shadows. Wearing an oversized, full-length tan leatherette coat and a Blue Jays' baseball cap, the man was hunched over, puffing fiercely on a cigarette. "He's a burned-out crackhead. He used to be a healthy kid. Look at him. He looks sick, strung out. He's lost fifty pounds. The guy lives for crack and will rip off anyone including his mother to get it."

A yellow Honda Civic slipped past us and stopped in the darkened driveway. The driver switched off the lights and waited. A second later, a butane lighter flickered in the distance. The driver responded by flashing his car lights, and a gangly youth romped over to take his order. The hustler then scurried over to the far end of the building and made a clucking noise. A head peered out of a window two floors up. The hustler made a hand gesture and, moments later, the dealer was lowering a red child's sand pail on a nylon rope. Inside was a piece of crack wrapped in aluminum foil. The deal was made. The driver sped away and the hustler jammed some bills into the pail, which was gingerly hoisted up to the darkened apartment window.

"Try busting that place," Payne said. "He's probably got the door fortified so if we ever tried to hit the place, he'd have the whole stash down the toilet or out the window before we could get in there."

Just around the corner, the undercover cop pointed to a pair of desolate-looking highrise apartment buildings on Jane Street. "We busted that place not too long ago. Arrested a South American woman who was selling high-grade cocaine. She would send her 12-year-old daughter to pick up the stuff from a dealer in that apartment building across the street. Can you believe that, using your kids to deal drugs?"

Payne drove for a while in silence. He looked troubled. "You know, a lot of good, hard-working people live in these complexes. A lot of good people are on welfare because of no fault of their own. But these Ontario and Metro Housing apartments have virtually fallen under the control of drug dealers. At night, the parking lots, the driveways, garages and the entrances to these buildings belong to the dealers. You've seen them. The good people are afraid to say anything because they believe they'll be beaten up or killed. They're afraid of reprisals so they lock themselves in their apartments every night until morning. That's no way to live but that's the way it is. It's a real shame. Let's call it a night. I can't take anymore of this."

Staff Inspector James Clark of the Metro Toronto Police Morality Bureau hesitantly confirmed that most of the dealers in the Jane-Finch corridor are black. The standard profile of a crack dealer given by many of his officers is "male between the ages of seventeen and twenty-six, illiterate, black, Jamaican." Clark is not so quick with those kinds of comments. "A lot of people tend to blame black people. That's bullshit. Especially when whites bring it in in the first place. The black community is being victimized."

For Clark, the issue is not black or white but how to rid the poorer communities of crack dealers and get treatment for young drug abusers. "Police can't look sideways at certain ethnic groups without creating suspicion and distrust, and what's starting to get lost in all this is we all want the same thing. Drugs will only be beaten if we work at it together. My worry is that a couple of years from now, while we're fighting among ourselves, we'll turn around and find a whole bunch of kids dead."

In the early morning hours of Sunday, October 9, 1988, Paul Davis was taken to an underground garage of a highrise subsidized housing project on Grandravine Drive in the Jane-Finch area and murdered. The 20-year-old black youth, who apparently had been warned earlier by drug dealers to stay away from the area, was shot in the head. The garage where the youth's body was found was a well-known crack drive-in. Police sources speculated that the killing was a message to independent dealers and other drug gangs that a new and extremely violent gang – a chapter of the notorious Jamaican gang known as the Posses (pronounced passees) – was vying for control of the lucrative crack trade in the corridor. Police had information that a Posse called the Strikers, with strong ties to a Posse in Miami, was setting up operations in the city. They also had intelligence that another Posse had been forged in Regent Park, a sprawling housing project on the eastern fringe of downtown Toronto.

For police forces across the country, the thought of Posse gangs gaining a foothold in Canada is extremely worrisome. The Posses have terrorized every city in the United Sates where they have laid claim to a piece of concrete for their drug-dealing enterprises. A classified intelligence report published in the United States in 1988 by the Bureau of Alcohol, Tobacco and Firearms states that forty Jamaican Posses with a membership of more than 10,000 are operating in the U.S., Canada, Great Britain and the Caribbean. The report also states that "since January 1, 1985, the Posses have been responsible for in excess of 1,000 homicides nationwide."

The Posses started out primarily smuggling marijuana from Jamaica into the U.S., but the cocaine and crack explosion of the 1980s offered the gangs more money than they had ever dreamed of. With the increased profits came increased violence. They have killed 12- and 13-year-old children and pregnant women. In February, 1988, four Jamaican women were shot, two critically, in an intended execution in Washington, D.C. When police arrived at the bloody scene, four children, from one to three years old, were crawling over the bodies in attempts to awaken their mothers. One of the victims was four months pregnant. The gangs also torture their victims. Some have been shot in the ankles, knees and hips before being shot in the head, and others have been thrown into scalding hot water in bathtubs. Their bodies were later dismembered and disposed of in the trash.

Intelligence compiled by U.S. drug enforcement agencies states that the Posses have their roots in the slums around Kingston, Jamaica. Of those that have been identified in the U.S., the largest, most well established and most violent is the Shower Posse. The second most prominent is the Spangler Posse. American drug enforcement officials say that all other Posses are simply offshoots of these two gangs. Both Spangler and Shower claim affiliations with Jamaican political parties: the Shower aligns itself with the Jamaican Labor Party of Edward Seaga, and the Spangler identifies itself with the People's National Party of Prime Minister Michael Manley. It is estimated that drug wars between the Spanglers and rival gangs are responsible for upwards of 350 murders in the last five years. The Spanglers distribute drugs on a wholesale and street-sale level. The gang virtually controls the cocaine and crack trade in a large section of Manhattan, and anyone selling drugs in that area who is not a Spangler member must pay a "tax" to the Posse.

The Posses get their cocaine supply from Colombians or Cubans living in Jamaica, the Bahamas and the U.S. Their purchases are usually made in small quantities of 4 or 5 kilograms, and then piecemealed and delivered by a large cadre of couriers to stash houses.

Although there is still some question over how organized the Posses are, there is no doubt in the minds of drug gang investigators that they are as disciplined as they are violent. The majority of members are convicted criminals who started their criminal careers in Jamaica and are fugitives from their homeland, living illegally in Jamaican-immigrant communities in the U.S. and Canada. Many Posse members have been arrested for murder in the U.S. but often the charges are dropped because the witnesses are found murdered or simply disappear.

U.S. Drug Enforcement Administration officials firmly

believe that Posse gangs have established themselves in Toronto, where there is a large Jamaican population. "Where you have crack and Jamaicans, you've got Posses," a DEA official stated emphatically. Yet, when the existence of Posse gangs in Metro Toronto was revealed in mid-October, 1988, in articles in the *Toronto Sun* and the *Toronto Star*, Metro's deputy chief of police William McCormack stated unequivocally that his investigators had not uncovered any Posse activity.

Over lunch at a sandwich shop in the city's north end, a top Toronto drug squad officer scoffed at McCormack's public denunciation. "We've been working Posses for over a year. We know they exist in Toronto and now we're being told to say they don't exist.

"The annoying thing is that this boils down to the issue of racism when it has nothing to do with racism and everything to do with a vicious bunch of criminals that are terrorizing and victimizing entire communities in the city. The brass are afraid of the Jamaican lobby in the city. They're paranoid that the department will be attacked as racists. This is really a highly sensitive issue with them. Everyone in the department is deathly afraid of a racial accusation so, to avoid it, we are simply told to deny the existence of Posses. So, on the record, they officially don't exist. Off the record, they do."

In November, 1988, Beale blanketed the Jane-Finch housing projects with his undercover officers for another major drug sweep. "We went right back in there after Project Return with Project Fall and started buying again off the very same people."

But this time, the situation was markedly different from past drug sweeps. During the two-month project, six of Beale's officers were robbed at knife-point; ten were assaulted while making undercover buys; and one undercover cop, 28-year-old Gordon Fritz, was attacked by a knife-wielding 17-year-old crack dealer. Fritz, who was wearing a concealed radio transmitter, had just bought some crack off the youth and told him he was under arrest. The dealer pulled a knife and the police officer warded off a blow aimed at his chest. The blade went through the palm of his hand. The struggle was picked up by a back-up team monitoring the transaction from a nearby van. They rushed to the scene and tackled the attacker as he was about to plunge the knife into the undercover officer's back.

In late January, Beale ordered "the take-down" of Project Fall after his officers had racked up more than 300 buys from 264 dealers. Ironically, two crack dealers busted in the drug sweep were back on the streets before the police announced what they described as "the biggest crackdown on street drug pushers in Metro Toronto" at a press conference on February 6, 1989. Leroy Carlester Elliston, 32, was handed a seven-day sentence by Provincial Court Judge Mary Hogan after he pleaded guilty to trafficking in crack cocaine. Both the Crown prosecutor and defence counsel had proposed a ninety-day prison term. Judge Hogan sentenced a second trafficker, Thomas Gerald Wick, 34, to two weeks on two counts of trafficking in crack, despite a joint submission by the Crown and defence counsel for a six-month term. The judge took into account the two months Wick had spent in custody await-ing the hearing.

The disparity in sentencing in the drug cases left Metro Police Chief Jack Marks fuming. "Some judges aren't in touch with the pulse of the community . . . don't feel the anger of the community," he said. Staff Inspector Jim Clark was less diplomatic. "That kind of sentence is really a joke if we are serious about cleaning up the distribution of crack cocaine."

Clark also said it was damaging to police morale to see criminals getting light sentences after the police put them-selves at serious risk to get evidence to arrest crack pushers. He offered to take Judge Hogan on a tour of the crack havens so she could have a first-hand look at the violence, devastation and misery caused by the drug dealing.

A week later, Staff Inspector Julian Fantino, the head of 31 Division, which includes the Jane-Finch corridor, sparked a furor when he told members of the city's committee on community, race and ethnic relations that while blacks make up 6 per cent of the Jane-Finch population, they accounted for 82 per cent of robberies and muggings, 55 per cent of purse snatchings and 51 per cent of drug offences in 1988.

"Police have an inordinate number of negative contacts with black youths," Fantino told the committee. "An inordinate amount of serious crimes involve blacks, particularly black youths. Many of the victims are black citizens." The officer maintained that he prepared his findings by poring over scores of arrest sheets and statements from victims of criminal acts. He added that police do not keep such figures, but he went through arrest sheets to put them together for the committee meeting. He also stressed that he presented the statistics not to show that blacks are criminals, but to make a point that there is a definite problem that must be addressed. "This community needs some attention. To attack the problem we have to understand it and get a commitment to tackle it," the balding 46-year-old officer maintained.

Black community leaders exploded with anger at the release of the statistics, which they hotly charged were intended to portray blacks as criminals. Wilson Head, a member of the Urban Alliance on Race Relations, said the figures would only fuel the petty minds of bigots. "There are people out there waiting for this. They want to get something to justify their bigotry."

Black Action Defense Committee spokesman Dudley Laws went further, describing the release of the statistics as "a racist and deliberate attempt to divide our community from the larger communities and for the police to obtain unlimited moral authority and action to harass and brutalize." Dan McIntyre, executive coordinator of Ontario's Race Relations Directorate, said the figures did nothing "to help the negative stereotyping of blacks and the Jane-Finch area."

Exasperated, Fantino reiterated that he compiled the figures "in light of criticisms that we pick on black youths." He stressed that now that the numbers were out, police and black community leaders must end the rhetoric and work to solve the problem. He explained that black youths in the Jane-Finch corridor are turning to crime, not because they want to, but because of the terrible social and economic conditions that exist there.

Fantino came loaded with even more statistics on the Jane-Finch community to buttress his arguments. They depicted an area with the highest population density of any area in Metro Toronto; the largest percentage of single-parent families, 21 per cent compared to the Metro average of 13 per cent; the largest concentration of newcomers to Canada in the city; one of the largest concentrations of subsidized housing; and the lowest average family income in Metro – $21,000 a year compared to the Metro average of $30,000.

When committee member Thomas Mininger asked Fantino for statistics compiled on the ethnic composition of the police staff in 31 Division, Fantino sheepishly replied that he didn't have them. "They should be on the tip of your lips," Mininger shot back. "You can't have it both ways."

More oil was thrown onto the fire with the release of a controversial report prepared by Metro's race relations department which concluded that police have contributed to a negative stereotyping of blacks in the Jane-Finch community through high-profile drug sweeps, and that black youths who simply "hang out" in the area are needlessly harassed by police. Fantino argued that the report lacked fairness and honesty, and questioned the motives of those interviewed for the report. He also said that literature had been distributed around the Jane-Finch community in November, 1988, accusing the police of fabricating the rampant drug dealing in the area. It went on to accuse police of racism and beatings of young blacks. Labelling some of the literature and reports on police-community relations "diabolical", the police officer countered that there has been "blatant discrimination directed against the police."

Looking drawn and tense, Fantino was trotted out the following day before an electrically charged meeting of the Jane-Finch Concerned Citizens' Organization to apologize for his comments. He said he did not know that a *Toronto Star* reporter was present at the meeting in which he released the statistics. "I, too, would have considered such presentation inappropriate and dutifully restricted my comments accordingly," the officer said, reading from a prepared text. "Obviously this is not the case, and harmful consequences have since surfaced to make the whole process regrettable."

Fantino added: "I realize the some members of the black community are angered as a consequence of my actions. I fully appreciate that the majority of black citizens are good, law-abiding and caring individuals whom I highly regard. I want those people to know that my comments were made in good faith, without prejudice, honestly motivated by a profound concern for the plight of all citizens who form a part of our caring community. I offer our black citizens my sincere regret for the unintended but troublesome repercussions that have taken place."

Fantino's immediate superior, Staff Superintendent Walter Tyrrell, suggested that, in future, meetings with members of the black community be closed to the press. "If we are going to reach a solution to a major community concern, then I think we are going to have to have in-camera meetings, and we're going to have to be very candid with each other to try and resolve our problems."

With the controversy now on simmer, Beale's undercover drug squad swooped down onto another housing project in neighboring Scarborough in Operation Bluff. By early April, the operation had yielded 100 arrests.

Raymond puffed nervously on a cigarette. He desperately wanted a hit off a crack pipe. Sitting in a smoke-filled, 24-hour donut shop in the city's east end, he hardly touched his coffee. He wanted to get going. He had arranged a visit to a crack house. It was 12:45 a.m. Outside, a fine drizzle blanketed the city. It was cool and damp.

"Everything is set up, I swear," Raymond pleaded. "It's cool. You just buy me some rock and we go in and I'll smoke it. You could just sit there and watch. I told the guy who runs the place that you're a friend of mine from Montreal. He knows me. I told him we were in the joint together. He believes me, I swear. I told him you're into smack, that I'm just going to do a couple of hits on the pipe and then we're on our way to my place. It'll be cool. I swear. You just buy me a 20 piece and I'll get you in."

Raymond knew the location of several crack houses in the city. The one he had selected was in a public housing highrise. The apartment was rented by a single mother, another crack-head, who allowed dealers to use her place in return for a constant supply of crack. Several months earlier, the woman had lost her 6-year-old daughter to the Children's Aid Society after social workers learned that the child was being abused and neglected.

As we approached the building, Raymond got incredibly anxious. He was anticipating getting high, and he could almost taste the crack. "Most times they got to know you before they let you in the place. They're paranoid of cops, man. So they test you. They make you do the stuff right there before they sell you any. You gotta use what you buy, and they know cops never use. You don't want to fuck with these people. If they think you're a narc, you're dead. But they know me, man. It'll be cool. I swear. You just buy me a 40 piece and we're in."

"A 20 piece," I reminded him.

"Yeah. Okay. Let's go. I'll do the talking."

Raymond pressed twice on a buzzer and waited. A gruff male voice crackled something inaudible on the intercom.

"It's Ray. I'm lookin'."

The door buzzed and Raymond scurried down the main-floor corridor to the stairwell at one end of the building. "We got to take the stairs," he advised.

At the first-floor landing, a whistler, who looked no older

than fourteen, stood lookout. He nodded at Ray and gave me a curt once-over glance. "It's okay, man. He's my buddy from Montreal," Ray explained.

The whistler made a clucking sound which was responded to by lookouts on at least two landings above. At the fourth floor, two more lookouts hustled us into the gloomy corridor. Half the lights had been either unscrewed or removed altogether. Raymond made his way to an apartment at the end of the hallway and rapped twice on the door. An eyeball peered through the peephole. There was a clunking of dead-bolt locks and the sound of a steel bar being removed from its wedges.

"Hey, Ray," a lanky, acne-scarred man shouted.

"How's it going?" Raymond asked as he slid into the apartment.

"Who's the dude?" the man asked, stepping in front of me.

"I told you about him. He's a friend of mine from Montreal. He's a frog. Doesn't speak much English but he's cool. I met him in the joint when I was busted a few years back in Montreal. He's got cash. He's going to score us two 40 pieces if I get him some smack. He's a junkie. Smokes the shit. I'll take a few hits off the pipe and then we're gone."

The door slammed behind us and the bolts clanked into place. The doorman pressed two vials into Raymond's hand. "That'll be eighty bucks, man."

Trying to conceal my anger at Raymond's antic, I pulled $80 out of my pocket. Raymond snapped open a vial and darted into the darkened living room. It was sparsely furnished with a few used mattresses and a half-dozen blue plastic milk crates strewn on the floor. Two gaunt-looking women and a man were sprawled on a mattress in one corner. The man sucked feverishly on a glass pipe while holding a butane burner over a glowing morsel of crack.

"I'll give you anything you want for a 20 piece," one of the women offered.

"No, thanks. Not the crack I'm into," Raymond shot back sarcastically. "I ain't into letting you suck on my pipe."

"Fuck you, asshole," the woman shouted.

I stared intently as Raymond prepared a pear-shaped glass bowl. With aplomb, he pushed a piece of crack into a mesh screen at the top of the bowl and lit a butane torch, which he held over the drug. In seconds, it began to glow and melt down into a brownish ooze. Raymond sucked back through a hole in the middle of the bowl, and a fine white mist began to fill the bottle. After two hits, Raymond sat back. He was flying. The neurons in his brain cells were crackling. His eyes looked crazed and a sinister grin covered his face. After fifteen minutes, he grabbed for the pipe and anxiously began to prepare it for another hit.

"We should split," I whispered urgently.

"I'm doing another hit," he snapped.

"After that let's go," I pleaded.

"You buy me another 40 piece and we'll go." He sucked back on the pipe and almost instantly began to soar.

A door at the other end of the room creaked open and a tiny, dark-haired woman emerged from a blackened bedroom. Her hands were trembling as she tugged at the doorman's arm. With a look of disgust, he handed her a vial and shoved her away from him. She disappeared into the bedroom and shut the door. A moment later, a buzzer over the door ignited. I shot bolt upright. The whistlers cleared the customers and the doorman welcomed two women, who were obviously prostitutes, and an emaciated man carrying a tote bag filled with stolen items. Regular customers, the hookers were in a hurry. They each passed the dealer a twenty-dollar bill, got their vials and left. The negotiations over the bag, which contained camera equipment and a ghetto blaster, were sharp but brief. A deal was struck for three 40-piece vials. The man picked out a spot along the wall and the doorman signalled to one of the whistlers to take the tote bag to some other location in the building.

By now, Raymond was hitting up a third time. When he was flying, I flashed two $20 bills. "I'll buy another 40 piece if we leave right now. I want to split," I whispered angrily.

As he reached cruising altitude, Raymond grabbed the money and scurried over to the doorman to make another purchase. With the transaction over, the doorman lifted the steel bar and unbolted the locks. On the way down the stair-well, we heard the familiar clucking sound of the whistler a few floors below. On the second-floor landing, we passed four more crackheads on their way up to the apartment.

Outside, Raymond broke out in a fit of laughter. "I told you I could get you in. You get to see what you wanted to see? What do you want to do next?"

7

Washing Dirty Money

Jeremy Lake and Norman Jackson (not their real names) were considered in some respectable circles of Toronto to be highly successful businessmen. Together, they had amassed an impressive real estate portfolio in Ontario and the United States, and they had done it all in just a few years. They owned a highrise condominium complex in downtown Kitchener, estimated in 1987 at $14 million. They owned a subdivision of 148 newly constructed homes in Barrie, a sports complex north of Toronto, and two sprawling farms in southern Ontario. They also owned two parcels of real estate in West Palm Beach, Florida, one consisting of 148 lots with an estimated value of $14 million U.S., and the other of 10 lots valued at about $800,000 U.S. These properties, and others, were maintained under numerous domestic and foreign corporations.

According to information gained during an extensive police investigation, these corporations, and others, were created by their Toronto lawyer for a sole purpose – to launder the more than $100 million amassed by the duo's marijuana and hashish drug distribution network in southern Ontario between the fall of 1983 and April, 1987.

The multi-million-dollar international drug dealings of Lake and Jackson began to unravel in April, 1987, when U.S. Drug Enforcement Administration agents stationed in San Diego, California, raided a farm in a nearby county and seized over 13 tonnes of Mexican-grown marijuana. The agents also seized more than $1 million in cash and took Jackson into custody.

Jackson, who was thirty-three years old at the time, made a deal with the DEA to be a witness for the State in return for

157

immunity from prosecution. If convicted in the U.S. under the charge "operation of a continuing criminal enterprise", he would have faced a mandatory sentence of life imprisonment with no chance of parole for forty years. Jackson chose to sing, and the tune he sang gave law enforcement officers in Canada and the U.S. the complete drug distribution network and money-laundering activities of the Canadian gang, and led to the arrests of more than a dozen people on both sides of the border.

Lake was fingered as the head of the syndicate and responsible for the acquisition of capital, collecting money from the sales of drugs and controlling the wholesalers at the distribution end. Court documents allege he had put together an impressive wholesale distribution network throughout southern Ontario, Calgary, Winnipeg and in several U.S. states, including Michigan, New York, Florida and Tennessee. Lake was also responsible for laundering and concealing the profits from drug sales in various offshore corporations and real estate acquisitions in Ontario, Florida and elsewhere.

Jackson told investigators that he joined forces with Lake as an equal partner in the fall of 1983. Jackson had key contacts in Mexico and California for obtaining large quantities of marijuana. His main supplier, who lived in Tijuana, also assisted in the transportation of the marijuana from Mexico to the stash site in California and the ultimate distribution of the drug in the U.S. and Canada. In addition, Jackson was responsible for paying the Mexican supplier and maintaining a set of various ledgers of payments and expenses.

Lake's lieutenant was Steven McDougall (not his real name), whose job was to handle couriers in the collection and delivery of money amassed from drug sales. He also assisted Lake in the concealment of marijuana and hashish in a farm in southern Ontario, the laundering of funds and the purchase of real estate.

Another key player in the organization was the Toronto lawyer, who had retired from his law practice in 1981 to work almost exclusively for the syndicate. The lawyer, the RCMP allege in court documents, became the principal contact for laundering drug profits for Lake and Jackson by creating and maintaining numerous offshore corporations.

After Jackson was arrested, he took Canadian and U.S. drug investigators through the entire operation, which began with purchases of large quantities of marijuana from the Mexican supplier. Jackson, who used the code-name Phil, would phone the Mexican, known as "the doctor", and using code words would arrange for a shipment. In turn, the Mexican would handle the transportation end, moving the marijuana to the farm in California. Jackson told DEA investigators that between April, 1986, and April, 1987, he had paid the Mexican about $25 million U.S. in cash for purchases of marijuana on behalf of the gang.

Jackson also fingered the Canadian truck driver who smuggled the marijuana from the States into Ontario. The trucker owned and operated an oil tanker tractor trailer with concealed front and rear bulkheads in which the drug was hidden. The trucker purportedly received $25,000 for each border crossing. The marijuana shipments were then taken to a farm in southern Ontario for concealment. That farm was owned by Jackson's brother-in-law, who was arrested in late 1986 when police found more than 400 kilograms of marijuana hidden on the farm.

Jackson identified several other key members of the gang for police and provided them with details of their relationships, roles and activities in the syndicate. He fingered the two men who were the gang's principal contacts with wholesale dealers in the southern Ontario region controlled by Lake and Jackson. He identified the men who arranged for the delivery of the marijuana to various dealers at predetermined times and locations around the province, and who were also responsible for the collection of money from these dealers. And he identified the women couriers who delivered drug profits to a money exchange on Bay Street in downtown Toronto, where Canadian tens and twenties stuffed into tote bags were converted into crisp, new $100 U.S. bills.

Jackson told investigators that in December, 1986, one of
the couriers was robbed of $580,000 at her former Missis-
sauga residence before the cash could be delivered to the
money exchange. And over a two-day period beginning January
ary 26, 1987, RCMP undercover officers watched the woman
rendezvous on at least four occasions at various industrial
and shopping complexes in Mississauga where she took delivery of tote bags from a key member of the gang. The woman
was followed to the money exchange on Bay Street where the
bags were deposited.

Steven McDougall's two daughters were also employed as
money couriers for the organization, Jackson said. The two
sisters smuggled converted drug money profits into the U.S.
inside cars outfitted with secret compartments to hide the
cash. Once across the border, they boarded a commercial
airline to West Palm Beach, Florida, or San Diego, California,
and delivered the money to its ultimate destination. Jackson
told U.S. investigators that Lake once dispatched one of the
couriers from West Palm Beach to Carlsbad, California, in
February, 1987, with upwards of $3.4 million U.S. to make a
payment to the Mexican supplier for a marijuana shipment.

In May, 1987, the two sisters were arrested at the Detroit
International Airport and charged with U.S. currency viola-
tions. The sisters had $468,000 U.S. in their possession and
were en route to San Diego to deliver the money to Jackson.
The Cadillac the women were driving belonged to their
father.

The DEA investigation found the Lake-Jackson organization awash in fraudulent identifications which, they were
told, were supplied by another key gang member, who operated a small hotel in downtown Toronto. The hotel was used to
launder and conceal drug money for the gang, Jackson said.
He also told police that the hotel operator had created more
than 100 sets of fraudulent identification for the organization, and showed police six sets of identification prepared for
him in the names of Robert W. Hughes, Robert Philip Burke,
Carl Robert Baker, Robert Holt, Robert Alan Babcock and

Philip Alexandre Lamoureux. Telephone records obtained by the RCMP show phone service at the hotel in September, 1986, in the names of Holt, Hughes and Lamoureux. Records on the fraudulent documents were hidden in a secret compartment behind a row of shelves on the ground floor of the man's downtown Toronto home. Jackson added that he helped him build a secret compartment in a cedar-lined closet located in the back of the hotel to store other fraudulent documents.

For six weeks from the time of his arrest in April, 1987, Jackson worked undercover as an informant for the DEA, participating in wiretapped telephone conversations with members of the organization. He supplied investigators with details, such as the corporate structure that was allegedly set up by the lawyer to launder the profits of the drug syndicate. He also agreed to participate in the shipment of more than 200 kilograms of marijuana by van from the farmhouse in California to Abbotsford, B.C. The RCMP and the DEA were aware that a Canada Customs officer was on the syndicate's payroll. He was arrested shortly after he waved the van through the Canada Customs inspection station. After the bust, the RCMP moved in on the entire organization, arresting fifteen people, including Lake, McDougall, and the lawyer. The Mexican, who was in Canada on a vacation, was arrested by the RCMP and returned to the U.S. to face drug trafficking charges there.

Drug trafficking in Canada and the United States has become a multi-billion-dollar industry. It is the largest single source of profit for organized crime. The RCMP estimate that the sale of illegal drugs in Canada in 1988 topped $10 billion. For drug dealers, who are amassing vast sums of dirty money, this poses a significant problem. They cannot spend their ill-gotten gains freely without attracting the attention of law enforcement officials.

Hard cash is the medium of exchange of the drug trade.

Street-level dealing brings in tote bags filled with five-, ten- and twenty- dollar bills. A large suitcase filled with $1 million in twenties weighs approximately 50 kilograms and cannot be lugged around easily. The million needs to be converted into something more portable, like $100 bills, which can fit into an attaché-case and weigh about 10 kilograms, or, better still, $100,000 bank drafts that can slip into an envelope.

In the course of drug busts, police across Canada have come across small mountains of tens and twenties that have been too big for dealers to count. Instead, they simply weighed the cash to calculate the total. In the summer of 1987, an RCMP officer stumbled on more than $1 million in small bills packed in boxes in a downtown Vancouver hotel room and another $800,000 in bags in the trunk of a car in the hotel parking lot after busting a drug gang that was attempting to smuggle 7 tonnes of marijuana by ship into British Columbia.

"Money laundering" is the term used to describe the process in which cash from illegal activities gets a thorough rinsing and is made to appear to originate from legitimate business enterprises. Organized crime has harnessed the financial and legal wizardry of a small army of money launderers – accountants, bookkeepers, lawyers and bankers – who have developed a host of sophisticated and intricate schemes to make the money look legitimate. The outlets they bring into play cover the entire financial spectrum, from banks, brokerage houses and foreign currency exchanges to legitimate businesses and offshore financial havens.

The first hurdle in the laundering of large amounts of raw currency is its physical movement. Dealers constantly worry about creating suspicion as to the origin of large cash deposits. In the United States, for example, deposits of more than $10,000 must be recorded on a Currency Transaction Report and reported to the U.S. Department of the Treasury within fifteen days. Violations are treated as criminal offences and are punishable by up to five years in prison and/or a fine of up to $500,000.

To avoid creating undue suspicion, traffickers employ

"smurfs" – nondescript couriers who make large numbers of small transactions, always under $10,000, at a variety of banks. The smurf will then buy bank drafts or money orders in specified larger amounts and turn them over to another person who is responsible for coordinating the movement of this money to another bank, usually in another country. The conversion of small denominations to large bills is referred to as "refining" dirty money.

Unlike U.S. banks, Canadian financial institutions are not subject to formal regulations requiring that large cash deposits be reported to the government, and this has given Canada a reputation in criminal circles throughout North America as an important first link in international money laundering. In recent years, the Canadian banking system has been directly linked to a number of illegal money-laundering schemes. All too often, their defence is that they are the unwitting dupes of sophisticated criminals in these schemes. But RCMP sergeant Marc Bourque, who heads the anti-drug-profiteering program in Montreal, doesn't buy the argument for a moment.

"There's just too much wilful blindness going on with a lot of these banks. How can you tell me that you don't suspect something fishy is going on when seedy-looking individuals come into your bank every second day carrying gym bags full of cash?" he asked sarcastically. Bourque cited a particular case in which managers of at least two major banks in Montreal helped a local syndicate of drug traffickers rinse truckloads of drug money through their branches and then make purchases of more than $40 million in bank drafts, which in turn were wired to, and deposited in, various foreign banks.

Even as the Canadian banking system becomes better informed about illegal laundering schemes, it is increasingly citing concern for client confidentiality as its defence for doing little to stop them. A document published by the RCMP in August, 1988, states: "Financial institutions often encounter cases of transactions obviously involving the proceeds of crime, but are reluctant to report these instances for fear of civil liability stemming from the breach of banking confidentiality. In some particularly blatant instances, members of criminal organizations were noted to have trundled dollies loaded with cartons containing hundreds of thousands of dollars into banks, secure in the knowledge their transaction would go unreported."

Canadian banking executives have fought pitched battles in the boardrooms of Ottawa to keep the federal government from imposing measures that would require banks or other financial institutions to disclose information that could help police detect money laundering by international narcotics traffickers. On January 1, 1989, when the government proclaimed Bill C-61, its legislation making money laundering illegal and allowing the courts to freeze and seize money and assets obtained from organized crime activities, there were no provisions obliging Canadian banks to record and report to authorities all large cash and foreign currency transactions. The powerful banking lobby had won.

Critics slammed the government for capitulating. New Democratic member of Parliament Howard McCurdy commented caustically that "the failure to include this kind of reporting requirement in any anti-money-laundering legislation is to load up the gun with blanks. In the absence of some facility by which one is able to detect transactions involving large sums of money that cannot be attributed to legitimate sources, you will have great difficulty enforcing a piece of anti-money-laundering legislation." Liberal MP John Nunziata accused the Progressive Conservative government of caving in to the banks. "If we do not have that legislation, and the Americans do, obviously, the illegal money is going to go the easiest route possible. One of the easiest ways, I suppose, is to use Canadian banks," the MP said. Critics from both opposition parties accused the Conservative government of being soft on the major banks, from which the Tory party receives substantial financial contributions.

A confidential document, titled "Enterprise Crime Study Report", prepared for the Department of Justice in June, 1983, stressed that without powers to track and identify the movement of profits earned by sophisticated criminals, it would be difficult for police and the courts to effectively use the so-called "freeze and seize" provisions of the proceeds-of-crime legislation. "Without clear powers to identify and track the proceeds of crime, it is difficult to connect the proceeds to a particular offence or to a particular criminal," the report said. "Given this obstacle, it follows that it would be equally difficult to apply provisions for freezing, seizure and forfeiture of criminal proceeds." The report concludes that a cash and foreign currency reporting system "would first of all make the identification and tracking of enterprise criminal profits much easier and, therefore, improve the success rate of financial investigations and prosecutions as well as support provisions for freezing, seizure and forfeiture."

More than two years later, those findings were reiterated by then deputy solicitor general Fred Gibson. In a four-page letter to William Kennett, then federal inspector general of banks, Gibson wrote: "Canadian legislation that would permit the freezing, seizure, and forfeiture of the profits from enterprise crime would have little effect unless there were mechanisms in place whereby these profits could be traced." Gibson went on to recommend, as did the Justice Department report, that the federal government, in cooperation with the provinces, examine the feasibility of introducing a cash and foreign currency transaction reporting system. That study was never carried out.

In an interview with *Globe and Mail* reporter Andrew McIntosh in late May, 1987, Ross Christensen, director general of police and law enforcement policy for the Department of the Solicitor General, defended the government's decision to exempt banks from recording and reporting all large cash and foreign currency transactions. "To impose that kind of reporting requirement on the banking community would be a major step. We are aware of that and we do not want any confrontation."

Christensen flatly denied accusations that political pressure from the financial community thwarted plans to include mandatory banking reporting procedures in the new law. He also noted that the reviews on the U.S. experience with its system were mixed, and that its implementation has "unreeled an enormous volume of paper and information" on federal law enforcement officials south of the border.

However, William Carter, a spokesman for the Federal Bureau of Investigation in Washington, D.C., countered that the U.S. transactions-reporting requirements have helped the police to spot money-laundering schemes and to make several big drug arrests. "We've had success in taking down a number of big drug operations as a result of that system being in place. And down the road, we expect to see many more significant cases of this type," he said.

In March, 1989, the U.S. Justice Department announced that it had smashed a $1-billion drug money-laundering ring, and added that it could not have been accomplished without the cash transactions reporting program. In a two-year undercover operation called Polar Cap, U.S. drug investigators sent the financial wizards of Medellin, Colombia's main cocaine cartel, scrambling to find new ways to launder their massive drug profits. U.S. authorities arrested and charged 127 individuals; seized a half-tonne of cocaine, some of it retrieved from the sewers of New York City, and $45 million in cash, jewels and real estate; and filed civil actions in an effort to seize as much as $412 million in assets of the Banco de Occidente of Panama and the Banco de Occidente of Colombia which had been deposited in U.S. banks.

The system, which laundered $1.2 billion in cocaine profits over two years, was both classic and complex. In October, 1987, undercover drug agents tracking cocaine shipments from Colombia to the U.S. stumbled onto a money-laundering ring called "La Mina", The Mine. During their investigations, they discovered that the cash generated from the drug sales in U.S. cities was being collected by the ring, packed into boxes and sent by courier to jewellery stores in New York, Houston and Los Angeles. At the stores, such as Ropex-L.A. and Ronel Refining in Los Angeles, and Andonian Brothers Manufacturing Co., a jewellery broker with offices in L.A., New York and Houston, the traffickers used high-speed money-counting machines to tabulate the bundles of loot. To conceal the source of the money, the store owners, who were working with the drug dealers, created false invoices for sales of large quantities of gold jewellery and bullion to fictitious customers who had paid for their purchases in cash. After the money was counted, it was then repacked. Brinks and Loomis armored cars were called in to truck the bags to local banks. Once the cash was deposited, the dealers asked that the funds be wire-transferred to other bank accounts in New York, London, Panama City and other cities around the world, including Toronto.

John Lawn, chief of the U.S. Drug Enforcement Administration, said the ring made substantial deposits, and the banks routinely filed currency reports, as required by law, on deposits of more than $10,000. But they raised few eyebrows because the gold business is cash-based. However, a suspicious bank teller alerted federal investigators when he noticed that Andonian Brothers had made cash deposits totalling $25 million over a three-month period. The banker simply did not believe a jewellery company could make that much profit in so little time, no matter how successful.

Lawn said the deposit slips, registered with the Internal Revenue Service, were used by undercover agents to verify the activities of the drug trafficking network. And a federal court affidavit filed in Atlanta, Georgia, states: "The purpose of these shipments, deposits and wire transfers was to conceal the nature, source, location and ownership of the cocaine proceeds, and to place the proceeds outside the United States, beyond the reach of law enforcement."

Combing through sheaves of currency transaction reports, DEA investigators traced $13.5 million (U.S.) to the Swiss Bank Corp. (Canada) in Toronto, which is a subsidiary of Switzerland's second-largest bank. The money had been deposited by Banco de Occidente (Panama). The DEA approached Canadian federal prosecutors for assistance,

claiming the money was part of the proceeds of the Colombian drug trafficking cartel in Operation Polar Cap. Using
the proceeds-of-crime legislation, Mr. Justice David Doherty
of the Supreme Court of Ontario ordered on April 6 that the
money be frozen for six months to give lawyers on both sides
of the issue time to resolve the matter.

Even Canadian banking executives agree that money launderers need the cooperation of the banks. Richard Marshall,
senior international counsel at the Bank of Nova Scotia,
noted in a *Globe and Mail* interview that "not just any bank will
do. Money launderers prefer banks that have an international
network of branches, including some in tax havens, and computers to shuttle money around the world. . . ." Canada's
banking system, international drug enforcement agencies
say, fits the bill to a tee. Added Marshall: "We are efficient at
what we do. As such, we're a good target of money launderers." The problem confronting Canadian bankers, Marshall
pointed out, is that they are used to dealing with honest
customers. "A money launderer doesn't come in wearing a
sombrero and trailing white powder. He is usually well-
dressed and passing as a businessman," he observed.

Canada's banking establishment remains vehemently
opposed to any mandatory transaction-reporting system, arguing that it will compromise the "duty of confidentiality" to its
clients. And in a move to counter criticism of its position, the
Canadian Bankers Association (CBA) announced in June,
1987, that its members have taken steps to reduce their expo-
sure to professional money launderers. In a policy statement
on money laundering, the CBA said: "Disclosure of account
information by a bank to enforcement agencies will occur
when the bank is compelled by law to do so. Such disclosure,
for example, may occur in cases involving legislatively con-
ferred authority, such as that which empowers the minister of
national revenue to obtain otherwise confidential information
from bank records. Account information is also legally dis-
closed pursuant to a court order such as a search warrant
authorized under the Criminal Code of Canada."

The statement acknowledged that banks and other financial institutions "are sought out by money launderers. . . . As such, we must constantly balance every person's right to financial privacy against society's right to be protected from criminal activity." It pointed out that every Canadian bank has internal policies that encourage employees to refer "doubtful transactions" to their superiors, who, if not satisfied about the source of the money, may decline the transactions or call in bank security officials. While detailed procedures differ from bank to bank, they all embody the common principle that a bank is under no obligation to conduct a transaction of any type or to operate an account when it has reason to believe that the funds involved are the proceeds of illegal activity.

A year later, the RCMP announced that it had embarked on a liaison program with a number of Canadian banks to discuss the legal avenues open to controlling money-laundering schemes. "The result of these discussions was that the major financial institutions have undertaken a proactive program in an effort to control money-laundering activities involving Canadian banks by establishing internal policy guidelines aimed at providing direction to employees who are faced with suspicious banking transactions," a 1988 RCMP intelligence report states.

It notes that "the principal thrust" behind the program, which relies heavily on self-regulation, is that bank employees should know their clients as well as their clients' business interests. They should be able to identify clients and ascertain the source of financial transactions and the legitimacy of the transactions. "The Canadian banking system is confident that this approach will result in criminal organizations having to seek out alternative means to launder their illicit profits," the RCMP report says.

Some of the more traditional businesses used as fronts to launder drug profits are retail stores, vending machines and pinball and video arcades. Through them, drug money is mixed with legitimate revenues. While the excess profit is now subject to tax, the dealers are at least able to spend the money, since it has been recorded as legitimate income. The major risk they face is that enforcement agencies can identify businesses making suspicious deposits or reporting unrealistic revenues.

Stephen Paul Pakodzy, an Edmonton businessman, used his business, Pine Village Quilts Ltd., which he and his wife bought in 1980, to launder the profits of marijuana trafficking. An audit of the company showed legitimate income from sales totalling $13,038 in 1981; $4,402 in 1982; $12,028 in 1983; and $219 in 1984. But Pakodzy and his wife lived very extravagantly. In fact, Pakodzy, who was described by the judge as "an obnoxious individual who brazenly flaunted his wealth," enjoyed a lifestyle well beyond what could be supported by his declared income. The investigation into Pakodzy's activities began in December, 1983, after he was arrested at Edmonton International Airport carrying a shoe box containing $145,290. A subsequent analysis of his finances, conducted by Revenue Canada and the RCMP, revealed unidentified income between 1980 and 1983 of $486,487.61 – profits which were eventually linked to drug trafficking.

Investigators found that the quilt company was set up primarily as a front to conceal the proceeds from a drug smuggling and trafficking operation. In addition to using the company to launder some of the drug money, Pakodzy also transferred money to the Grand Caymans through five branches of the Bank of Nova Scotia. The money was deposited into an account registered to Fall Enterprises, a trust account of A.M.E. Management Limited. Pakodzy used the money from the trust account to maintain a lavish lifestyle and to finance further marijuana shipments.

A unique aspect to this case was that no drugs were ever seized, but other evidence proved beyond reasonable doubt that Pakodzy was involved in drug trafficking. Investigations revealed that he used a courier to transport marijuana from

the U.S. to Edmonton in a pickup truck. The marijuana shipments, which ranged from 45 to 70 kilograms, were concealed
in a false ceiling in the canopy of the vehicle. Once in Edmonton, the marijuana was sold on the streets through a network
of local dealers. Pakodzy ultimately pleaded guilty to a variety
of charges brought against him and was sentenced in April,
1986, in Alberta Provincial Court to six years in prison – four
years for trafficking and two years consecutive for possession
of property obtained by crime. He was also sentenced to two
years and six months concurrently for income tax evasion. In
addition to the prison sentence, he was fined $32,000 for
disposing of a Porsche sports car during the course of the
criminal investigation.

After Revenue Canada investigators and the RCMP got
through with him, Pakodzy was left almost penniless. All his
assets, determined to be obtained through profits from drug
dealing, including a large log home, cars, fur coats, jewellery
and gold bullion, were confiscated.

Across Canada, police investigations have revealed that foreign currency exchanges are often set up as storefront operations for the laundering of dirty money from major crime
syndicates. They have also found that drug traffickers are
increasingly rinsing their cash through these enterprises,
since few exchanges keep records that would lead to the identity of a customer. For drug dealers, these outlets are ideal for
exchanging large quantities of cash in small denominations
for foreign currencies in large denominations or bank drafts.
At this point, any possible audit trail is broken.

In 1985, Gary Hendin, a 36-year-old St. Catharines,
Ontario, lawyer, pleaded guilty to charges involving the laundering of $12 million for organized drug traffickers over a
three-year period from January 1, 1978, to December 31, 1980.
He was sentenced to five years in prison, fined $1,122,512 for
tax evasion, and ultimately disbarred by the Law Society of
Upper Canada. Hendin had set up a company known as
M&M Currency Exchange Ltd., which he used as a front to
convert the piles of small bills earned from street-level drug

deals into large denominations of U.S. currency. Proceeds of illegal drug sales were brought to Hendin's office on King Street in St. Catharines by couriers carrying cash stuffed in attaché-cases, gym bags and even grocery bags. The lawyer personally took delivery of the cash and locked himself in the library of his office where he ran the bills through a $6,000 Pitney-Bowes money-counting machine. He then took the "rinsed" money to a branch of the Bank of Nova Scotia in town where it was converted into U.S. currency, which was on occasion delivered to his office in an armoured van. Couriers then picked up the U.S. cash from his law practice and delivered it to Miami, where some of it was used to finance further drug deals. The rest would be channelled into banks or secret, numbered corporations in the Cayman Islands.

Another popular laundering method is the use of offshore financial havens. The key here is to move drug profits to these countries in a way that will distort or destroy any audit trail that authorities could track. In their selection of an offshore haven, drug-trafficking syndicates look for specific features that include strict secrecy laws governing banking and corporations; the ease of setting up a foreign-based company or dummy corporation; a stable political and monetary climate; minimal restrictions on the movement of currency both into and out of the country; and little or non-existent taxes of foreign-controlled corporations.

A key consideration for launderers is the haven's secrecy laws, which are used to cloud the real ownership of a foreign corporation wishing to invest in legitimate businesses in Canada. Often referred to as daisy-chaining, multiple layers of corporate ownership are set up to obscure the true ownership. A recent RCMP investigation into a Canadian money-laundering racket revealed more than ninety domestic and foreign corporate entities which made up a convoluted web specifically designed to thwart police efforts to trace the flow of millions of dollars of drug profits.

Offshore havens are a continuing source of anxiety to Western governments concerned with the incredible profits reaped by international drug-trafficking gangs. With some forty or so such countries in existence, they have become the most important and notorious link in money-laundering schemes. On virtually every day of the week, couriers carrying attaché-cases filled with hard currency arrive by executive jet to make their bank deposits. No questions asked. Investigations into money-laundering operations have taken police to havens on every continent of the globe.

Many countries have actively courted the infusion of foreign capital, and to accomplish this they have structured a climate to attract individuals wishing to place their money outside their home country. In the case of smaller countries, the provision of financial-haven facilities is often the principal industry on which the entire economy is based. Some of the more popular financial-haven countries are Panama, the Bahamas, the Cayman Islands, Vanuatu, Hong Kong, Singapore, Switzerland, Liechtenstein, the Channel Islands, and even Canada. Some East Bloc countries, such as Hungary, are now joining the club in their pursuit of badly needed foreign exchange.

No doubt the best-known financial tax haven in the world is Switzerland. For decades, the secretive Swiss banks have cultivated an image of hushed respectability. But in recent years, this gilded citadel has been tainted by one embarrassing scandal after another. The proud Swiss have seen their arcane bank laws used to create stashes for the vast fortunes of deposed Third World despots like Ferdinand Marcos of the Philippines, who is said to have kept up to $5 billion (U.S.) in Switzerland during his twenty-year rule, and Jean-Claude Duvalier of Haiti, who funnelled several hundred million dollars into numbered Swiss accounts. Some of the most violent international drug barons have deposited or moved billions of dollars through the austere, fortress-like banks. In one case involving a Mafia heroin-smuggling family based in Montreal, the RCMP traced millions of dollars laundered by the clan through Swiss banks. These sensational revelations have inspired uncomplimentary comparisons between the Swiss banks and the country's famed multi-holed cheese.

The most damaging revelation surfaced in December, 1988, when the nation was rocked by a huge money-laundering scandal and what is widely regarded as its worst political scandal. It prompted the resignation of Justice Minister Elisabeth Kopp, who was also serving as the nation's vice-president. And she was not alone in disgrace. Two weeks earlier, Rudolf Gerber, the government's chief prosecutor for sixteen years and head of its secret service, was dismissed for his failure to follow up leads about Mrs. Kopp's alleged breaches of official secrecy and for being lax in an investigation into the activities of an international drug money-laundering syndicate operating in Zürich.

The first ripples were felt in the summer, when prosecutors in Ticino, a canton in southern Switzerland, arrested Barkev and Jean Magharian, two Lebanese brothers, on charges of using Swiss banks and currency trading companies to launder as much as $1.3 billion from 1985 to 1988. The money – a good portion of it from the drug trade – had come from the United States, Colombia, Turkey, Italy and elsewhere. The long and winding tale, according to U.S. and Swiss investigators, began in a greasy Philadelphia pizza parlor in 1983. Police learned that the restaurant was a front for heroin dealing, part of a chain of heroin franchises run by the Mafia in a number of cities throughout the country. The discovery led to the arrest and imprisonment of scores of Mafiosi in the U.S. and Italy in what has been dubbed the Pizza Connection.

A key link in the Pizza Connection was a heroin refinery in Palermo, Sicily, which was shut down by Italian police. It was used to refine Turkish morphine base into heroin. According to U.S. drug investigators, the dismantling of the Palermo refinery left a number of Turkish opium and morphine wholesalers holding hundreds of kilograms of morphine base with no place to process it. One such trafficker was Haci Mirza. Desperate to unload his product, the Turk contacted Nicola Giulietti, an underworld associate, for help in finding a buyer. Giulietti put the word out on the drug underworld pipeline, which was picked up by Swiss police, who in turn asked for the assistance of the more experienced U.S. Drug Enforcement Agency. A DEA agent, masquerading as a drug buyer, eventually managed to link up with Mirza and Giulietti in July, 1986, and, in February, 1987, a $4-million deal was struck for 80 kilograms of morphine base and 20 kilograms of heroin. The Swiss police moved in, seized the drugs and arrested the duo. What they hadn't expected to find was an electronic address book belonging to Giulietti. After breaking the code, they found the phone numbers of the Magharian brothers and the number of one of their secret accounts at Crédit Suisse, one of Switzerland's largest banks.

The Magharian name rang a bell with DEA investigators. Three months earlier, customs agents at Los Angeles International Airport had seized three suitcases containing $2 million in cash. According to a U.S. indictment brought against the Magharian brothers in California and New York in early March, 1989, the money, which was being shipped to Barkev Magharian in Zürich, was the profits from cocaine trafficking. During the course of the investigation, the name of Shakarchi Trading A.G. of Zürich, which specializes in handling large quantities of cash and gold bullion, popped up. The currency trading company is owned by Lebanese businessman Mohamed Shakarchi. Two of its major clients are the Magharian brothers, and Mrs. Kopp's husband, Hans, was a director and vice-chairman of Shakarchi Trading at the time. He resigned abruptly from the company on October 27, 1988, citing personal reasons.

In announcing her resignation, the 51-year-old justice minister admitted phoning her husband that day, urging him to step down after learning from her officials that the company was a target of a major money-laundering police investigation. In a terse statement, Mrs. Kopp, the first woman member of the Swiss Federal Council, said she had given her spouse no official information but merely passed on unconfirmed rumors. "It was brought to my attention in my department, in an unofficial way, that Sharkarchi might be implicated in the Lebanon Connection affair. I then advised my husband to immediately resign from the board. I repeat that at the time I neither possessed nor used any documents or information from my department," she insisted.

Ironically, while she was Justice Minister, Mrs. Kopp had pushed for a tough law making money laundering a crime. A draft of a strict new law outlawing money laundering was begun at her request in 1986. The scandal forced Swiss authorities to retrieve it from a back shelf in the justice department and dust it off.

Once drug profits are safely deposited in an offshore haven, the next step in the laundering process is repatriating the loot in a way that makes it appear to come from legitimate sources. One method is the "loan-back". A drug trafficker sets up a corporation in a financial haven, usually by placing it under the name of a local lawyer to conceal the true owner-ship. The trafficker will then buy a business or some real estate at home with a loan from his secretly held offshore corporation. In effect, he is borrowing his own money. The key is to continue to make scheduled payments on the loan as if it were legitimate; otherwise, the transaction could raise questions by authorities at some future date. Gary Hendin's downfall came when he used the loan-back scheme by pre-tending to lend $324,802 for the purchase of a property to a company which involved a known organized-crime figure. The loan was recorded as a mortgage on the property but Hendin never collected any payments.

The loan-back not only allows cleansed drug profits to be repatriated, but it also gives the launderer the right to claim interest payments on the loan as legitimate business expenses.

Under another popular laundering technique called dou-ble invoicing, a domestic company buys goods from an off-shore corporation at inflated prices, and the difference between the inflated and the real value is deposited into an offshore account. In this way, the domestic company shows a very low profit, which reduces its taxes at home, and the corporation in the offshore tax haven shows a "legitimate" profit.

In the real estate market, launderers use what is known as the reverse flip scam. It somewhat resembles the double invoicing scheme to the extent that two scales of pricings are used, one real and one artificial. A dealer purchases a $3-million property for an official stated price of $1.5 million. The vendor receives the other $1.5 million under the table. Ironically, the vendor then faces a problem in laundering that money. After holding the property for some time and possibly making some improvements to it, the new vendor can sell it for its true value and be quite willing to pay taxes on his "windfall" profit.

Sergeant Bruce Bowe, who heads the RCMP's anti-drug profiteering squad in Ottawa, firmly believes that Bill C-61 will deal a crippling blow to drug traffickers by taking away their accumulated wealth once they have been arrested and convicted – no matter where the spoils are hidden or how the cash was laundered. He refers to his program as the third dimension to drug enforcement. The first two dimensions are the arrest of the trafficker and the seizure of illicit drugs. "The drug trade is a three-dimensional activity. It involves people, drugs and money. For this reason, any enforcement program directed against the drug trade that does not include an attack against the proceeds is destined to fail in the long run," Sergeant Bowie wrote in a report entitled "Asset Forfeiture, The Third Dimension to Drug Enforcement", published in August, 1988.

"As long as the trafficking organization is permitted to retain the profits accumulated through the sale of drugs, individual members will be able to finance their re-entry into the drug trade at their former levels upon release from prison. If the organization is deprived of these financial resources, and thereby denied the means of maintaining the organization structure, the traffickers will be forced to start at lower levels, where the chances of detection are much greater," Bowie pointed out.

In an interview at RCMP headquarters in Ottawa, Bowie lauded the provisions of Bill C-61, proudly boasting that it will be the mainstay in the government's war on drugs. "If we can't seize it because it is in some numbered foreign bank account," he noted, "the courts will have the power to levy fines equal to what we believe are the hidden profits of drug organization. And if the convicted traffickers refuse to pay, then they will get more jail time added to their sentence. It's either pay the fine or do the time, so I'm sure they'll think twice about the prospect of doing more time." What's more, after they are released, convicted drug dealers will be under constant scrutiny, unable to spend their ill-gotten gains on toys, trinkets and towers because they will be required to prove they bought them with hard-earned money and not with the profits from drug dealing.

Despite the lack of regulations requiring Canadian banks to report large cash deposits to the government, Bowie maintains that Bill C-61 is a tough law. It provides for court-ordered procedures to seize, freeze and forfeit proceeds of crime, and it also provides for new offences dealing with money laundering. When former Justice Minister Ray Hnatyshyn introduced the legislation in Parliament in the spring of 1987, he stressed that its intent "is to attack enterprise and drug crime and the laundering of monies obtained through illicit channels. This government intends to take the profit out of crime."

Until C-61, law enforcement authorities faced the grim fact that the threat of imprisonment or the loss of a large drug shipment was looked on by traffickers as a mere irritant, an annoying aspect of doing business. In Canada, as in the United States and elsewhere around the globe, greed and the potential for profit far outweigh the risks presented by traditional judicial sanctions of a fine, a few months or even years in prison. The inescapable conclusion reached by many justice critics was that for any enforcement action directed at lucrative classes of crime to be truly effective, it had to include an attack against the proceeds.

For decades, investigators had been sorely hampered by the lack of adequate and effective legal tools to seize and forfeit money and assets obtained by criminal activities. Canadian laws contained some measures dealing with the proceeds of crime. Section 312 of the Criminal Code makes it an offence to be in possession of property or proceeds which were obtained by, or derived from, the commission of an indictable offence in Canada or elsewhere. However, Canadian laws did not adequately address the problems of freezing, seizing and ultimately forfeiting of the proceeds of crime. Without the ability to freeze assets once they had been identified as having been obtained by criminal acts, police were powerless to stop a suspected drug dealer from selling off and transferring his wealth to a foreign jurisdiction. Investigators had also been seriously hampered by a lack of adequate seizure provisions in Canadian law. For example, search warrants issued under Section 443 of the Criminal Code allowed only for the search and seizure of "tangible things" that were the objects of, or would provide evidence of, a criminal offence. In proceeds of crime investigations, this provision proved wholly inadequate because two important classes of assets could not be seized: real estate and intangible assets, such as money deposited in a bank account. It became clear to authorities that for proceeds of crime to be subject to forfeiture, additional legal provisions had to be developed.

Bill C-61 also contains a provision that would give a court of superior jurisdiction the power to issue an order permitting the disclosure of income tax records, but only in cases of serious drug offences. In his report, Bowie noted that, in the past, criminal organizations have been "shielded" from prosecution by secrecy provisions in the laws governing Revenue Canada tax records "which were designed to protect law-abiding citizens from unwarranted intrusions into their private affairs." Another significant feature of the law is a provision that would protect a source of information, such as a bank teller, from any criminal or civil liability resulting from the disclosure of information concerning a suspected case of money laundering, as long as the disclosure was based on reasonable grounds.

As might be expected, C-61 does not sit well with criminal lawyers and civil libertarians. Many have slammed the legislation, claiming that it makes a mockery of the presumption of innocence. They are particularly concerned that the police can now "seize first and prove later." In an article published in *The Globe and Mail* on April 28, 1988, criminal lawyers Clayton Ruby and Frank Addario argued that the confiscation of property in criminal proceedings "has not been part of our law for several hundred years. The combination of greed and the power of the state made for bad criminal law and mistrustful relations with the citizenry." The lawyers described the powers set out in C-61 as "breathtaking. The legislation permits police to seize and freeze citizens' assets – jewelry, cash, real estate, clothing – before anyone is convicted of a crime." They maintained that the legislation "is vague and frighteningly wide, and creates a significant extension of our present law. . . . The police are jubilant. They know that, without stretching the law at all, they will have authority to do things they could only dream about before."

While these concerns are not negligible, numerous stringent safeguards have been incorporated into the law which appear to strike a proper balance between the protection of legitimate property rights and the quest to confiscate the profits of crime. Forfeiture orders must be scrutinized by the provincial attorney general and approved by a senior judge. The law also sets out a number of comprehensive review and appeal procedures to ensure that innocent parties are not deprived of the use of their property. In addition, it allows money to be released for reasonable living, business and legal expenses. The government is also liable to damages if the accusations prove unfounded. Furthermore, while the law does violate the presumption of innocence, the question is whether such violation may be justifiable. A person charged with a crime is sometimes held without bail because there is fear that he might be dangerous to public safety or that he might flee. A similar principle could be applied to the money and assets from the commission of crimes that might otherwise be hidden or sold off.

The bottom line is that without the provisions for seizure of Bill C-61, any legislative action against money laundering in Canada would be futile.

8

Omertà

At the well-travelled Pacific Highway border crossing separating British Columbia and Washington State, a flatbed truck rumbled into the Canada Customs inspection station with a bonded shipment of seventeen "jade" rocks. Packed in five wooden crates, the seemingly nondescript load, which originated in Bangkok, Thailand, weighed 420 kilograms. It was being trans-shipped from Seattle, where it had arrived by cargo plane on May 9, 1988, and was on its way to Vancouver's International Airport for re-shipping by Air Canada cargo plane to Montreal. Customs agents were about to wave the load through when they noticed irregularities in the bill of lading. A cursory check found that the jade importer had not paid the excise tax of about $500 on two previous shipments in June and July of the previous year. More information was punched into a Canada-wide computer network and in seconds it spewed out an urgent alert. The RCMP drug unit in Montreal had posted a lookout on the importing company.

The Mounties were called in immediately. They tried to track down the shipper but found that the name and address on the shipping documents were bogus. The address was that of a nightclub in east-end Montreal. The shipment was taken to Vancouver Airport where it was X-rayed, revealing hollowed-out cavities in each of the rocks. One rock was broken open. Inside, investigators found a cache of high-grade heroin. The smugglers had bored holes into the boulders, filled them with heroin and carefully resealed them. In total, the RCMP extracted 20.5 kilograms of 87 per cent pure China White heroin from the jade rocks worth more than $150 million on the streets. They then carefully replaced the drug with baking powder before resealing, repacking and sending the load by cargo plane to Montreal.

For three weeks, RCMP undercover agents patiently and discreetly watched the crates as they sat in a Canada Customs warehouse at Dorval airport waiting to be picked up. Back in Thailand, RCMP Sergeant Ken Kelly reviewed the visa application of the suspected Thai heroin trafficker who shipped the jade rocks. Kelly enlisted the cooperation of immigration officials at the Canadian Embassy, and a visitor's visa was issued. The Thai supplier arrived in Montreal in late May, and, after checking out the Canada Customs site on repeated occasions, he finally cleared the rock shipment on June 2. An independent trucking company picked up the load and took it to a deserted lot, where it was transferred by three men to a rental truck. The truck, which was rented under a phony name, sat for three days in a parking lot almost a kilometre from a hotel where the trio had booked a room. Every day for almost a week, individual gang members circled a four-block radius around the truck looking for police surveillance. They didn't detect any and decided to move the load to Windsor, Ontario.

In unmarked cars bearing Ontario licence plates, a squad of RCMP surveillance teams from Montreal tailed the truck along Highway 401 to a farm outside Windsor. The next day, one of the men headed back to Montreal to return the rented vehicle. The other two stayed behind with a fourth man, who owned the property. Police kept the farm under surveillance and moved in on June 7 when the men began smashing open the rocks. They arrested Giovanni Laudicina of Maidstone, Ontario, and Joseph Guaragna, 24, and Antonio Zambito, 46, of Montreal. Joseph Dennis Cuffaro, 28, was arrested later in Montreal. Suchart Areephan, 40, of Lopburi, Thailand, was picked up in Texas in the fall of 1988 and extradited to Canada six weeks later to face drug trafficking charges in Windsor.

On the property, the police discovered a 1982 Chevrolet that had been modified to smuggle heroin to Detroit across the U.S.-Canadian border at Windsor. They also found broken pieces of "jade" rock buried on the property from two previous shipments that had come from Thailand through Dallas, Texas, and then on a Pan Am flight to Montreal. Based on Canada Customs records and the size of the cavities in the rocks, RCMP investigators estimated that those shipments contained at least $300 million worth of heroin.

But this particular bust went much deeper than just a single seizure of heroin in the seemingly endless war on drugs. For police, it demonstrated the tenacity and ingenuity of a Montreal-based Mafia syndicate with strong links to Mafia families in New York City, Sicily and Venezuela. Four of the men arrested in the jade rock caper were of Italian background with close ties to the Cuntrera-Caruana family, a Mafia clan which police claim ran an international heroin and hashish smuggling operation from Montreal from the late 1970s to 1988. The clan smuggled numerous multi-million-dollar shipments of heroin and hashish out of India and Thailand through England to Montreal. The ultimate destinations were New York and New Jersey. The RCMP drug squad maintains it can prove that between 1978 and 1984 the gang moved 800 kilograms of China White heroin to New York via Montreal. U.S. drug enforcement agents have identified the Cuntrera-Caruana mob as a key link in the notorious Pizza Connection in which powerful Sicilian Mafia mobsters in several U.S. cities used family-owned pizza parlors to traffick tons of heroin.

The Cuntrera-Caruana clan's roots are in the impoverished, sun-baked town of Siciuliana in southwestern Italy. Pasquale Cuntrera and his brother Gaspare left Sicily and immigrated to Canada in the early 1960s to escape the violent internal feuding between Mafia families. At about the same time, Alfonso Caruana and his brothers Gerlando and Pasquale also left Italy for Canada. The Cuntreras and Caruanas had blood ties through intermarriage in Sicily. In 1961, Paolo Cuntrera, a third brother, married Antonina Caruana, Alfonso's first cousin.

In Montreal, Pasquale Cuntrera allied himself with Nicolo "Nick" Rizzuto, a reputed Mafia leader from Sicily, and soon established himself as a ranking member of the Montreal Mafia. Cuntrera appointed Alfonso Caruana as his lieutenant. Widely regarded as somewhat of a financial wizard by Mafia chieftains, Caruana handled the banking and money-laundering side of the operations for the gang.

Police intelligence states that by the mid-1970s, the Cuntreras, the Caruanas and the Rizzutos had established an international base of operations in Canada, Britain, Italy, Switzerland and Venezuela. Today, drug enforcement investigators in Canada, the U.S., Britain and Italy claim that the Cuntrera-Caruana family, along with their ally Nick Rizzuto, have smuggled almost $2 billion worth of heroin, hashish and cocaine into the United States, most of it through Montreal. The RCMP anti-crime profits unit in Montreal has also unearthed an elaborate money-laundering scheme involving several city banks and tens of millions of dollars in U.S. currency from illicit drug sales in New York.

In 1984, Tommaso Buscetta, a Mafia *capo* turned police informant, who defied *omertà*, the legendary Mafia code of silence that members swear under pain of death, told Italian organized crime investigators that he met the Cuntrera brothers in Montreal in 1969. Buscetta, who lost several members of his family, including two sons, to Mafia internecine warfare in Sicily, described the Cuntreras as "men of honor" in the Mafia who were involved in heroin trafficking. Canadian investigators said that while Buscetta was in Montreal and Toronto in the 1960s, he was involved in heroin smuggling. Buscetta was arrested as an illegal alien in New York in 1972 but skipped the country for Brazil after posting a $40,000 bail bond. He was extradited to Italy from Brazil in 1984 on drug charges and charges of criminal association with the Mafia and was sentenced to three years. His testimony was instrumental in the convictions of 338 Mafia members in Italy and 22 in New York in 1987.

The unravelling of the Cuntrera-Caruana clan's drug smuggling empire was not the result of an informant or police investigation. Ironically, it was sparked by a wily black Labrador dog named Ben. On December 2, 1984, Ben's sensitive nose sniffed out a 250-kilogram shipment of hashish at a massive customs warehouse in London, England. The hashish had been concealed in compartments carved into the bottoms of thick walnut table tops. The manifest indicated that the furniture had been imported from Bombay, India, by a London company called Elongate Ltd., which, it turned out, was set up in 1982 by two Montrealers, Antonino Zambito, who was arrested in the 22-kilogram heroin bust in Windsor in June, 1988, and Francesco Siracusa. Elongate was transshipping the tables to Santa Rita Imports Inc. in Montreal. British customs immediately telexed the RCMP in Montreal for information on Santa Rita Imports and were told that it was linked to a suspected Mafia family. The company had been registered in October, 1982, by Emmanuel Guaragna.

Police investigations later revealed that Siracusa was the man who arranged all the drug shipments in India and Thailand. In late 1982, Siracusa flew to Bombay, where he spent several weeks setting up a furniture shipment, which arrived in England in early May, 1983. On May 15, the furniture was trans-shipped by Elongate to Santa Rita in Montreal, where it cleared Canada Customs a month later.

In the early fall, Siracusa was back in India arranging a second shipment, which arrived in England in February, 1984. A few weeks later it was trans-shipped to Santa Rita, clearing Canada Customs without incident. Then in April, 1984, the arranger flew to Thailand, and in late June, a container of teak furniture departed Bangkok for a company called Ital Provisions Ltd. in England. Ital Provisions, which was set up in 1982 by Antonino Luciani and Filippo Monteleone, was originally a food importing outfit but it soon switched to importing furniture from the Far East. The Thai furniture shipment arrived in England on August 20 and, within a few days, was on its way by cargo freighter to Santa

Rita in Montreal, where it cleared customs in late September.

Another furniture shipment that was sent from India to Elongate in early November, arriving on December 2, 1984, was randomly selected by British customs for a more detailed inspection. Within seconds of skirting around the packed container, Ben began barking frantically. A score of customs agents swarmed over the shipment and soon discovered the stash of high-grade hashish concealed in the table tops. The agents carefully repacked the shipment and allowed it to be delivered to Elongate's warehouse in London. There, under a blanket of tight security, police surveillance teams watched as Siracusa and Alberto Gualtieri, another Montrealer, painted over the Indian markings on the crates and stencilled in English markings. This, they hoped, would give Canada Customs officials the impression that the goods originated in England. Both men were arrested as they left the warehouse. In Siracusa's car, police found airline tickets to Montreal and other papers which they eventually traced to Pasquale Caruana. They also discovered that the car's servicing bill had been paid by Alfonso Caruana. Alfonso and Pasquale Caruana had moved to England in 1982, leaving brother Gerlando in charge of the clan's affairs in Montreal. Siracusa had also been identified by witnesses during his trial as a frequent visitor to the posh country estates of the Caruana brothers south of London.

After Siracusa was arrested, police raided his home and found files of shipping documents. Their curiosity was piqued by a particular bill of lading for a furniture shipment that had gone through Ital Provisions. They wondered what a food importing company was doing in the furniture business. A lookout was immediately posted for any shipments going to, or originating from, this company.

The arrest of Siracusa dealt a serious blow to the Cuntrera-Caruana clan. He was a loyal and trusted soldier. The syndicate's operations were also stung by the discovery of two of its key front companies – Elongate and Santa Rita. They had been rendered useless. The gang desperately needed a safe dummy company in Montreal and another in London to continue operating.

In March, 1985, Filippo Vacarella set up Thermo Import and Export Inc. as the front company in Montreal to replace Santa Rita. Unwisely, the gang leaders concluded that Ital Provisions had gone undetected and was secure. But to be on the safe side, they arranged for a "clean" shipment of furniture to be sent to Ital from a company in Bangkok which had supplied an earlier drug load. It arrived in England in February, 1985, and was thoroughly searched by British customs agents before being cleared. It sat unclaimed on the dockyard for eight weeks.

In the meantime, another furniture shipment for Ital Provisions left Bangkok in late January for England, arriving on May 26. Customs agents scoured it and found 58.2 kilograms of China White heroin worth several millions of dollars concealed in honeycombs of compartments in teak tables. The shipment, with the drugs still hidden in the furniture, was cleared by British customs and closely monitored by surveillance teams after it was picked up and taken to a warehouse leased by Ital Provisions.

Francesco Di Carlo, a close friend of the Caruanas and a ruthless and trusted *capo* in the clan, arranged for the part of the furniture load containing 22.6 kilograms of heroin to be shipped to Montreal on a Yugoslavian cargo ship. British authorities promptly notified the RCMP that the shipment was on its way across the North Atlantic Ocean. In the meantime, the "clean" shipment of Thai furniture was picked up and delivered to the elegant and spacious homes of Alfonso Caruana and Di Carlo.

On June 19, the furniture destined for Montreal arrived and was quickly cleared by Canada Customs. It was immediately picked up by a cartage company and delivered to the Thermo Import and Export warehouse on Halpern Street in Ville St. Laurent. The next day, Gerlando Caruana was spotted by undercover police surveillance teams driving around the warehouse looking for police surveillance. Later RCMP phone taps picked up a conversation between Gerlando and his brother Pasquale, who had moved back to Montreal some months earlier. Gerlando informed his brother that everything appeared to be okay at the warehouse.

Unknown to the gang, the RCMP had placed microphone transmitters in the warehouse, and when Gerlando, Vacarella and Luciano Zambito entered the building on June 21, the surveillance teams listened with Cheshire cat grins plastered on their faces as the threesome, using saws, drills and hammers, took apart the furniture. When the signal was given, the RCMP moved in and made their arrests. Once they had the men in custody, the Mounties informed Scotland Yard, which in turn arrested Di Carlo and Monteleone.

In 1986, the three gang members in Montreal were found guilty of possession of heroin for the purposes of trafficking and were each sentenced to twenty years in penitentiary. The British courts sentenced Di Carlo, Siracusa, Monteleone and Luciani to twenty-five years each.

The day after Di Carlo's arrest, Alfonso Caruana boarded a flight to Caracas. He sold his estate for $827,962 and wired the proceeds to his bank account in Montreal, but before he could retrieve it, Revenue Canada froze the account on May 20, 1986, for back taxes.

Poring over a mountain of documents seized in raids on the homes and businesses of gang members involved in the heroin ring, investigators managed to piece together an elaborate scheme set up by the Cuntrera-Caruana syndicate to launder millions of dollars in drug profits through various banks in Montreal. The first step in the laundering scheme was to send gang members to various bank branches throughout the city to test their willingness to accept large cash transactions without asking too many questions.

Sergeant Marc Bourque, who heads the RCMP anti-drug-profiteering unit in Montreal, winced at the thought of the amount of drug profits laundered by the Cuntrera-Caruana syndicate in Montreal. "We can prove that in two years, the Cuntrera-Caruana gang physically laundered $34 million in

U.S. currency and $20 million in Canadian currency. We know of money couriers pulling up to the back of the Montreal City and District Savings Bank branch on St. Jean Boulevard in Dollard-des-Ormeaux with trucks loaded with tote bags of cash. Now who comes into a bank with suitcases and gym bags filled with $600,000 and $800,000 in small U.S. bills that can say the money comes from a legitimate business?" Sergeant Bourque asked sarcastically.

Investigators said that Aldo Tucci, the manager of the Dollard-des-Ormeaux branch, was very helpful to his new-found clients. Always eager to serve, he even established a special account called the Caruana International Department. Documents show, for example, that on January 10, 1981, Tucci accepted a single cash deposit from Caruana for $1.1 million. Sergeant Bourque noted that when Tucci, an Italian immigrant from Sicily, was asked by the bank's security division to explain the deposit, which was made in American fives, tens and twenties, he replied that he was told that the money came from casino and oil profits in Venezuela. "Firstly, U.S. currency is not the official currency of Venezuela," Sergeant Bourque pointed out wryly. "Secondly, the oil industry is state-owned, and, lastly, there are no casinos in Venezuela."

Investigators also identified a major money mover working for the Cuntrera-Caruana outfit. Affidavits filed in the Federal Court of Canada Trial Division in Montreal by Sergeant Bourque on September 23, 1988, named Giuseppe Cuffaro, 56, as "a member of the Mafia" and linked him directly to money-laundering activities for the gang. Cuffaro's son, Joseph, was arrested on September 9, 1988, in connection with the 22 kilograms of heroin seized in Windsor in June. The affidavits state that from January 1, 1979, to December 31, 1985, Giuseppe Cuffaro made numerous cash deposits and international money transfers involving millions of dollars to banks in Switzerland, such as Crédit Suisse and Union Bank of Switzerland. For example, the documents show that from May 21, 1981, to June 29, 1984, Cuffaro transferred

$1,734,299.11 to Pasquale Cuntrera's Swiss account through the Canadian Hellenic Trust on Avenue du Parc in Montreal. In ten separate banking transactions from the Montreal City and District Bank in Dollard-des-Ormeaux from January 10, 1979, to September 16, 1980, he tranferred $1,887,824 to a company called Aceros Prensados in Switzerland, which is controlled by the clan. And in twenty-four separate transactions from the National Bank of Canada branch on St. Michel Boulevard in east-end Montreal from October 19, 1981, to September 28, 1982, Cuffaro transferred $9,556,791.32 to Alfonso Caruana's Swiss account. He also transferred $2,035,621.42 in U.S. drafts to his own account in Switzerland.

With a fine-tooth comb, a Revenue Canada team sifted through Cuffaro's business dealings from 1979 to 1985, and in 1988 hit him with a bill for $6,312,041.42 in unpaid taxes and penalties. Revenue Canada concluded that he had not declared earnings of $8,277,000 for that period. Cuffaro, who immigrated to Canada from Sicily in 1953 and became a Canadian citizen in 1959, is fighting the tax assessment, contending that he has not been a resident of Canada since 1978, when he moved to Venezuela, and is therefore not subject to Canadian tax laws. However, court documents indicate that he had been carrying on business and real estate transactions using his St. Réal Street address in north-end Montreal during that entire period.

In November, 1988, Cuffaro crossed into West Germany from Switzerland to do a little gambling at a casino in Baden-Baden where he purportedly lost $200,000. As he was leaving, he was promptly arrested by West German police and held on arrest warrants issued by the Italian authorities charging him with being a member of the Mafia and with drug trafficking. Three months earlier, in August, Pasquale Caruana was arrested in West Germany and held on a similar warrant. In mid-February, 1989, both men were extradited to Italy. They were taken to Palermo, Sicily, where they joined more than 300 other defendants in the country's notorious Mafia trials. The charges against Cuffaro and Caruana mark the first time two Canadians, alleged to be top-ranking members of the Mafia, will be brought to trial, and the case against them in Italy is based almost entirely on RCMP evidence.

In the meantime, the Cuntrera-Caruana clan, through its association with Nick Rizzuto, showed signs in 1987 that they were expanding into the cocaine and hashish market. On February 8, 1988, Rizzuto, who fled to Caracas in the early 1970s after the Violi Mafia clan put a contract out on his life, was arrested with Gennaro Scaletta in Venezuela and charged with drug trafficking and conspiracy to smuggle a large shipment of cocaine into the U.S. market via Montreal. Rizzuto, who maintains a home in Montreal, was in possession of a money belt containing samples of five grades of cocaine totalling almost a kilogram. Scaletta, who lived illegally in Montreal for several years in the 1970s, was carrying a similar belt. In the summer of 1988, Canadian authorities seized a bank account with $250,000 and a house in north-end Montreal belonging to Scaletta.

Rizzuto has also been plagued by family troubles. His son Vito was arrested in mid-November, 1987, in Newfoundland after the RCMP seized a ship that was off-loading over 13 tonnes of hashish. Investigators believe the ship was off-loaded in two stages, and that a first load of 15 tonnes managed to slip into the country. Vito Rizzuto was given a $100,000 bail and ordered not to leave the province. A year later, in November, he was arrested in Sept-Îles, Quebec, and charged with conspiracy to import around 30 tonnes of hashish into Canada. Through a telephone wiretap, the RCMP discovered that a captain of a Quebec fishing trawler had accepted $54,000 to off-load a "mothership" in international waters that was laden with Lebanese hashish. The boat captain pleaded guilty to a reduced charge of accepting a bribe and was sentenced to four years in prison. The reduced charge was in exchange for his cooperation. He supplied the police with the names of the other people involved in the conspiracy and agreed to testify against them.

Meanwhile, international drug investigators are keeping a

close eye on the activities of the Cuntrera-Caruana syndicate in Venezuela. They have recently discovered that gang members have purchased substantial land holdings on the duty-free island of Margarita off the coast of Venezuela. U.S. Drug Enforcement Administration officials are concerned that these farms and other properties will be used as remote landing strips for small aircraft bringing in large shipments of cocaine from Colombia for repackaging and export to the North American and European markets.

9

Pot Luck

From the outside, the sprawling complex looked very much like a theme park with its fire-engine red turrets jutting into the azure sky. A dusty camper van with Georgia licence plates wound its way along the narrow, black-top road leading up to the entrance of the fantasy-land castle, which was enclosed by six-metre high concrete walls. The vehicle sputtered to a stop outside the imposing centre doors and disgorged a plump American family in matching wide-striped, yellow-and-orange golf shirts and Bermuda shorts. While Mom and her teenie-bopper son and daughter gazed up in excited expectation of the good times they would soon have behind the imposing grey walls, the balding, jelly-bellied leader of the expedition jammed his thumb into a protruding brass buzzer. Moments later, an eyeball peered out of a peephole in the middle of the door. A rattling of bolts followed and the silhouette of a burly man in a pale green uniform appeared in the blinding mid-morning sunlight.

"This all some sort of Disneyland or somethin'?" the man asked in a southern drawl. He squinted his eyes to get a better look at the towering figure in front of him.

The well-built, uniformed man shook his head and chuckled. "This is no Disneyland. It's Collins Bay. This is a maximum-security federal penitentiary."

"Huh? A prison. It looks like a sort of . . . Never mind. C'mon kids. Hon, let's go. I'll explain. . . "

In the cool, dimly lit foyer, the guard, still chuckling to himself, asked for some identification before he signed me in. Sitting on a wooden bench, I wondered about the convict I had come to see. What he looked like, how he would act, what he would say and whether he would be forthcoming or beat

194

around the bush. A week earlier, Jay Durie was a suspicious voice on the telephone, wondering why I wanted to talk to him. My reason, I explained, was simple. He was the main player in a major liquid hashish smuggling operation, and I wanted to get his story.

Durie wasn't keen on granting an interview until I dropped the name Jim Leising, the Crown attorney who prosecuted him and succeeded on July 10, 1987, in putting the drug trafficker behind bars for ten years for importing and trafficking in narcotics. Leising, a relentless prosecutor and meticulous investigator, virtually jailed Durie's entire gang through sheer dogged determination. To Leising, Durie was the prize catch, the prime mover in an elaborate international drug-smuggling operation. In a submission to the District Court of Ontario, Leising likened the antics of Durie and his gang to "a script from a 'Miami Vice' episode." This man, he argued forcefully, conceived and executed "one of the largest importations of a cannabis drug [namely 318 kilograms of hash oil] that has ever been achieved in Canada."

After a twenty-minute wait, a social worker appeared on the other side of an electronically controlled steel door and ushered me in. I followed her to her office. Five minutes later, a young man dressed in green fatigues, a grey sweatshirt and running shoes appeared at the door. Durie looked nothing like what one would expect of a drug dealer. In fact, he looked like the typical, middle-class boy next door whom every mother of a wayward son has admired from behind a kitchen screen door. Short, with a slight build, Durie had wavy, California blond hair and an infectious Huckleberry Finn grin. He looked younger than his twenty-nine years and didn't seem to be the worse for wear at having spent more than a year at Collins Bay, and eight months in Florida fighting extradition to Canada.

It quickly became apparent that Durie liked to talk. He had a gift for the gab and loved reminiscing and offering opinions on a range of topics, mostly related to prison life, the law, the legal system and the legalization of marijuana. He began chatting amicably about his teenage years at Erindale High School in Mississauga, Ontario, and his initial involvement with marijuana. "I began smoking grass when I was thirteen. It all started out as sort of a high-school thing. Very innocent. It certainly didn't affect me or harm me. I flew through high school with a B-plus average and graduated from grade 12 in 1979. But I did drop out for a year after grade 11, bought a motorcycle and got into sky diving. I even jumped with the Canadian sky diving team. Then I realized I needed that piece of paper for all the years I put into high school. So I went back and got my high-school diploma."

Durie was introduced to marijuana by school chums. "Everyone was doing it, and just about everyone who smoked pot has sold a little," he noted, handing over a two-page article he had written and published in a prison monthly. Entitled "Why All the Fuss?", it was his official position on marijuana use. The article began: "As I see things, the campaign against pot is one our government's most contemptible and superfluous pursuits. It's an exercise in idiocy! I've never understood why all the fuss. I've indulged in this delightful pastime since I was 13 years old. I'm 29 now, my health is excellent, my intelligence is about average, and I haven't suffered any debilitating side effects, mental or physical, from an occasional joint.

"I remember my smug indifference at the urging of teachers, parents and other experts warning me of the dangers of pot. They lumped all mind-altering substances into the same dishonorable category. I didn't try to defend the worthy pot plant. There was no point. The authorities had decreed marijuana an evil. I could find no words to describe its stimulating effects that induced deep, peaceful contemplation. There was no way of sharing the tranquil feeling I had experienced, and I dared not offer one of my cigars as a testimonial! I asked myself, 'Why are they demanding prohibition?' What exactly are the terrible traumas that result from the use of this mild herb? I've experimented with hard drugs and I can see why they're so dangerous and why they're forbidden. Their addictive and seductive nature brings misery and eventual destruction to the user. We have hospitals and addiction centres filled to capacity with emaciated, burned-out heroin and cocaine addicts. Alcoholism has permeated all levels of our society and is steadily rising.

"But where are the marijuana addiction centres? How many deaths or overdoses have occurred from the use of this stimulating plant? I see no reason for the insistence on this absurd law when there has never been any real basis to damn its use. I'm not the only one who uses marijuana with this insolent manner. I've smoked this illegal booty with doctors, lawyers, university professors and many other respected, and otherwise law-abiding, people. Sure, marijuana is a drug. So is coffee and cigarettes. And what about the government's tight-fisted control on the distillation and sales of alcohol? There's never an excuse for prejudice, except to spur on the bleeding hearts of millions, united in a cause. But for what, and for whom? And who started all this fuss anyway?"

Durie grinned. "Nobody can change my mind about pot. I think everyone should smoke it. I think if you're going to get off on something because you have some need to get a buzz, then pot is all right. It doesn't make you steal or want to get into a fight. But the law is the law and it takes a dim view of middle-class gangsters.

"But I'm absolutely against acid. I've done coke. I consider it dangerous. I've been offered to do coke runs. It's a dirty business operated by dirty people. The thing with coke is that it changes your nervous system. I've done it with lawyers and all kinds of upper-class people. Your mood really changes. It gives you verbal diarrhea. First it's yappity yap. It starts out as fun and then you start getting paranoid and your orbit begins to decay very quickly. Your lines keep getting bigger to achieve the same orbit. I've had a dozen friends die on coke or become severe epileptics. In six months, I've seen very intelligent people degenerate into complete nervous wrecks. It's disgusting. I think it's even more deadly than heroin. You'll do it till you die because you want the high. As for heroin, from what I hear it's extremely dangerous and lethal. Pot is laid back, mellow. The only side effect is you get the munchies. Pot cures glaucoma and anorexia."

Durie drifted into drug dealing by happenstance. His friends relied on him for their supply and he got ambitious. By the time he was nineteen, he had a $150,000 line of credit with pot wholesalers. But selling marijuana was not his full-time job. He was variously a real estate salesman for Century 21, a car salesman and a roofing salesman. "I was always interested in business," he explained.

In his entire drug-dealing career, Durie said he never carried or used a weapon or saw any guns, and he was never ripped off. The only time there was violence and threats, he said, "was when the police kicked in my door, stuck a gun in my head and trashed my house looking for drugs."

He shook his head and gazed down at the cement floor when asked about his prison sentence. "Ten years. When I was sentenced I thought to myself, 'These people are ridiculous. This is absurd'. I'm not saying this as a cop-out and I'm not about to get on this like some crusade like Save the Whales. I just think they were a little hysterical giving me ten years."

Durie's zest for the high life began in early 1980 when he visited Jamaica for a winter holiday. He was sitting at a beach bar at the Sea Winds Hotel in Montego Bay when he was approached by a local and asked to join a few people at a nearby table. Rita Marley's voice boomed from two stereo speakers, singing "One Draw", he recalled.

"There were a bunch of Americans and Jamaicans at the table. They were animated characters. Laid back and having a good time. I noticed this one Jamaican was wearing a gold Rolex watch. He had an aura around him that he was doing all right, not like a pimp who needs a big car to show off. But these people had money and they had some interesting sailing stories. They took me to their villas. They had cooks and maids and yachts in the harbor." His blue eyes sparkled and a smile covered his boyish face as he reminisced about the old days. "At the time I was selling real estate. I wasn't suffering.

Then you see all that, and suddenly the listing you wanted to get for the next week just didn't mean much anymore."

He wanted what he saw and made up his mind to go for it. The men he met were looking for someone to unload a stockpile of "weed oil". There was virtually no market for the product in the U.S., but there was a demand in Canada. "I told them I would take all the weed oil they had in stock. I proved to them who I was and that I could market it."

Over the next few years, Durie smuggled numerous shipments of weed oil into Canada. He had established a tight and trusted network of couriers and dealers to sell the product at the street level. The money poured in and he shifted gears into the fast lane. It was glitz and glamor. All-night parties, beautiful women, fast cars, luxury yachts, five-star hotels, first-class air travel and the finest restaurants.

In January, 1984, Durie vacationed with friends at a ski chalet in Blue Mountain just north of Toronto. "We were up there for a few weeks. We had a blast. Lots of parties, airplanes, skidoos." Crown attorney Jim Leising maintained that the winter interlude was a working vacation during which Durie was introduced to Robert "Sunny" Coltraine, who also went by the names of Gregory Chase and David Johnson.

"Mr. Durie and Mr. Coltraine discovered that they had something in common in that at that point in time they were both fairly successful drug dealers and importers," Leising recounted at Durie's trial. "It was at that time they decided to form a partnership. Mr. Durie and Mr. Coltraine each brought certain unique assets to this partnership. Mr. Coltraine in his drug-importing business had become the owner of various airplanes and boats and, as well, had in place certain corporate vehicles that he had utilized in business. Mr. Durie, on the other hand, because of his involvement in drug dealing in the past, had connections in Jamaica to purchase drugs and, as well, he had in place at the time a distribution network in Canada which included both traffickers and experienced drug couriers," Leising said.

The federal prosecutor maintained that the two men com-

bined their particular assets and planned to import 315 kilograms of cannabis resin in liquid form, commonly known as
hash or weed oil. "The plan they hatched was this. Mr. Durie
would utilize his connections in Jamaica to obtain the 700
pounds [318 kilograms] of hash oil at a low price. The drugs
would then be put in a boat, which was owned by Mr. Coltraine, and shipped from Jamaica to Florida. From there, the
drugs would be transported overland to an airport near the
Canadian border. At that stage, they would be loaded on an
airplane, flown into Canada and then put in the hands of
various drug dealers who would sell them," Leising said.

Some time in early March, after forming the partnership
and agreeing on the plan to smuggle a large cache of drugs
into Canada, Coltraine left the country, leaving behind a
twin-engine Cessna 206 Skywagon.

At Collins Bay, Durie became agitated at the mention of
Coltraine's name in connection with the 318-kilogram weed
oil venture. "Sunny had fuck all to do with this," he interjected abruptly. "He did his trip and I did my trip. Sunny was
bebopping up north in Blue Mountain. We partied and after
the vacation was over, he went back south to wind down at his
home on Paradise Island in the Bahamas.

"I'd drop by from time to time and stay with him. His
kindness is what screwed him up. He liked me and trusted me.
There may have been other matters we were discussing but he
had nothing to do with the 700-pound deal. Now Leising is
making him out to be this mysterious character. It's true he
had an airplane he wanted to get rid of and my friends were
looking for a no-heat, no-problem airplane. But me and
Sunny never hatched any plan. He may have been doing
something else. I don't know." He paused and grinned. "Well,
I may know but I'm not going to say anything."

After the winter romp in Blue Mountain, Durie got to work
on a detailed plan to bring in the big shipment. He recruited the
foot soldiers he would need to carry out the various stages of the
operation – the boat crew, offloaders, truckers, pilots and street
distributors. Once they were in place, he approached his con-

nections in Jamaica and gave them instructions to amass the weed oil for a pickup sometime in late January, 1985.

By now, Durie was living on the edge and he loved it. He savored the thrill of each moment and decided to push it to the limit. He had become good friends with the major suppliers in Jamaica and asked if he could oversee the "cooking operation" or preparation of the weed oil. "I was quite happy up in the hills," he recalled. "The Rastafarians were great people. Scary-looking but great. They were quite mellow and fun to be around. We would smoke joints as big as cigars and I would sleep on 20-pound bales of grass in little wooden shacks that leaked when it rained. It was unreal. One day I would be in a first-class hotel in New York or Miami and the next day I would be up in the hills. Both were a real trip."

Making the weed oil was really quite simple, Durie explained, but it was also extremely dangerous. "Collie weed", or marijuana which had gone to seed, was the principal ingredient. Once the female marijuana plant goes to seed, it is virtually useless as a saleable commodity. The level of THC, the active ingredient, drops significantly and as a result it will not give as good a high as resin-laden female plants harvested just as they begin to flower.

The collie weed, Durie said, was stuffed into huge drums and cooked for six to ten hours in a toxic mixture of about 90 to 140 litres of exane or acitane. "The heat and the chemicals help in extracting the juice with the THC in it from the plants. But you have to be very careful because if the heat is too high, the chemicals could ignite and blow up. I've seen it happen. The final product is a slime green. Not very appealing, so we throw red berries into it to make the oil brown."

The Jamaican side of the operation cost $70,000. That included buying the marijuana plants and the chemicals, and paying off bribes. Durie always carried a shoe box filled with Jamaican $100 bills for those occasions. "I had to pay the guy at the chemical plant to give me a licence so I could buy the chemicals, and then I would pay the local police to allow me to truck it up to the hills."

On the way down to the coast with the finished product stored in 90-litre plastic drums, Durie got an army escort. "There's road blocks all over Jamaica. Mostly, they're looking for guns. When they find you with pot, it's a joke. You just pull out the hundreds and they let you through."

In early December, Durie left Toronto for Florida, where he met with a master carpenter who was recruited to customize a cabin cruiser called the *Scotch and Water*. The carpenter built a concealed compartment into the hull of the boat, which was renamed the *Danbar II*. Later that month, Durie flew to Puerto Rico, where he transferred the ownership of the boat to a company called Danbar Enterprises Limited. On January 20, 1985, Durie took the cruiser to what he described as a "ma and pa marina" near Montego Bay, where the 318 kilograms of weed oil were secreted into the hidden compartment. He then met two Canadian associates, William Kenneth Pinto and Ronald Warren Osborne, at a local bar. Pinto, 30, who is from Toronto, and 34-year-old Osborne, who is from Thornbury, Ontario, were using aliases and forged identification papers supplied to them by Durie. The duo took possession of the *Danbar II* and, shortly after, set off for various ports in the Caribbean on their way to Miami.

Meanwhile, Durie returned to Canada. "I found out that the U.S. Coast Guard boarded the boat twice and searched for drugs but they didn't find any. The second time they boarded, the boat had taken on water and one of the plastic containers had broken open and was leaking weed oil. The liquid was floating on top of the water in the boat and the coast guard guys got it all over their boots. They must have thought it was diesel oil. That was a close call."

On February 11, the boat docked in Port Canaveral, and Durie flew to Florida to meet with Pinto and Osborne, and with Clement Ebanks, one of the Jamaican suppliers, at the Cocoa Beach Holiday Inn. Durie gave the offloaders instructions on what was to be done with the weed oil and immediately left for Coltraine's villa on Paradise Island. There, he made arrangements to have the ownership of the Cessna, which was in his friend's common-law wife's name, transferred to a company called Champagne Tours.

After this was completed, Durie called Pinto and Osborne and instructed them to divide the shipment into a 135-kilogram and a 183-kilogram load. The first load was concealed in a secret compartment in the ceiling of a Winnebago camper van and driven to Romeo, Michigan. Durie then contacted Drew Taylor and Robert Manson, two Toronto-area pilots, and instructed them to fly the Cessna, which was sitting at an airport just north of Toronto, to Romeo. On February 19, the pilots linked up with Pinto and took possession of the first shipment. The weed oil, which was packed in two suitcases, was casually loaded onto the airplane in broad daylight and flown into Canada. That day, Durie flew back to Toronto from Florida and issued instructions to a number of street dealers on the disposition of the weed oil. The entire load was sold within days.

Following the successful disposal of the first shipment, Durie gave the order to move the second load. Two couriers were recruited to drive the load from Miami to an airport in Flint, Michigan. On March 7, Taylor and Manson landed in Flint and carried two suitcases onto the Cessna. It took off late at night for Maple Airport north of Toronto. But the aircraft never made it to its final destination. It crashed near King Township. "The plane wound up in the trees," Durie recounted. "I guess you could say it was a bad day at the office." He laughed.

"The pilots were flying at 400 metres when the weather suddenly turned bad. There was a blizzard. The visibility was zero and they had to fly on their instruments. They were following Highway 400 heading north to Maple at full throttle when the plane hit a tree and split in two. It's incredible, it's a miracle that Taylor and Manson came out alive. That was a brand-new Cessna with only twenty hours on the engine. It cost me $50,000 U.S.

"But it didn't turn out to be an entirely bad day at the office. The cargo wasn't lost. I got a call from the pilot. He was shaken up and totally in shock. He had been squashed like a weed-oil sandwich when the load flew forward into the cockpit on impact. He told me he tossed the product from the airplane to the ground and the two of them had dragged the shipment through four feet of snow to the edge of the highway. All this time the transponder [an emergency transmitter] is going, sending out an SOS signal that a plane had crashed." Durie immediately dispatched a van to retrieve the pilots and the shipment. "We got it out of there before daylight. The next morning I pick up the *Toronto Star* and see this big picture of a plane in a tree with a headline saying: Who walked away from this?"

The entire week was spent jockeying the hot load to underground garages in expensive condominiums in downtown Toronto. The shipment was then repackaged in a clandestine warehouse. Using a horse syringe, Durie's men injected the weed oil into one-dram plastic vials which sold for $50 each. The entire 318-kilogram shipment worked out to 63,000 vials. Durie chuckled. "That's a lot of dope. I never realized it. In ten days, it was all dumped. Gone. Sucked up by the thirsty lungs of bored factory workers in Hamilton." And for his efforts and organizational skills, he got upwards of $900 per kilogram. "I wasn't really interested in the money. It was the game that intrigued me," he said.

After the Cessna crashed and the vials were in the hands of pushers, Durie, his "manager" Randy Hollwey, Taylor and Manson flew to Paradise Island to meet with Coltraine to work on alibis in the event the downed Cessna was traced to any of them. Taylor later told the court that the foursome were warned by Sunny that "if anyone ever implicated him he could be killed."

Durie felt everyone was home free. The police traced the ownership of the airplane to a phony U.S. company, and then hit a brick wall. The two sets of footprints and marks in the snow leading to the edge of Highway 400 told investigators that something heavy had been dragged from the downed Cessna. They were baffled and stuck with an investigation that was heading nowhere. Then in the late-night hours on

March 14, a chance traffic violation gave police the key that would unravel the entire drug-smuggling operation.

Driving a sports car, Paulo DeSouza, a small-time Toronto drug dealer, was pulled over by Peel Regional Police for speeding near his home in Mississauga. DeSouza, 26, had $11,000 in cash in his possession and a business card in his wallet. Scribbled on the back was a telephone number and a room number at the Constellation Hotel near the Pearson International Airport. The police brought him in for questioning. "He flipped right there," Durie said angrily. "I never thought he would stoop so low. On the scale of things, DeSouza was a nickel-and-dime dealer. I could have cut him off but I didn't. I should have."

DeSouza babbled on into the night, telling his interrogators everything he knew. He also told them that he was collecting money for Durie and two Jamaican men who were holed up in a suite at the Constellation Hotel. Early the following morning, a search warrant was obtained and the police raided the hotel room. They arrested Durie and Ebanks, and a third man, who was later acquitted. Police also seized about $150,000 in cash. Durie was charged, released on bail and took off for Florida. Ebanks, who police say has family ties to corrupt police officials in his homeland, fled to Jamaica.

In November, 1986, Durie was arrested on a luxury yacht in Fort Lauderdale by U.S. marshals. He was travelling under the name Alex Goodbrand. The arresting officers weren't convinced that Durie was Goodbrand and took him in. He was positively identified and spent the next eight months in an air-conditioned detention centre that was equipped with tennis courts where "ninety-nine per cent of the inmates were high rollers. Coke dealers," Durie said. He was then brought back to Canada to face trial, and rather than drag a foregone conclusion through the courts for months and possibly years, Durie decided to get it over with and pleaded guilty to a variety of drug-trafficking charges. "I was sick and tired. I wanted out and I wanted it over with. I didn't want to roll over on anybody so I pleaded guilty."

On July 10, 1987, Durie was jolted into reality when he appeared in Ontario District Court in Brampton for sentencing. Before pronouncing the ten-year sentence, Judge Martin Morrissey told the accused: "I consider that the term of years which I am about to give you will be a deterrent to other persons who are like-minded, who wish to, perhaps through the promise of gain, engage in the illegal exercise of importing and trafficking in drugs."

Durie slumped in his seat, looking helplessly at his devastated parents. "I felt bad for my mother and father that they had to see their son sentenced. They had no idea at the time what was going on. They may have seen some running around and heard some rumors. When I was seventeen, my mother caught me with a wheelbarrow with 100 pounds of compressed marijuana in it. She started screaming and yelling at me. Telling me how stupid I was. Then she told me to get it off the property. So I stashed the stuff from then on at a retreat house in Mississauga where old priests go to contemplate their navels for two or three days. My mother also caught me smoking but I wasn't about to stop just 'cause she told me to."

After he was sentenced, Durie said he felt incredible relief. "This whole trip was a wild fantasy, a hiatus, and now I'm on another hiatus in this shadow land. I kind of knew one day I would go to jail. It had to end. You just can't go through life being a criminal and not get caught, especially when you're playing with something this dangerous. Now it's over."

He swears vehemently that he is flat broke. "I spent a lot of the money I had, and what I didn't get around to spending, the lawyers got." Revenue Canada has slapped him with a bill for $490,000 in back taxes for undeclared earnings in 1985. "They figure I made $1 million in that year. And the police are convinced that I've got millions stashed somewhere. That's a joke. I've got nothing. I had a beautiful house, but they took that away from me. I also owned a magnificent 53-foot sailboat. The U.S. marshals pinched it on me. I was living on the boat in Coconut Grove in Florida when I was arrested. I bought it the day the Space Shuttle blew up. I should have taken it as a bad omen."

Court cases against various members of Durie's gang dragged through the legal system. Most were not about to plead guilty to get it over with. In all, thirteen of twenty-three indicted co-conspirators were found guilty. Several others were acquitted after agreeing to testify for the Crown, and warrants are still outstanding on Ebanks and Coltraine, who are in hiding outside Canada.

According to the National Drug Intelligence Estimates, released by the RCMP in June, 1989, cannabis derivatives – marijuana, hashish and liquid hashish – continue to be the most prevalent drugs of abuse throughout Canada, and they remain in "abundant supply".

"In general, marijuana, hashish and liquid hashish were readily available from the gram to the multi-pound levels in all regions of Canada, including the more isolated and rural regions," says the report. And that popularity, which may be news to people who think smoking pot had gone the way of the long-haired hippies of the 1960s, is reflected in the number of Canadians arrested every year for possession of cannabis products – about 50,000, and most of them under the age of thirty. Every year since 1985, the RCMP have been seizing shipments involving several tons of marijuana and hashish. In 1987, the Mounties and Canada Customs seized 26 475 kilograms of marijuana, an increase of 218 per cent from the 8 314 kilograms seized in 1986. Hashish seizures increased from 17 837 kilograms in 1986 to 23 968 in 1987, while seizures of liquid hashish rose significantly from 99 kilograms in 1986 to 439 in 1987, an increase of 340 per cent.

RCMP intelligence has found that "sea conveyance" has become the principal mode of transportation to smuggle large quantities of both marijuana and hashish into the country, and it warns that Canada's Atlantic and Pacific coastlines will be increasingly used in the future in what has been dubbed "mothership operations". "All of Canada's vast coastline is vulnerable to this type of operation," an RCMP report states, particularly with stepped-up enforcement by U.S. authorities along the American coastline. The Mounties have snagged a number of motherships off each coast, but their intelligence shows that many more shipments got through the vast, rugged Canadian coastline.

On a sticky, humid evening, in a dingy discothèque called the Superstar in the heart of Bangkok's raunchy sex district, a small band of former U.S. Vietnam veterans and drug dealers met to hatch a plan that would come to be one of the biggest marijuana shipments in North American history. The leader of the group, Brian Peter Daniels, a wealthy New York native who had lived in Thailand for many years, had more than 90 tonnes of high-grade Thai marijuana stockpiled in a warehouse in nearby Laos, and he desperately wanted to move it.

Daniels, 43, had been identified by U.S. Drug Enforcement Administration investigators as the top supplier of marijuana in the world. For almost two decades, Daniels' organization had eluded police around the world as his drug empire smuggled hundreds of tonnes of marijuana into the United States, Canada, Britain and Western Europe. In Southeast Asia, he was almost untouchable, receiving protection from high-level connections in the military commands of Thailand, Laos and Vietnam.

Attending the meet in early February, 1988, were Philadelphia-born twins Robert and Samuel Colflesh, two former Green Berets who stayed in Bangkok after the Vietnam war. They operated the Superstar disco bar as a cover for their smuggling operations. Also in attendance were Raimundo Angel Rabreau-Pacheco, a large-scale importer of marijuana on the west coast of North America, and Donald Burton Taylor, a high-rolling investor.

Unknown to the group, a police informant was at the table.

He would eventually lead Daniels and the twins into a trap that would bring down the operation. The informant, who was working for the DEA, arranged a meeting in a posh Hong Kong hotel on May 5, 1988, between members of the Daniels gang and a man who would off-load the marijuana shipment when it reached the shores of the United States. That man was an undercover DEA agent.

Over the next few weeks, several clandestine meetings took place in various hotel rooms in Hong Kong. Daniels decided that he would send out two shipments – 65 tonnes and 18 tonnes which would be dropped off at a scheduled spot along the coast of Washington State near Seattle. Daniels began amassing several millions of dollars in seed money for the operation. Some of the cash was earmarked to bribe military officials, but the bulk of it would be needed to buy two "motherships" to carry the loads.

Vacuum-packed in 8-kilogram bales and stuffed in water-proof canvas tote bags, the marijuana made its way overland from Thailand to Laos and then into North Vietnam, where it was taken to Da Nang Harbor and loaded onto the *Meridian*, one of Daniels' ships, by Vietnamese Army soldiers. In late June, the ship slipped out of the harbor and made its way to a rendezvous point on the South China Sea where 65 tonnes were transferred onto the *Encounter Bay*, a 55-metre oil rig supply vessel, and 18 tonnes were loaded onto the *Lloyd B. Gore*, a west coast tugboat.

On July 4, the U.S. Coast Guard cutter *Boutwell* intercepted the *Encounter Bay* several hundred kilometres off the Washington coast in international waters. After repeated attempts by radio failed to stop the ship, the *Boutwell* fired more than sixty rounds into the engine room of the *Encounter Bay*. Out-gunned, the 17-man crew of the *Encounter Bay*, including the Colflesh twins, surrendered.

The crew of *Lloyd B. Gore* had instructions to off-load its cargo onto a ship identified as the *Old Grandad*. But the skipper of the *Old Grandad* discovered he was under surveillance by a Coast Guard patrol boat and signalled the mothership to abort the plan. Under a veil of darkness, the *Lloyd B. Gore* entered Canadian waters and, at 4 a.m. on July 27, it cleared Canada Customs at the Steveston Petro-Can dock site in Richmond, B.C. The ship's cargo hold was empty.

Meanwhile, in San Diego, California, Donald Taylor was arrested and charged on July 29 for his part in financing the 65-tonne marijuana-smuggling conspiracy. Sitting nervously in a police interrogation room, Taylor was told in graphic detail what lay in store for him should he be convicted. He didn't need much convincing. Taylor agreed to cooperate with the DEA and the RCMP in their joint investigation of the missing 18 tonnes; after all, he had $1 million invested in that load.

On August 1, Taylor phoned someone called "Big Don" in Vancouver who instructed him to go to the Coach House Inn in North Vancouver on August 4 at 6 p.m. and sit in the cocktail lounge. "I'll be wearing a blue flannel shirt and you wear a red baseball cap," Big Don said. When Taylor arrived, Big Don was sitting in the lounge but he wasn't wearing a blue flannel shirt. It was draped on the seat next to him. In his early forties, he was 1.8 metres tall and heavy-set. Across from him was a second man, identified as John, a former Hell's Angel.

In hushed conversation, the trio discussed the adventures of the *Lloyd B. Gore*. Big Don told Taylor that the 18 tonnes were off-loaded in the Queen Charlotte Islands. Taylor was then taken to the Capilano Motor Inn in North Vancouver, where he was shown a nautical map of the islands. Big Don mentioned Rose Inlet and Nagas Point in reference to the off-load site. He also suggested that they rent a float plane to fly the marijuana from the cache site to the distribution areas in California. Taylor said he had someone who would move the marijuana to the mainland and then by truck across the U.S. border. That person was an undercover RCMP officer, code-named HQ 626.

With the general area of the cache site now identified, the RCMP began an intensive aerial and shore search, isolating possible landing locations on remote shores and beaches of the Queen Charlottes.

The following day, Taylor and HQ 626 met with Big Don and John at the Lynnwood Hotel in Vancouver at 4 p.m. Big Don was suspicious of HQ 626 and his plan to use a tug and barge to move the 18 tonnes to the mainland. Instead, he insisted that a better proposition would be to fly the load out to a lake in the interior of British Columbia. It would be carried out in a total of forty flights, with approximately 350 to 450 kilograms of marijuana per flight.

Big Don also told Taylor that he needed $200,000 up front to pay for the plane and the pilot, but Taylor said he couldn't afford to pay the up-front money. Having reached an impasse, the group agreed to another meet for the following day at 6 p.m. Big Don and John then left the Lynnwood and headed for the Keg Restaurant on West Esplanade Street, North Vancouver, where they met with the captain of the *Lloyd B. Gore*. RCMP surveillance teams noticed that Big Don was using a calculator.

On August 6, Taylor met with Big Don and John in a room at the Coach House Inn where they discussed the breakdown of the 18 tonnes. A total of 2,610 bales of marijuana were hidden on the Queen Charlotte Islands. The off-load crew would get 783 bales, and Taylor, Daniels and Rebreau-Pacheco would each get 609 bales. Each bale weighed 8 kilograms and would sell to street dealers who carried large weights at $5,400 a kilogram. A deal was reached whereby HQ 626 would be paid $3.5 million to move the entire 18-tonne load.

The following afternoon, Taylor and HQ 626 met Big Don and his sidekick at the Coach House Inn in North Vancouver. HQ 626 was told he could use a tug and barge, bring the load to a beach on the mainland and truck it from there to an abandoned logging camp in the B.C. interior. The foursome met again at 6 p.m. at the Cannery Restaurant in Vancouver, where they spent almost three hours discussing details of the transfer.

Over the next few days, there were more meetings during which HQ 626 managed to extract more precise information about the location of the stash site which he passed on to his handlers. On Thursday, August 11, an RCMP search team radioed headquarters. A shore search conducted in Sperm Bay within Flamingo Inlet on Moresby Island turned up more than 2,000 navy-blue canvas tote bags stuffed with marijuana.

Meanwhile, final preparations were still being made by gang members and HQ 626 to move the load. The date to move the cargo was set for Monday, August 15. With enough wiretap information and taped conversations picked up on the undercover agent's bodypack, and the informant in hand, the RCMP moved in and rounded up six gang members. They were charged with conspiring to traffic in marijuana. At the time of publication, the trial had not been held.

Jamaican, Colombian and Thai marijuana are the most popular among Canadian pot puffers, each cornering 20 per cent of the market, according to the RCMP. Mexico is in fourth place with 15 per cent of the market; and the United States has 5 per cent. The remaining 20 per cent is domestically grown in secret gardens, and indications are that this method may soon supply a much more significant portion of Canada's demand.

"The short growing season in Canada, when compared to the major cannabis source countries, as well as access to more sophisticated equipment, are factors that will increase employment of hydroponic indoor growing operations in Canada," says a 1989 RCMP intelligence report. "This cultivation method is more difficult to detect and results in greater profits for growers, yielding up to three crops per year with less risk of detection than conventional outdoor growing operations. Indicators suggest an increase in indoor marijuana operations across Canada."

British Columbia was identified as the "most active" region in Canada for indoor cultivation using the hydroponic method. "There has been a consistent increase in the number of growing operations for personal consumption and for major trafficking networks," a Mountie report states. But the practice, the report adds, is spreading right across Canada. Indoor operations have been found in Alberta, Manitoba, Ontario, Quebec and New Brunswick. "This is believed to be a growing trend," the report notes.

A fleet of cars and vans screeched to an abrupt stop on a quiet, tree-lined street in suburban Surrey, British Columbia, and disgorged a small platoon of what appeared to be football players in street clothes. These men were members of the RCMP Vancouver drug squad, and they were on a marijuana-hunting expedition. But they weren't looking for a few bedraggled plants growing in someone's vegetable garden or in a flower box by the back window, or a stash of pot smuggled in from South America or Thailand. They were on the prowl for a secret garden – an indoor marijuana-growing operation.

The officers approached a modest, unassuming bungalow and rapped on the door. No "Miami Vice" type tactics here. No SWAT teams with battering rams. No assault rifles or bullet-proof vests, and no megaphones. Just a simple police raiding party. A nervous-looking man pulled back a curtain covering the rectangular window in the middle of the door and swallowed hard. "We're the police. We have a warrant to search the house for narcotics," the RCMP sergeant said flatly.

Within seconds, the raiders found what they had come looking for in the adjoining double-car garage – a "grow lab" with more than $100,000 of high-grade marijuana being cultivated with the latest, state-of-the-art hydroponic technology.

Since joining the RCMP in 1969, Sergeant John Abbott has spent virtually all his working time looking for pot. At first, he used to look for the imported variety – Acapulco Gold, Mexican Red and Thai Sticks. Then his attention turned to marijuana crops being cultivated in outdoor patches throughout British Columbia. Now, he spends much of his time hunting for pot plantations in the basements, attics and garages of middle-class homes in the province.

"This grow-lab phenomenon has spread right through B.C. From the rural areas to the cities," Abbott said in an interview in the fall of 1988. "My estimate, and I think it's extremely low, is that there are anywhere from 500 to 1,000 grow labs in the province right now with an annual yield of about 4 tonnes of high-grade marijuana."

Abbott said he saw his first grow lab in 1981 in the Nelson region of the Kootenays. "By 1984, they began to crop up all over. I've seen an epidemic in the grow-lab phenomenon with an almost total switch from outdoor to indoor cultivation, and it is spreading across Canada as more and more people become aware of what is involved and the money that can be made."

The Mountie noted that while the international war on drugs has made it tougher, riskier and costlier to smuggle drugs into the country – especially bulky drugs like marijuana – improved technology has made it possible for local growers to pick up the slack. The Mountie estimated that by the early 1990s, more than half the marijuana consumed in Canada will be grown in secret gardens around the country.

Unlike other dealers involved in the illicit drug trade, marijuana cultivators have an uncontrollable urge to share their knowledge with other fellows of the soil. They take pride in their crop somewhat as a farmer takes pride in growing the biggest pumpkin, the juiciest tomatoes or prize-winning cucumbers. Their experience and know-how are disseminated in pro-marijuana magazines like *High Times*, which offers tips on the latest technology, where to buy equipment and seeds, and the best concealment methods.

While many growers swear they are simply in it for the challenge of growing the "best weed", the real draw is money. For an initial investment of between $7,000 and $10,000, virtually anyone can set up a secret garden in a basement and make from $50,000 to more than $100,000 a year tax free.

One former grower, who was arrested and convicted in early 1987 for marijuana cultivation, recounted how he first began growing pot in his bedroom in the mid-1970s. "I did it for fun. I didn't think too much about it at the time. It was for my own use. The most I ever had was half a dozen plants. But I got good at it and when I took in my second crop, my friends came over for a taste. It was like a wine tasting. They all told me how great this shit was so I started growing more and more, always trying to get a better crop than the year before. Before I knew it, I was really into it. My basement literally became an underground marijuana jungle and I was harvesting three crops a year and clearing about $85,000 a year tax free."

Then came that fateful knock on the door and arrest. "I pleaded guilty and got two years and a $10,000 fine. I served nine months, and now I'm out of this business for good. Man, the stress was just too much. I used to almost crap my pants when the doorbell rang. I lived in a constant state of paranoia thinking the police were going to bust down the doors at any minute, or that I would get ripped off by some punk gang. I mean, who needs to live like that? A couple of months before I was busted, I really thought the police were at the door. It was really early. There was this persistent knocking. Well, my heart was pounding in my chest. It took all the energy I had to crawl to the window and when I looked out, I saw these two middle-aged women. They were Jehovah's Witnesses. Can you believe that? I nearly had a heart attack over two Jehovah's Witnesses! Maybe it was some sort of omen. Who knows. Anyway I finally did get caught and now it's over and I'm out of the business for good."

Abbott said that the common line he hears from busted indoor farmers is that they are growing for their own personal use. He recalled one raid where the drug squad netted 7.13 kilograms of marijuana. "Being extremely liberal at a half a gram a joint, that would yield 14,260 joints. That works out to a 39-year supply of personal use at one joint per day and a 19-year supply at two joints per day. Another grow lab we hit recently had an annual yield that would give the grower a 57-year supply of personal use at one joint a day, so this refutes the personal-use defense. These people are drug dealers. They are in it for the money."

The advantages of indoor cultivation are many. Fewer

plants are needed to obtain a greater and more potent yield than those grown outdoors, and that improved quality is reflected in the street cost. Indoor pot will run from approximately $4,500 to $9,000 per kilogram, whereas marijuana from Mexico or Thailand will fetch only approximately $3,000 to $5,500 per kilogram. The irony is that, just a few years ago, an indoor cultivator couldn't give his product away without lying about its origins. Users wanted to think it was from some far-off exotic place like Thailand or Colombia. They wanted to see twigs and seeds and a brownish-green hue in their plastic, one-ounce baggies. They didn't like the unfamiliar dark green color and virtually seedless and twigless look of the indoor product. So the indoor growers added seeds and twigs and gave their products titillating names, such as Hawaiian Gold.

But today, hydroponically grown marijuana has come into its own. Under ideal growing conditions, it goes from seedling to mature plant in just three months, allowing the cultivator to bring in up to four crops a year. It is high in demand and is far more potent than any marijuana grown outdoors. The active ingredient THC (tetrahydrocannabinol), which produces the high, runs anywhere from less than 2 per cent to 7 per cent in plants grown outside. Indoor grass grown hydroponically in secret basements has been tested and found to have THC levels reaching a mind-numbing 22 per cent.

In the Surrey raid, the RCMP stumbled on one of the best, state-of-the-art hydroponic operations ever uncovered in Canada. When they approached the double-car garage, they noticed that the windows had been covered with dark curtains to prevent anyone from seeing in. But as they got nearer, they could hear the classic sound of a secret garden: the low hum of the fans and the muffled buzz of electrical equipment.

The garage was segregated into four areas. The first was the workshop equipped with an electronic scale, a phone and packaging materials. The other areas were used for the three growing stages. The first was the starter room where new plants were propagated from seed or cuttings under fluorescent lighting. When they reached the seedling stage and were firmly rooted, they were moved to the "grow room" for the vegetative stage. Here, under eighteen hours of constant light, the plants can grow seven to ten centimetres a day. In this cycle, which lasts about two months, the plants will not flower. In effect, they have been tricked into thinking that the long hours of light mean it is summer. They will then be moved to the third-stage maturing room, where the daylight will drop from eighteen to twelve hours, triggering the plant into thinking autumn is coming. In the next four to six weeks, the plant will flower and reach maturity, and the harvest will begin. The real technology in hydroponics comes into play in these final two stages.

At the back of the garage, a sophisticated electrical panel controlled the entire growing and maturing cycle of the plants in these two areas, which were covered entirely with reflective foil. That panel, which was illegally connected to an underground B.C. Hydro cable, thus bypassing the hydro meter, ran a network of 1,000-watt halide and sodium lights on tracking systems that moved back and forth. The lights are the key to any grow-lab operation and produce the equivalent light and warmth of a tropical rain forest. The panel also controlled canisters of carbon dioxide, which increases the growing rate of the marijuana, air filters and ionizers to cleanse the air and keep out unwanted pollen, bug zappers, electrostatic precipitators to vent the pungent odor of marijuana up the chimney, a heat exchanger to keep the room at a constant temperature, and a series of pumps to push the right balance of air, water and nutrients through a labyrinth of plastic hoses into pots filled with lava rock and water.

The raiders found dozens of cuttings rooting in the starter room. They seized forty-one plants in the grow room and another forty-one plants in the maturing room. Almost 2 kilograms of buds taken from an earlier crop were drying on a screen table, and another four half-kilogram packages were retrieved from a freezer. Police estimated that at 85 grams of smokable product per plant, the forty-one mature plants would yield about 3.6 kilograms. The marijuana from this bust was also found to have an exceptionally high THC content – 22 per cent. Abbott figured the grower could have commanded top dollar: at least $8,000 per kilogram.

What was unique about this particular secret garden was that the cultivator, Gyula Julias Szalontai, had perfected a technique to grow sinsemilla marijuana, the most potent strain of pot. The term sinsemilla is Spanish for "without seeds". Growers would rather cultivate only female plants because it is in the female buds and flowers that the THC-laden resin collects when it is maturing and about to seed. However, the sex of plants cannot be determined by the seeds, or even at the seedling stage. The sex becomes known at the flowering and pollinating stage, and female plants stop producing resin once they have been pollinated by a male plant. In a sinsemilla environment, the female plant frantically oozes resin right to its death hoping to be pollinated. To guarantee a crop of sinsemilla, the cultivator must first isolate a female plant and propagate new seedings by rooting cuttings from it. He must also hope that his filters will keep stray male pollen from entering the grow lab.

Abbott shook his head in amazement at how the grow-lab phenomenon has taken hold in B.C. "We've run into families, husband and wife teams, growing pot. Mothers and fathers with children growing marijuana to make money. We've run into hardcore drug addicts growing the stuff to pay for their heroin or cocaine habit. Cultivators cover the whole spectrum from bikers to daddies."

Increasingly, undercover drug cops throughout the province are encountering homegrown marijuana on the streets. Grow labs have become a highly profitable hometown industry in B.C. And the major hurdle confronting drug enforcement officers is that the secret gardens are not easy to find. Virtually the only way they can be detected is through informants. On the other hand, the danger for anyone who sells homegrown is that he is automatically suspected of having a grow lab or of being close to someone with a secret garden, making the trail easy to follow.

Furthermore, there is nothing illegal about owning any of the equipment used in hydroponic gardening. At a gardening centre outside Surrey, anyone can go in and buy 1,000-watt halide and sodium bulbs, canisters of carbon dioxide, plastic tubing, timers, nutrients, lava rocks, all the necessary para-phernalia for setting up an indoor garden. Chances are that many of the 20-year-olds frequenting this gardening centre are not spending thousands of dollars on equipment to grow prize orchids or hothouse tomatoes. At the gardening centre, a long-haired salesman chuckled knowingly when asked if he has ever seen any of the vegetables and flowers his clients purport to grow.

10

LSD *on a Harley*

Benjamin Hayward did not come home after a Pink Floyd concert at Exhibition Stadium in Toronto on Friday, May 13, 1988. Several times during the early morning hours, the 14-year-old's mother, Sandy, frantically phoned police to check whether they had any information on her missing son. It was not like Benji to miss his curfew.

At 3:40 a.m., Toronto police picked up the boy's best friend, Eric Hutcheson, who was wandering aimlessly along a downtown street. The spaced-out 15-year-old was wearing only pants and socks. Two hours later, Constable John Evans arrived at the Hayward home and prepared a missing-person report. He also phoned the Hutcheson home, but Eric's mother said her son was asleep and not in an emotional or physical state to be interviewed. Hesitantly, Sandy and Gordon Hayward informed the police officer that they thought their son might have experimented with drugs that night.

"My reaction was maybe he had gone home with someone else and gone to sleep without expecting his parents were waiting up all night," Evans later testified at an inquest. "In all my experience in missing persons, I never had one that hadn't turned up in a short time – hours or a day."

A deep anguish descended on the Hayward home. Gordon was sure something terrible had happened to his son. He tried to force the worse fears from his mind but the anxiety kept jabbing at his gut. Over the weekend, there was still no news about Benji. Family friends, school chums and neighbors dropped over to the Hayward home to offer support. Urgent phone calls were placed to anyone who knew the boy – friends, classmates, neighborhood kids. But no one had seen Benji.

220

It seemed that only Eric, who went with Benji to the Pink Floyd concert, might hold a vital clue to the boy's whereabouts. That Sunday, during an interview with police, he admitted that he and his best buddy had purchased some LSD and marijuana outside the stadium before going in for the concert. He said he last saw Benji just as the concert was ending. "I suggested beating the crowd so we headed out some stairs. Then the band started playing again and Benji must have gone back in. I thought I'd meet him at the exit."

At the request of investigating officers, the teenager agreed to be hypnotized in an effort to trigger a memory that might give the police a clue. While in a hypnotic trance, Eric recalled, "Benji has a big smile on his face. He's really confused. He's about four or five feet [away]. I wave to him, tell him we better leave. [The rock fans] are pushing really hard. Then Benji's gone. I turn around because I want to see him laughing, but he's not around."

The effects of the LSD were pleasant at first, Eric remembered, but then his trip began to disintegrate. "I felt myself getting weirder and weirder . . . I was totally absorbed in a total loss of reality." He wandered down an alleyway and encountered a bag lady. "I remember all these voices in my head . . . weird ones about death and reincarnation . . . I felt I could die. I asked this lady to help me and her eyes looked really sorry for me. I got scared looking at her 'cause she was so ugly. I could see her face changing. . . . I could remember looking at myself: green, grey, pasty, slimy. I remember thinking I was the only person in the world who knew we were really these creatures, space things." The next thing he remembered was being helped into a car, but he didn't realize the driver was a police officer. He thought that the man in the uniform would "take me back to the real world."

Earlier, Eric told investigators that he had used drugs for about a year. He also said that he and Benji had taken LSD three times, including once while they were at the Hayward home and once while they were spending the night at Eric's home. He said he began using marijuana and hashish and then acid because his friends were using drugs and seemed to be enjoying them. "I didn't want to be naive about the whole thing. I just wanted to find a way to have fun."

Benji's ex-girlfriend, Starr Williamson, told police that she saw the boy during the show. She said he showed her two hits (pieces of blotter paper) of acid under his tongue. "He was really messed up. He was falling down. I'd seen him stoned on acid before but I don't think he could have made it home in that condition."

Fed up with sitting around for two days waiting for news about their son, the Haywards began their own search. Enlisting the help of their friend Henry Goodman, an advertising executive, they printed posters of Benji, asking: "Have you seen this boy?" Benji's 18-year-old sister, Miranda, and dozens of school chums fanned out across the city tacking the posters on telephone poles and trees.

Late Monday, police turned up at the Hayward home with their first hard lead: Miranda's school jacket. It was found by a cyclist on the park grounds two days earlier outside the Exhibition Stadium. Benji had borrowed the jacket to go the concert. The search intensified.

Then just before noon on May 18, two police constables arrived at the Hayward home once again. Gordon met them at the door. From the sombre expression on the officers' faces, he knew his son had been found. He knew in the pit of his stomach that Benji was dead. Inside the house, the officers told the couple that the body of a teenage boy fitting Benji's description had been pulled from Lake Ontario a few hours earlier. Gordon asked Henry Goodman to accompany him to the morgue to identify the body. Outside, on the tree-lined street, Gordon approached a small group of reporters. He was grateful to them for the publicity in trying to help find his son. "The police are 99.9 per cent sure it's Benji," he said.

After he came back from the morgue, Gordon again met with reporters. "He's gone . . . it's an end. That was the feeling his mother and I had from day one. Even if I didn't know the other things, I knew about my son – that if he had been physically able to call, he would have. That's all I have to say, except that I hope other parents take a little more time, a little less father in front of the TV set, and that they listen. No one wants to think that their kids are into drugs. . . . And kids, don't be afraid of your parents. They're not as bad as you think. Sometimes, they do know a little better than you."

News of the heartbreaking discovery of Benji's body sent shock waves through Toronto the Good. Parents, neighbors, friends, schoolmates struggled to understand what had happened. How and why it happened. Benji was not some low-class young offender. He didn't come from the wrong side of the tracks. He came from the respectable side of town: from a fine Jewish family that cherished family values, that loved and deeply cared for each other. Benji was an intelligent, typical, fresh-faced, middle-class kid. He was full of energy and ideas. According to his friends, Eric included, Benji wasn't a "drug-gie". Robbie Kane, a high-school friend, said Benji "didn't do drugs for attention. He was one of the clean-cut kids. He always wore his hair short. He always dressed appropriately. It's just that drugs are all over the place."

Exactly what happened to Benji after the concert will probably never be known. Footprints leading up to a fence at the edge of Lake Ontario have led the boy's parents to speculate that he walked onto a breakwall, slipped and fell into the frigid waters early on the morning of May 14.

At a coroner's inquest in late July, a jury of three women and two men learned that Benji and Eric had been stopped by police on March 24 after they were observed by a police officer "in an apparent drug transaction" on Yonge Street in downtown Toronto. The officer, Constable Andrew Dobro, sternly lectured the panic-stricken boys for about a half-hour and then let them go. Dobro recounted that Benji had dropped a crumpled scrap of newspaper onto a sewer when Dobro and his partner, Constable Jim Hutcheon, stopped the boys. The officer said he and Hutcheon left the two teenagers "quaking in their boots" and didn't call their parents because "we thought we scared the boys enough." He noted that, according to police regulations, parents must only be called if the youths are charged. Nonetheless, Dobro later filed a "172" form, an internal document which is filled out when someone has contact with police but no charge is laid.

The jury also learned that Benji and Eric were among thousands of teenagers who smoked dope, dropped acid, drank alcohol or snorted cocaine at the rock concert. A police officer told the jury that "bike gangs control the acid [LSD] trade in Ontario" and have been a "much-felt presence" at rock concerts over the years.

Sergeant James Lee, who is attached to the Metro Toronto Police biker enforcement unit, noted that 15 of the 208 security employees hired by Concert Productions International for the Pink Floyd concert were affiliated with biker gangs or had been the subject of police drug investigations. There was also strong suspicion that another ten employees were involved in biker gangs.

He testified that 90 per cent of motorcycle gang members have criminal records, and that entire clubs are sometimes hired by concert promoters in various North American cities for crowd control. "Basically, they're in charge, they make their own rules . . . you get the world right where you need it. It wouldn't be in their interests to stop kids bringing [drugs] in. They're more likely to sell it to them." Lee later told a throng of reporters that motorcycle gangs almost exclusively control the manufacture, distribution and sale of chemical drugs, and that most LSD comes from gang-run labs in Southern California. Bikers hired as "peer security" guards at rock concerts "have the best of both worlds," he said. "They have the entire distribution ring sewn up – they have manufacture, distribution and security."

Outlaw motorcycle gangs have been labelled by police as the largest organized crime threat in Canada, bigger than even the Mafia. Deeply immersed in criminal pursuits, biker gangs have reached a new and more dangerous level with their increasing national and international activities. They are involved in every conceivable criminal enterprise, ranging from contract murders to sophisticated white-collar crime. But their most intensive pursuit is the trafficking of illegal drugs. One of their seedy sidelines is the manufacture and distribution of chemical drugs and their customers are chiefly high schoolers, street kids and dropouts.

Biker gangs virtually control the black market in illicit chemical drugs and are directly involved in the financing of clandestine chemical drug laboratories across Canada for the production and distribution of PCP (phencyclidine), MDA (methylenedioxy-amphetamine), and speed (methamphetamine). From 1982 to 1986, police have busted more than fifty clandestine laboratories in isolated communities right across the country.

In British Columbia, gangs have set up labs to produce MDA, PCP and methamphetamine in remote locations from Quadra Island to Coquitlam and Nanoose. In Quebec, motorcycle gangs are responsible for a significant proportion of PCP production. Police have raided and dismantled PCP labs in such out-of-the-way Quebec towns as Ste-Marguerite, St-Sauveur, St-Hilarion, Fossambaut-sur-le-lac, St-Ubald and Lac Sergent. PCP, which is also known as angel dust, elephant and hog, was originally developed as an anaesthetic for use in veterinary medicine. With effects lasting from three to eighteen hours, it produces a state of pleasurable intoxication; a sense of separation from surroundings; perceptual distortions; and difficulty in concentrating and communicating. Users may also become highly confused, paranoid, terrified and aggressive. Bad trips are more common with PCP than with any other drugs. In Ontario, biker gangs are involved in the production of MDA and methamphetamine, also known as STP and DOM. Police drug squads have shut down clandestine labs in such towns and cities as Madoc, Peterborough, London and Hamilton.

In March, 1988, Gerald Lukaniuk was sentenced to six years in prison for operating a clandestine drug lab. Police raided a laboratory used by the 37-year-old Toronto man to create theatrical special effects for his company, Art Effects. They found 1,200 grams of methamphetamine "cooking" and 10 grams of MDA. The court was told that Lukaniuk was a self-trained chemist and a respected special effects artist who was coerced into "a flirtation with illegality" by motorcycle gang members. "There is no evidence that the accused was involved in distribution but I can't help but think that his involvement was the first link in an evil chain," District Court Judge Alexander Davidson said in passing sentence. He said the stiff sentence was necessary because speed is "a mind-destroying drug" and others should be deterred from manufacturing and selling it. Judge Davidson noted that although Lukaniuk, a father of three young children, was a first-time offender, his drug laboratory was no amateur undertaking but, rather, "an operation conducted for financial gain in a commercial manner."

LSD (lysergic acid diethylamide) is largely produced in underground labs controlled by motorcycle gangs in California, and is smuggled into Canada by bikers, often for an even swap of Canadian-made chemicals.

Ironically, many people had thought LSD and other mind-altering, psychedelic drugs had disappeared with the hippies. "Turn on, tune in and drop out," the rallying cry during the 1960s of Timothy Leary, the high priest of LSD, is now a faint echo in the minds of greying flower children.

Today, Leary, the defrocked Harvard University professor and former holy prophet of hallucinogens, is still unrepentant about exhorting his students to expand their minds on acid. But he stresses that he deplores the use of LSD – or any other drug – by immature, naive teenagers. Leary continues to maintain that the use of mind-altering drugs is a helpful tool for intellectuals who want to explore and expand their intellectual capacities, and counters that if anyone is to blame for giving LSD a bad rap, it is in large part the morons who devour drugs as if they were candy-coated M&Ms and then freak out on a bad trip, and the manufacturers who produce a product that is too potent.

"Drugs, like computers, are ways for an intelligent person to activate new brain circuits," he once said in an interview with *The Globe and Mail.* "Ninety-five per cent of the people who use illegal drugs, you never hear about them. They're silent, hard-working, intelligent people starting out to get control of their brain and their mind. It's the other five per cent that causes the trouble. They're losers. If you want to self-destruct, you can use sex, booze, money, gambling. One way is drugs. But the problem is not drugs. The problem is recognizing, anticipating and preventing drug abuse by this five per cent."

While Leary advocates intelligent drug use, he abhors drug abuse and strongly disapproves of young people using any kind of drugs. "I encourage students and young people to keep their brains alive and sharp. They must be totally committed to intellectual excellence. I deplore young unprepared people using any kind of drug – alcohol, LSD, whatever. The problem is that in the context of the war and propaganda that the government is doing [against drugs], everything gets confused. Kids today are so disgusted and frightened by doom and gloom that they blindly strike back in rebellion."

But the worrisome reality today is that kids are experimenting with mind-altering drugs, and these substances are more powerful and dangerous than they were in the 1960s, in part because of the biker connection and because they are mixed in dirty kitchens by amateur chemists. In most Canadian high schools, students know where to get a hit of LSD, and it is relatively cheap. For $5, they can buy a blotter or micro-dot of Red Laser, Purple Mike, Strawberry, Around the World or California Sunshine. The most popular outlet for chemical drugs is rock concerts, and it is in this venue that biker gangs unload large quantities of chemical drugs on a naive teenage clientele.

In late 1986, at a trial in Toronto of several members of the Outlaws biker gang charged with conspiracy to traffic in LSD, speed and cocaine, testimony was given by a former gang member which provided the public with a rare glimpse into the drug dealings of the club. Steven Caretta, a former Outlaw, testified that the gang's clubhouse had been fitted with chicken wire to deflect hand grenades that might be tossed by rival bikers. It was reinforced with sandbags, shuttered and barred windows, watchdogs, a 2.5-metre fence and security cameras. Each Outlaw was required to contribute to the security of the clubhouse. Caretta detailed a scheme instigated by the president of the Outlaws which involved the distribution of 1,000 hits of LSD to each member, who in turn would sell them to pay for a handgun and clubhouse security. All drug sales had a built-in "kickback", and that money went to the president so that he could order drugs in larger quantities.

Caretta had originally been a member of the Iron Hawgs. That gang amalgamated with the Outlaws in September, 1984, because, he said, it wanted to keep the Quebec Hell's Angels from spreading its wings into the lucrative Ontario drug trade. In an unrelated, seven-month trial in 1988, seven members and associates of the Outlaws were found guilty by a jury in Toronto of trafficking in LSD and speed between October, 1983, and January, 1985. In passing sentence in July, 1988, on two gang members, Ontario District Court Judge Hugh O'Connell labelled the duo "merchants of misery".

"What a terrible, terrible crime . . . the suffering and misery it's brought on people who use [drugs]. I have no compassion or sympathy for those who sell it," Judge O'Connell said, adding that the sole purpose of the Outlaws was "to distribute and sell huge quantities of drugs. It's not just living on the profits of drugs, it's the misery you have caused. It's the disease of the seventies and eighties and it costs the taxpayers millions in health care."

On a warm summer night in early August, as the Benji Hayward inquest was drawing to a close, the rock group Aerosmith arrived in town. It was almost three months to the day that Benji had died. Thousands of teenagers converged on Exhibition Stadium for the concert. Outside the gates, dozens of undercover police officers fanned across the exhibition grounds to hunt for drug pushers. They collared scores of dealers that evening, including two teenage girls. One had 144 hits of LSD in her possession, the other 65 hits.

11
Narco-Terrorism

It has been dubbed "an unholy alliance", a malevolent association of two of the most dangerous forces plaguing society today – drug traffickers and guerrilla revolutionaries. In a once unthinkable move, scores of violent terrorist organizations and jungle insurgencies around the globe have compromised their ideals and principles by forging links with powerful crime syndicates in order to provide themselves with the funds to sustain their various causes.

For the greedy drug barons, these alliances have become part of the price tag of doing business. They are a minor irritant, and the additional cost of paying for protection is simply passed on to the consumer. But for international law-enforcement agencies battling on the front lines of the drug war, this alliance, which has been labelled "narco-terrorism", is yet another difficult hurdle in the seemingly endless war on drugs.

"Narco-terrorism, the involvement of terrorist organizations and insurgent groups in the trafficking of narcotics, has become a problem with international implications," a confidential FBI document, prepared in October, 1987, states. "In Third World countries, narcotics traffickers, terrorist organizations, and insurgent groups are alleged to use the wealth they obtain from the sale of illegal drugs to exert economic, political and military pressure on the governments of the countries in which they operate. The activities of these groups, particularly in Latin America, can threaten the stability of the various countries' governments."

The document, prepared by the FBI's Terrorist Research and Analytical Centre in Washington, D.C., points out that in a number of Third World countries contact and cooperation between insurgent groups and drug traffickers comes about because the former maintain "base camps and infiltration routes in remote rural areas where narcotics traffickers cultivate their crops." It notes that while most insurgent groups are not directly involved in the cultivation and processing of illegal drugs, they obtain cold, hard cash from the drug barons through "extortion, typically by charging fees for protection of growing areas, processing facilities, or distribution routes."

In Alto Huallaga, a mountainous jungle valley some 880 kilometres northeast of Lima, Peru, the fanatical Maoist faction Sendero Luminoso (Shining Path) protects the peasant growers of coca, the tropical bush from which cocaine is extracted, by intervening in price negotiations with drug traffickers. In early March, 1989, Sendero, whose nine-year guerrilla campaign has claimed 14,000 Peruvian lives, teamed up with the *narcotraficantes* in attacking a police post in the heart of the coca-rich valley. The raid, in which ten policemen and three civilians were killed, gave Peruvian authorities and U.S. drug enforcement officials the first clear evidence of a link between Sendero and the traffickers.

Next door in Colombia, the notorious 2,000-strong M-19 movement and the 7,000-member Revolutionary Armed Forces of Colombia (FARC) have been accused by the Colombian authorities and the U.S. Drug Enforcement Administration of providing safe passage to caravans transporting coca paste through jungle roads en route to clandestine refineries deep inside the country. The billionaire cocaine barons in Medellin and Cali pay handsomely for the service, and the leftist guerrillas get money to buy more weapons and ammunition to continue their struggle. The U.S. has used the so-called "FARC-narc" connection to buttress its claim that leftists and traffickers are in league. FARC rebels are known to receive payoffs from Medellin intermediaries who buy coca base from peasant farmers in the lowlands region it controls. FARC "allows" the peasants to cultivate coca because they simply cannot subsist with ordinary crops. And since the rebels are intent on establishing a strong base in the region, they control the marketing and pricing of the raw product. They also set the wages of the coca leaf pickers and mete out harsh penalties for anyone caught pushing or taking drugs.

No episode better illustrates the frightening potential of narco-terrorism than the attack by M-19 guerrillas on the Palace of Justice in Bogotá in November, 1985. Concealed in a van, about forty heavily armed insurgents entered the building through an undergound garage. According to the Colombian military and U.S. DEA officials, the objective of the M-19 force was to destroy the court records of some 200 drug traffickers as part of a "contract" with the cocaine bosses. As the army counterattacked, eleven of the nation's twenty-four Supreme Court justices were killed, along with the entire M-19 attack squad.

Halfway around the world, Beirut continues to be senselessly pounded into near oblivion by warring factions. In the heaviest fighting in years, hundreds of Lebanese men, women and children were killed or maimed in April and May of 1989. Yet in the midst of this bloody carnage, there is one area where this nation's opposing forces cooperate: the Bekaa Valley. The mainstay of the economy of the valley, a 160-kilometre-long, 16-kilometre-wide strip of land that lies between Syria and the war-torn Lebanese heartland, is the illegal drug trade. In the shattered economy of Lebanon, drugs pay for the weapons that have wreaked destruction and misery on this once prosperous and peaceful country. Aside from the occasional Israeli air strike, the Bekaa Valley is the most peaceful region in the entire country. Only there do Christian, Sunni, Druze, Shia and Palestinian factions coexist without constant bloodshed.

DEA officials in Cyprus estimate that drug profits account for 50 per cent of the entire Lebanese economy. Lebanon has traditionally been the world's major supplier of hashish. The RCMP estimate Lebanon's share of the Canadian hashish market at 85 per cent. An RCMP drug intelligence report states that Lebanese hashish trafficking is largely controlled by brokers who take orders and then contact the cannabis farmers. "Once they agree on a price, the brokers make arrangements for transportation, delivery and payment. Intelligence reveals that most brokers are Lebanese, although there are reports of European, Egyptian, Tunisian and Canadian brokers. Their European and North American trafficking connections are frequently of Lebanese background, often with family ties in Lebanon," the report states.

International drug experts agree that hashish, and increasingly opium and heroin, production is inextricably and strategically intertwined in the complex political situation of Lebanon. "Here you have a country devastated by war, and yet the drugs keep flowing to market," a DEA agent commented caustically. "Bombs are going off everywhere and warring factions find time to wave through a drug convoy, taking their cut of the profits as it moves through their sector on its way to a port city. What a crazy world! I would venture that not one of these fanatical religious gangs would last a month without the drug trade."

Narco-terrorism has so far been a problem whose impact has been felt only in drug-producing countries – Burma, Thailand, Afghanistan, Pakistan, Iran, Lebanon, Peru, Bolivia and Colombia. But there is mounting concern in Canada, the United States and Western Europe that certain insurgency groups and terrorist organizations are increasing their profit margins through expanding their involvement with drug trafficking by trading with their sympathizers in the West. In recent years, drug investigators in Canada have uncovered cases involving contacts between established North American drug syndicates and individuals and gangs linked to terrorist organizations and causes abroad. Police in Montreal and Toronto have arrested several drug traffickers from Iran, Sri Lanka and Lebanon who have confessed to being involved in the trade as a means of raising money for their causes back home. RCMP assistant commissioner J.J.M. Coutu makes a passing reference to narco-terrorism in the force's National Drug Intelligence Estimate released in June,

1989, noting that "there is growing evidence that proceeds from the international drug trade support terrorism."

However, Jim Warren, who heads the terrorism analysis and investigation section for the Canadian Security Intelligence Service (CSIS), prefers to believe that people who deal in narcotics "are first and foremost out there for their own financial benefit." Warren says he has wondered whether drug traffickers purporting to back or support insurgency or liberation struggles in some far-flung land "are insurgents, terrorists or revolutionaries first and drug lords second in order to finance their political agenda. Or are they first and foremost drug lords out there to fill their own pockets and kind of veiling or cloaking it all with [the] respectability of a political agenda. I guess my suspicions lie more often that not with the latter. But that is more a matter of opinion than proof."

Warren says he has heard comments from individual drug dealers "in the Tamil community" stating that the drug profits were being sent back to Sri Lanka to support rebel groups. "I wonder if those kind of comments are not attempts to legitimize what is recognized by everybody as being an especially dirty business by tacking on some kind of a laudable end to it – 'the freedom of my people' – that this is what this is really all about."

Warren admits that while CSIS has not identified a clear and definite narco-terrorist link in Canada, "We also have had our suspicions too that from time to time some people in Canada might be involved. . . . One of the suspicions we know is [that] some of the people involved, whether it's the Sikh terrorist movement, or the Iranian dissident movement or the [various] Middle East movements, are also involved in drugs. We've seen that. Now whether they're doing that as a matter of policy is in considerable more doubt. I can think of at least two Sikhs where we concluded after looking at it very closely that it was not a matter of policy. They belonged to the Sikh Youth Federation. In fact, one of them was a fairly senior officer in the federation. But our conclusion was their activities were not sanctioned by and not even acquiesced by the Sikh Youth Federation. These people were first and foremost out there for their own financial benefit.

"We've seen it in the Middle East too where people who come across our radar screen . . . they're also involved in the drug trade. We look at those kind of connections and wonder, but to date, I can't think of one case I can really nail down, get a hold of and say there's a documented example of an organization using the drug trade to finance its political agenda."

Informed of Warren's assessment of the situation, two top drug investigators in Toronto and Montreal wonder aloud whether a CSIS agent has ever been "on the street", or in a position to really know whether drugs and politics are sometimes one and the same in major Canadian cities. "I'm out on the street doing drug busts," the Toronto investigator said. "I've talked to the Iranians and the Tamils we've busted, and they've told us straight up that they're buying arms with the drugs they sell. We've traced money going right back to Madras, India, where some of these Tamil rebel factions have their headquarters. When has a CSIS officer ever gone out on the streets to see just what the hell is going on out there? They sit in their offices and read the newspapers and make informed guesses. The street end is where the intelligence is, and that's where they should be."

In late December, 1987, undercover officers with the Metro Toronto Police drug squad arrested several Tamil refugee claimants from Sri Lanka and seized 700 grams of almost pure heroin. The investigation, dubbed Operation Cheap, began in the summer months and focused on a particular Tamil gang that was attempting to sell heroin to organized crime rings in Toronto. After the bust, Staff Sergeant Larry Hovey told reporters at a press conference that the investigation found that some of the money from the heroin sales was "definitely" going to India. Meanwhile, immigration documents indicated that most of the drug dealers who were arrested were connected to Tamil insurgency organizations battling the Sinhalese-majority government in Sri Lanka for an independent state. In August, 1988, six members of the drug ring pleaded guilty to conspiracy to import heroin and were sentenced to prison terms ranging from four years to ten years. Interpol investigations in Western Europe have also found links to Tamil drug rings in West Germany, France and Britain, and various liberation fronts in Sri Lanka. Hovey suggested that it was possible that the Toronto ring could have raised millions to finance the struggle back home. "The methods of operation ... are similar to Tamil organizations in Europe and England who have set up importation and distribution of heroin operations," he said.

Arul Aruliah, a member of the Tamil Eelam Society of Canada, hotly denies any connection between heroin drug dealers and the Tamil Tigers. "The Tigers would not ever get into this type of immoral activity to fight an immoral regime," he maintains.

In an effort to find out whether a narco-terrorist link existed in the Tamil community in Western Europe, Mazher Mahmood, a reporter for the *Sunday Times* in London, England, managed, in August, 1987, to infiltrate a heroin racket run by Tamil terrorists in West Germany. The ring had been using London's Heathrow airport as a staging post in a multi-million-dollar drug-smuggling operation. Mahmood was told by the gang's leader that the money from the drug dealing was being used to continue funding the Tamil resistance in Sri Lanka.

The *Sunday Times* investigation unearthed a highly sophisticated network purportedly run by members of the Liberation Tigers of Eelam. "Last week, Sooriyakumaran Selvadurai, the head of the militant Tigers organization in West Germany, offered to supply two kilos of heroin in Britain to a *Sunday Times* reporter who infiltrated the ring," Mahmood wrote. He noted that in the past eighteen months, at least ten Tamils carrying heroin had been caught at Heathrow and several more were detected in transit, each carrying three kilos, and had been followed to their final destination before being arrested.

Mahmood learned that the first leg of the Tamil heroin trail began in Bombay and involved smuggling the drugs into West Germany, where there are more than 25,000 Tamils claiming political asylum. "In West Germany, representatives of the Tigers negotiate wholesale deals with buyers throughout Europe. The drug is then smuggled to order, supervised by Tiger bases in each country, or smuggled direct to local markets by the Tamils. The main destinations include Britain, Switzerland, Spain, Italy, France and Canada."

Mahmood also wrote that once he convinced Sooriyakumaran that he was a genuine customer the Tamil admitted the Tigers' involvement in the drug trade. "Unlike you, we don't do it for personal profit. We are only interested in making money to buy arms to help our fight for justice back home," Sooriyakumaran stated.

Sitting in a booth at the back of a greasy restaurant in Montreal's west end, an Iranian police informant puffed nervously on a cigarette. It was obvious he didn't want to be in the company of the burly detective or of the stranger from Toronto. Staring out onto the street at the cars driving by, he offered only terse replies to a few questions. Yes, he said, some Iranians he knew were involved in heroin dealing to raise money to fight against the regime of Ayatollah Khomeini. "They send the money to Paris. I don't know anything more."

Jacques Duchesneau, who heads the drug squad for the Montreal Urban Community Police force, said wiretaps on certain Iranian drug gangs indicated that money was being sent to help finance Iranian political factions. "That was the deduction we made but we don't have the manpower to chase it. We're working at a different level here." Two of his investigators confirmed that they had been told by Iranian dealers that money from heroin sales had been earmarked for "the Iranian cause".

On July 23, 1987, the People's Mojahedin of Iran, the main opposition group to the Ayatollah Khomeini's regime, claimed it had evidence linking Iran's chief justice to a drug smuggling operation to help finance the war effort against Iraq. According to the Mojahedin, Iran netted upwards of $40 million from heroin sales outside the country from March, 1986, to May, 1987. The group stated that the drugs were sent out in diplomatic pouches to the Iranian Embassy in Rome, and from there distributed to a network of drug traffickers.

Meanwhile, a circumstantial link between Iranian drugs and weapons purchases became public in 1983, when a former Iranian deputy prime minister was caught carrying about two kilograms of opium into West Germany. The man, Sadegh Tabatai, was related by marriage to Ayatollah Khomeini. He fled the country hours before his court appearance and was sentenced in absentia to three years. That same year, Swiss authorities indicted three Swiss nationals for swindling Tabatai by promising him fifty American-built tanks, which were never delivered.

In a Montreal courtroom, a bizarre tale of Sikh extremists using drugs to further their separatist movement in India unfolded in late December, 1986, and early January, 1987. Two Sikhs, Santokh Singh Khela, 25, and Kashmir Singh Dhillon, 42, were accused of offering an undercover agent 20 kilograms of heroin to blow up an airliner in the United States. During the trial, it turned out that the person the two had approached to obtain explosives was a Quebec police force informant, and the man they plotted with to place the explosives on the aircraft was Frank Miele, an agent with the U.S. Federal Bureau of Investigation, who was brought into the case by the RCMP. Miele was introduced to the two men as George, a New Yorker and Vietnam veteran who was an explosives specialist.

The conversation, which took place in room 2101 at Le Grand Hôtel in downtown Montreal, was secretly taped by the RCMP. Miele was handed a piece of paper with code words listed on it, such as "mobile home" for airplane and "ship it" for destroy it. On the tape, a voice says: "When we talk we'll use those words. We don't want anyone to get into trouble." A little later the same voice says: "We want a big one, fully loaded." During the conversation, Khela says: "I want it ready in June, can you do anything about that?" In a series of responses to questions by Miele, Khela pointed out that the invasion of the Sikh Golden Temple in Amritsar by Indian soldiers occurred on June 5, 1984. He also noted that the crash of the Air India Boeing 747 in which 329 people died off the coast of Ireland happened in June, 1985.

A document seized by the Mounties at Dhillon's home outlined the need to set up a Sikh youth association for North America under the World Sikh Organization to achieve the establishment of Khalistan, an independent nation which many Sikhs are fighting to carve out of India. In a footnote, Dhillon, an elder in Montreal's Sikh community, urged martial arts and weapons training for Sikh youth.

A jury found both men guilty of conspiring to blow up an airplane. At the pre-sentence hearing, Crown prosecutor Claude Parent argued that the two accused should receive a sentence of life imprisonment. But Michael Code, the lawyer for Khela and Dhillon, compared his clients' case to that of the Front de Libération du Québec (FLQ) terrorists who got much lighter sentences for their crimes. Code cited the case of FLQ supporter Pierre Vallières, who was sentenced in 1968 for his part in the bombing of a Montreal shoe factory that killed one man. His sentence, for manslaughter, including the time he spent in jail during the court proceedings, was "effectively nine to ten years," the lawyer argued. "The FLQ and Vallières concerns were analogous to their [the Sikhs'] concerns for a homeland." And like Vallières, the two accused had no criminal records before their convictions, and their political views would probably change over time, he added.

Code also drew a parallel with two other FLQ terrorists, Louise and Jacques Cossette-Trudel, who pleaded guilty in 1978 to a charge of conspiracy to kidnap British diplomat James Richard Cross in October, 1970. The charge carried a maximum sentence of life imprisonment, but the couple's guilty plea, after eight years of self-imposed exile, got them a sentence of two years less a day. "These were machine-gun-wielding terrorists in 1970 when they committed the crimes," Code said. "And yet eight years later, the Cossette-Trudels returned completely reformed."

Notwithstanding Code's arguments, on January 28, Madame Justice Claire Barrette-Joncas of the Quebec Superior Court sentenced Khela and Dhillon to life imprisonment for conspiring to blow up a jetliner. Judge Barrette-Joncas told the two men, "The fact that you chose to conspire to kill hundreds of innocent people for terrorist purposes has brought you [into] the category of worst offenders."

Yet another link between drug trafficking and terrorist activities in Canada came to light a week after an Armenian group attacked the Turkish Embassy in Ottawa in March, 1985. Michael Gunter, an expert on Armenian terrorism, said the Armenian Revolutionary Army, which claimed it was behind the attack, was partly financed from the proceeds of drug trafficking. Gunter, a professor at Tennessee Technological University in Cookville, Tennessee, identified Noubar Soufoyon as the financial kingpin of Armenian terrorism. Soufoyon, an alleged drug trafficker indicted in New York in 1981 on charges of importing heroin, is wanted in the United States by the FBI and was last reported to be in Beirut. He has also been cited in U.S. congressional testimony as the conduit for funds for both the Armenian Liberation Army and the Armenian Secret Army for the Liberation of Armenia.

Some allege that the narco-terrorist threat is a deliberate conspiracy against Western nations by their most ardent foes – the Soviet bloc and some of its allies, with the goal of undermining the decadent West with drugs. For more than two decades, defectors from Bulgaria, Czechoslovakia, Cuba and Nicaragua have spun intriguing yarns about a well-orchestrated Soviet-inspired plot to destroy the West by poisoning its youth with dope.

CSIS official Jim Warren says he is wary of the grand conspiracy theory: "I'm a bit skeptical of it. That's not to say that somebody didn't think of it somewhere along the line." Moreover, he notes that in the era of *glasnost*, the Soviets would likely be hesitant to get involved in such a venture. "More importantly, they are worried themselves [about] a mounting drug problem in the Soviet Union and [the] East bloc. The sense we have is they are just as worried as the West about the spread of drugs in their country."

One of the most startling revelations about the so-called grand conspiracy theory came in 1968 when General Jan Senja, secretary of the Czechoslovak Defense Council and chief of staff at the Defense Ministry, defected to the West. In an interview with *U.S. News*, Senja recounted a top-secret meeting he attended in Moscow with high-ranking members from the eight-member-nation Warsaw Pact which had been called by Soviet Premier Nikita Khrushchev. During the meeting, Senja said, the Soviet leader unveiled a bizarre plan in which he saw drugs leading to the ultimate destabilization of the capitalist nations while generating much-needed foreign capital. The program was to be directed by the KGB, with the assistance of the secret service agencies of the other Warsaw Pact members. Senja recalled that Khrushchev mentioned the concerns harbored by some at the meeting that the strategy he was proposing might be immoral. However, he countered, "Anything that speeds up the destruction of capitalism is moral."

The theory got a jolt of credibility when Stefan Sverdlev, a high-ranking officer in the Bulgarian Committee for State Security, defected in Greece in 1971 with his wife, two young children, and a suitcase filled with hundreds of top-secret documents. Among them was a directive dated July 16, 1970. Coded M-120/00-0050, the document was drafted at a meeting of the chiefs of the secret services of the Warsaw Pact in Moscow in 1967. The subject was to discuss ways of exploiting and accelerating the "inherent corruption" of Western society. "We all knew what it meant," Sverdlev told Nathan Adams, a senior editor with *Reader's Digest*. "The movement of narcotics from the

Middle East through Bulgaria to Western Europe and North America was well-known to us. It was, of course, illegal, and drugs were seized when found. Now it would be a weapon."

The outcome of the directive was to use Kintex, the Bulgarian state commercial trade office, as a front to smuggle narcotics into Western Europe and the United States. Colonel-General Grigor Chopov, deputy minister of the interior and head of the Bulgarian secret service, controlled the clandestine operations of Kintex. When the notorious French Connection was smashed in the 1970s, a top Kintex agent was identified as a key link to the heroin-smuggling ring.

After a series of mishaps and internationally embarrassing revelations, the Bulgarians took on a very low profile, passing on much of their covert drug operations to the Cubans. In the late 1970s, the DEA began to pick up intelligence that the Cubans had struck a deal with key Colombian drug lords which would allow boats laden with marijuana to use Cuban waters and to sail to its ports for refuelling and repairs. The money from this venture, which was estimated at several million dollars a month, was earmarked for the purchase of weapons to be supplied to Marxist rebel groups throughout Latin America.

With a sheaf of intelligence in hand, the U.S. State Department flatly accused Cuba in January, 1982, of using Colombian drug gangs to funnel arms and money to guerrillas in Colombia. In exchange for this service, the department said, Havana gave sanctuary in Cuban waters to ships carrying marijuana bound for the U.S. market.

"It is the first firm information we have which implicates Cuba in drug trafficking," a State Department official said, linking the regime of Fidel Castro to the activities of Jaime Guillot, identified as a drug trafficker who had been arrested in Mexico. Guillot had admitted acting on behalf of Cuba since 1980, channelling both weapons and money to M-19 guerrillas in Colombia. State Department officials said they had information that Guillot had travelled to Cuba twice since October, 1981, "and on the second visit received

$700,000 from the Cuban government" to buy arms for M-19. "In return for Mr. Guillot's services, the Cubans facilitated the ring's trafficking by permitting motherships carrying marijuana to take sanctuary in Cuban waters while awaiting feeder boats from the Bahamas and Florida," a State Department official said.

In April, 1983, Mario Estebes Gonzalez, a Cuban defector, told the FBI and New York State law enforcement officials that agents of the Cuban government were actively involved in drug trafficking in New York and Florida in 1980 and 1981. He said his mission on behalf of the Cuban government was to distribute cocaine, marijuana and methaqualone tablets in New York, New Jersey and Florida, and that in that period he earned more than $7 million for the cash-starved Castro regime.

Carlos Lehder Rivas, the arrogant and high-living Colombian cocaine drug baron who was sentenced to life imprisonment in the United States in July, 1988, once declared that drugs are the Third World's "atomic bomb" and boasted that "coca has been transformed into a revolutionary weapon for the struggle against American imperialism. The Achilles' heel of imperialism [is] the *estimulantes* of Colombia."

There have also been allegations that the Sandinistas in Nicaragua established themselves in the drug trade at the urging of Raúl Castro, Fidel Castro's brother. DEA intelligence revealed that the Sandinistas swiftly established themselves in the cocaine trade by importing coca paste from Colombia and refining it into cocaine in their own refineries using precursor chemicals supplied by Cuba which they had obtained in Europe. While the U.S. State Department and former President Ronald Reagan fired salvos at their Marxist adversaries, they in turn were embarrassed by revelations that the CIA, the Israeli Mossad and the Honduran military were involved in an arms deal to supply millions of dollars in weapons to the Nicaraguan *contras*. High-level U.S. government documents indicate the weapons were bought in part with drug money.

According to Richard Brenneke, an arms dealer with connections in the Soviet bloc, the Medellin cartel put up financing for an operation to supply weapons to the *contras*,
believing that it would ensure safe entry of its drug flights
into the U.S. Brenneke, who has done work for the Mossad
and the CIA, said the cartel used its own planes to fly arms to
the *contras* and then fly cocaine shipments into the U.S. Testi-
fying before a Senate Foreign Relations subcommittee in
April, 1988, he admitted that he flew with one such drug
shipment into Amarillo, Texas. Brenneke also told the committee that the Israeli connection was run by a former Mossad
agent who had become a close friend and advisor to Panama-
nian strongman General Manuel Noriega. The agent advised
Noriega to cooperate with the network to win favor in
Washington.

On April 13, 1989, a Senate report released by the U.S.
Congress said the U.S. government had allowed the war it
backed between the *contras* and the Nicaraguan government
to obstruct its fight against drugs. The report, prepared by the
Senate subcommittee on narcotics, terrorism and international operations, noted that U.S. agencies' first priority was
to support the *contra* rebels, even though that interfered with
efforts to halt drug trafficking by them, by Noriega and by
Honduran army elements. In some cases, the U.S government
went so far as to block law enforcement efforts to stop drug
shipments. "U.S. officials involved in Central America failed
to address the drug issue for fear of jeopardizing the war
effort against Nicaragua," said the report, which is based on a
two-year investigation.

Subcommittee chairman Democratic Senator John Kerry
of Massachusetts, told reporters that "law enforcement personnel were demoralized" by what they encountered. "Again
and again, we found agencies with foreign policy responsibil-
ities failed to provide law enforcement . . . with the support
or information they need to make arrests."

The report also noted that foreign policy priorities toward
the Bahamas, Honduras, Nicaragua and Panama "at times

delayed, halted or interfered with U.S. law enforcement's efforts to keep narcotics out of the United States." It said the foreign policy priority in all those countries was the Nicaraguan effort, except for the Bahamas, where it was the continued presence of U.S. military bases. The subcommittee said that it found no evidence that *contra* leaders were involved in drug smuggling, but stated that individual rebels, suppliers, pilots and supporters did smuggle narcotics. It added that U.S. policy makers "were not immune to the idea that drug money was a perfect solution to the *contras'* funding problems."

While Canada may appear to be far removed from these sordid events, it nonetheless plays a role in the complex and dangerous web of narco-terrorism. The vast amounts of money spent by Canadians to satisfy an insatiable demand for drugs do go in part toward funding activities which have frightening implications. The presence in Canada of sympathizers to a host of national liberation groups may provide a small but important link in the narco-terrorist chain.

Appendix

Appendix: Price Lists (1988) for Illegal Drugs, from Grower to Street Level

HEROIN

Figure 1

Representative prices for Southeast Asian and Southwest Asian heroin at successive stages of trafficking, 1988

Southeast Asian Heroin

Farmer — 10 kilograms of opium* — $1,000–$1,600
Laboratory (Golden Triangle) — 1 kilogram of No. 4 heroin (pure) — $4,400–$5,000
Distribution Centre (Bangkok) — 1 kilogram of No. 4 heroin (pure) — $6,000–$8,000
Canada — 1 kilogram of No. 4 heroin (pure) — $120,000–$200,000
— 1 ounce (28 grams) of No. 4 heroin (pure) — $6,000–$15,000
— 1 gram of No. 4 heroin (pure) — $650–$1,000
— 1 point* of No. 4 heroin (30% pure) — $75–$100

Southwest Asian Heroin

Farmer — 10 kilograms of opium — $1,400
Laboratory (Golden Crescent) — 1 kilogram of heroin (pure) — $4,400–$4,800
Distribution Centre (Europe) — 1 kilogram of heroin (pure) — $50,000–$90,000
Canada — 1 kilogram of No. 4 heroin (pure) — $120,000–$200,000
— 1 ounce (28 grams) of No. 4 heroin (pure) — $3,000–$15,000
— 1 gram of No. 4 heroin (pure) — $200–$750
— 1 point* of No. 4 heroin (25–65% pure) — $75

*It takes 10 kilograms of opium to make 1 kilogram of heroin. One point is one-tenth of a gram.
Source: RCMP National Drug Intelligence Estimates

COCAINE

Figure 2

South America

Farmer — 250–500 kilograms of coca leaves — $200–$750

Laboratory — 250–500 kilograms of coca leaves = 2.5 kilograms of coca paste — $900–$1,000

— 2.5 kilograms of coca paste = 1 kilogram of cocaine base — $1,300–$1,600

— 1 kilogram of cocaine base = 1 kilogram of cocaine hydrochloride — $3,000–$6,500

Canada

Wholesale — 1 kilogram of cocaine hydrochloride (pure) — $22,000–$55,000

Retail — 1 ounce (28 grams) of cocaine hydrochloride (pure) — $1,300–$2,000

— 1 gram of cocaine hydrochloride (pure) — $85–$130

Representative prices for cocaine at successive stages of trafficking, 1988

Source: RCMP National Drug Intelligence Estimates

MARIJUANA

Figure 3

Level and Weight	Source Area				
	Colombia	Jamaica	Thailand	United States	Mexico
Source 1 pound (450 grams)	$115–$135	$25	$25–$70	Sinsemilla $350–$1,450	$600
Trafficker (Canada) 1 pound (450 grams)	$700–$2,200	$400–$1,400	$3,800	Sinsemilla $2,100–$3,300	$1,800–$2,500
Street (Canada) 1 ounce (28 grams)/ unit	$60–$250	$35–$165	$25–$40 per stick	Sinsemilla $210–$300	$200–$250

Source: RCMP National Drug Intelligence Estimates

Representative prices for marijuana at successive stages of trafficking, 1988

HASHISH

Figure 4

Representative prices for hashish at successive stages of trafficking, 1988

	Source Area	
Level and Weight	**Lebanon**	**Pakistan/India**
Source		
1 pound (450 grams)	$20–$35	$18–$34
Trafficker (Canada)		
1 pound (450 grams)	$1,600–$3,500	$1,600–$3,500
Street (Canada)		
1 ounce (28 grams)	$150–$550	$150–$550
1 gram	$10–$30	$10–$30

Source: RCMP National Drug Intelligence Estimates.

LIQUID HASHISH

Figure 5

Representative prices for liquid hashish at successive stages of trafficking, 1988

Level and Weight	Source Area	
	Jamaica	Lebanon
Source		
1 pound (450 grams)	$1,125–$1,250	$290–$320
Trafficker (Canada)		
1 pound (450 grams)	$3,000–$6,500	$3,000–$6,500
Street (Canada)		
1 ounce (28 grams)	$250–$500	$250–$500
1 gram	$10–$40	$10–$40

Source: RCMP National Drug Intelligence Estimates.